Dale
Hedman

IMS PROGRAMMING TECHNIQUES

A Guide to Using DL/I

INCLUDING THE IMS DB/DC ENVIRONMENT

IMS PROGRAMMING TECHNIQUES

A Guide to Using DL/I
INCLUDING THE IMS DB/DC ENVIRONMENT

Second Edition

Dan Kapp
Joe Leben

 VAN NOSTRAND REINHOLD
New York

Copyright © 1986 by Van Nostrand Reinhold

Library of Congress Catalog Card Number 85-22609
ISBN 0-442-24655-2

Manufactured in the United States of America

Van Nostrand Reinhold
115 Fifth Avenue
New York, New York 10003

Chapman & Hall
2-6 Boundary Row
London SE1 8HN, England

Thomas Nelson Australia
102 Dodds Street
South Melbourne, Victoria 3205, Australia

Nelson Canada
1120 Birchmount Road
Scarborough, Ontario M1K 5G4, Canada

15 14 13 12 11 10 9 8 7 6

Library of Congress Cataloging-in-Publication Data

Kapp, Dan.
    IMS programming techniques.

    Bibliography: p.
    Includes index.
    1. Data base management.   2. IMS (DL/I) (Computer
system) I. Leben, Joe. II. Title.
QA76.9.D3K36 1986   005.75   85-22609
ISBN 0-442-24655-2

For Pat and Carol

Preface to the Second Edition

IBM has made many changes to IMS since this book was first published. We have added significant content to the present edition. Some additional content reflects the changes that apply to application programming in the IMS environment, including coverage of the fast path feature and field-level sensitivity. We have also expanded the original material on some IMS facilities, such as secondary indexing and logical relationships, that we felt were not originally covered in sufficient depth.

The entire book has also been extensively edited to make it easier to read. For example, most short coding examples have been included inline in the text itself rather than being placed out of line in separate figures. This makes it easier to follow coding examples, which are sometimes complex.

We have also taken the opportunity to correct the technical errors that cropped into the original edition and have attempted to improve the style of presentation.

DAN KAPP
JOE LEBEN

Preface to the First Edition

An important topic currently of interest to people in the computing industry is data base technology. Many publications in the data base field try to be all things to all people and present information which has wide application to many different software implementations of data base techniques.

This book takes a different approach and deals specifically with techniques used in writing application programs in ANS COBOL, PL/I, or Assembler Language in an IMS DL/I data base environment. While some of the techniques may apply to other data base management systems, we decided to focus specifically on the IMS family of data base management systems supplied by IBM. We feel that there is a real need in the industry for such a book.

This book assumes no prior knowledge of IMS or any other data base management system. However, a basic knowledge of one of the IBM operating systems that supports IMS is assumed. This basic knowledge includes concepts and terminology used in describing the IBM access methods: QSAM, BSAM, ISAM, and VSAM.

We use a central case study, a data base for a hospital system, to present key concepts and programming techniques. While the main orientation of the book is toward the application programmer, it can be used by anyone who will work with IMS. Analysts, designers, operators, and managers can use this book to learn what IMS is all about and how application programs interface with it.

Exercises follow each of the chapters and answers are provided in Appendix F. Some of the exercises consist of assignments to write entire programs. Many sample programs are included that can be used as models in coding new programs. The organization of the book allows it to be used by individuals in a self-study environment, as a supplement to an in-house training program, or as a text in a college-level data base programming course.

DAN KAPP
JOE LEBEN

Contents

IMS PROGRAMMING TECHNIQUES

A Guide to Using DL/I

INCLUDING THE IMS DB/DC ENVIRONMENT

Part I
Concepts

1
IMS Systems and DL/I

In this book, we discuss programming techniques for IBM's IMS (*Information Management System*) data management system software. Most of the book focuses on the data base interface of these systems.

In this chapter, we look at some of the main purposes and objectives of data base management systems, particularly the two specific systems this book applies to: IMS/VS (*Information Management System/Virtual Storage*) and DL/I VSE (*Data Language/I—Virtual Storage Extended*). Both IMS/VS and DL/I VSE are program products available from IBM for a license fee.

The IMS/VS program product contains a teleprocessing monitor, generally called IMS-DC (*Information Management System—Data Communications*) as well as a data base interface, generally called DL/I (*Data Language/I*). Both the DL/I and the IMS-DC components of IMS/VS are available separately from IBM. The DL/I VSE program product implements a DL/I data base interface only.

THE OBJECTIVES OF DATA BASE MANAGEMENT SYSTEMS

The main objectives of most data base management systems are *to increase data independence*, and *to reduce data redundancy*. Many data base management systems also *provide data communications* facilities. We next discuss these three objectives briefly.

Data Independence

One of the objectives that data base systems attempt to accomplish is to reduce the application program's dependence on the format and physical characteristics of the data it processes. Data independence allows application programs to be written with little regard to how data is physically stored. With IMS, data is stored in a centralized collection called the *data base*. The IMS software accomplishes data independence by handling all requests that programs make for accessing the data base. Data independence allows application programs to request specific pieces of data by name, so they do not have to be aware of the stored format of the data.

Data Redundancy

In a traditional data processing installation, the same data tends to be repeated in many places. For example, customer information might be contained in several application files. If each file is keyed on customer number, the customer number would be carried in every file. Data base systems attempt to reduce the need for data redundancy by giving the data base designer tools for controlling data redundancy.

Data Communications

In addition to providing ways of organizing and accessing data, a third objective of the IMS/VS program product is to provide data communications capabilities. Data communications functions are handled by the IMS-DC *teleprocessing monitor*. The DL/I VSE program product does not include a teleprocessing monitor. Many DL/I VSE installations (and many IMS/VS installations as well) use the CICS program product for this purpose. The installation can implement only the data base manipulation portion of IMS/VS. The data base interface and the teleprocessing monitor are available separately from IBM. Using only the data base portion of IMS/VS allows application programs to access data bases in a batch environment. Optionally, the installation can implement both the data base facilities and the data communications portion. The IMS/VS teleprocessing monitor provides programmers with an easy-to-use method for transferring data between the data base and remote terminals.

Most of this book deals with DL/I, the data base component of the IBM data base management systems, but the two chapters in Part III of this book provide an introduction to IMS data communications facilities.

THE IMS SOFTWARE ENVIRONMENT

There are a number of ways that we can approach the IMS software. For the purposes of this introductory chapter, Figure 1.1 divides into the following five categories the data and software that work with the operating system to form the IMS software environment:

- IMS application program
- IMS data base

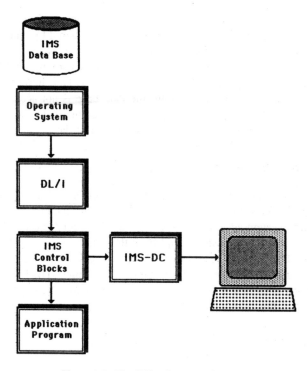

Figure 1.1. The IMS software environment

- IMS data base software
- IMS control blocks
- IMS-DC software

Application Program

The application programs are those parts of the system that are designed and coded by the installation's data processing staff. An IMS application program uses a standard interface between it and the other components of the system. Those interfaces are described in detail in this book. In general, IMS application programs use standard CALL statements and parameter lists to communicate with IMS. Because IMS uses standard operating system interfaces, application programs can be written in COBOL, PL/I, or Assembler Language.

IMS Data Base

The IMS data base itself is the heart of any system using IMS. In general, an IMS data base is organized differently from a traditional file or data set. A file is generally used by one or a small number of programs and serves the needs of a single application area. A data base is generally shared by many programs and often serves the varied needs of many application areas.

IMS data bases are normally stored in direct access storage, but under certain circumstances, sequential data sets can be used. One important thing to remember is that in a data base system, the data base is not accessed directly by application programs. Instead, application programs make calls to IMS to request data. IMS performs the actual manipulation of data in the data base.

IMS Data Base Software

IMS consists of a set of program modules that intercepts all requests that programs make for accessing the data base. IMS program modules use both standard operating system access methods and a set of specialized physical access methods to handle data transfer to and from the data base.

IMS uses DL/I, which stands for *Data Language/I* to provide a set of programming standards for interfacing with DL/I modules. DL/I programming standards form what is sometimes called an *interface language*. The main purpose of most of this book is to describe, in detail, this interface language.

IMS Control Blocks

The application program uses the DL/I interface language in communicating with the system. The person who sets up IMS data bases uses two IMS control blocks in describing the data base structure and identifying how the data base can be accessed. These two control blocks are called the *Data Base Description* (DBD) and the *Program Specification Block* (PSB). These control blocks are normally maintained by the *data base administration staff*. We will talk more about the function of this group in Chapter 3.

The DBD is used to describe the physical nature of an IMS data base, including the way in which data is stored on the storage device and the way in which it is accessed. The PSB describes the data base as a particular application program views it. The PSB identifies which pieces of data a program is allowed to access and describes the type of functions it can perform on each collection of data, such as read only, update, or delete.

The IMS-DC Teleprocessing Monitor

As we mentioned above, IMS-DC is the IMS/VS teleprocessing monitor. IMS-DC consists of a set of program modules that allow an application program to communicate with remote terminals. These data communications modules allow application programs to communicate with remote terminals through a standard interface language using CALL statements and parameter lists. The way in which the program communicates with remote terminals is similar to the way the program accesses the data base.

IMS Terminology

It is perhaps unfortunate, but in this introductory chapter we have been forced to use the term DL/I for three different purposes:

- DL/I is IBM's name for the collection of software modules that provide access to the data stored in a DL/I data base.
- DL/I is IBM's name for the interface language that programmers use in accessing the data base in an application program.
- DL/I is part of IBM's name for the DL/I VSE program product available for users of the VSE operating systems.

Throughout most of this book, we use the term IMS to refer to the IMS data base software and to the DL/I interface language. When we use the term DL/I in this book, the context makes it clear which of the above we are referring to.

EXERCISES

1. List the three main purposes and objectives of the IMS data base management system.

2. Match each of the IMS components below with the statement that best describes it. Each component matches one statement.

COMPONENTS	STATEMENTS
A. Application program	a. Written by the installation.
B. IMS data base	b. Communicates with remote terminals.
C. IMS data base software	c. Handles data base access.
D. IMS control blocks	d. Pool of data shared by one or more application programs.
E. IMS-DC software	e. Maintained by the data base administration staff.

2
IMS Terminology

The purpose of this chapter is to define the terms used to describe IMS data bases. As we introduce IMS terminology, we also introduce the HOSPITAL data base used as a central case study throughout this book. We show how IMS terminology relates to our central case study example.

THE HOSPITAL DATA BASE

The HOSPITAL data base is used by a series of applications to keep track of patients, hospital beds, and special facilities in a group of hospitals. Before we go any further, we must offer an apology to those familiar with medical applications. Our sample data base is not meant to be a solution to any real problem. Any data base which might actually be used in the real world for a similar purpose would be much more complex. Keep in mind that our data base is designed to illustrate important concepts about IMS, and is not designed to be used in a real medical application.

Data Base Contents

Following are the types of information we are storing in the HOSPITAL data base. Notice we have organized the information in the form of an outline.

I. Hospital General Information
    A. Wards and Rooms in Each Hospital
        1. Patients in Each Ward
           a. Symptoms
           b. Treatments
           c. Doctors
    B. Special Facilities Available at Each Hospital

At the highest level, we are maintaining general information about each hospital, such as the hospital's name, address, phone number, and administrator's name. At the next lowest level, there are two types of information stored for each of our hospitals. First, we keep track of the wards and rooms in each hospital. (Our example makes the overly-simplistic assumption that each hospital is divided into a series of *wards*, each made up of a number of *rooms*.) Information stored for each ward includes ward number, total number of rooms, total number of beds, and the number of available beds. The second type of information we are storing for each hospital is about each special facility available at the hospital, such as a pump-oxygenator.

Dropping down yet another level, for each ward in a particular hospital, we are storing general information about each patient in that ward, including the patient's name, address, and the date the patient was admitted to the hospital. Finally, at the lowest level, we store more detailed information about each patient's symptoms, treatments, and doctors. As in the real world, our HOSPITAL data base allows a patient to have multiple symptoms, treatments, and doctors.

Record Descriptions

Next, we will look at the information stored at each level. Rather than show in a tabular form the details concerning the information stored in the data base, such as in a traditional record layout, we show the format of each piece of information in the form of COBOL DATA DIVISION statements. Figure 2.1 shows these statements.

Notice that there is very little redundant information in the COBOL statements in Figure 2.1. Any attempt to organize this information into a series of interrelated files would probably require some data redundancy. For example, to construct a file of patient records, we might have to carry the patient's ward number and hospital identification in each record. Notice the COBOL statements that define general patient information (under the 01 level name PATIENT) do not contain that information.

Also notice that if we attempted to organize the HOSPITAL data as a set of interrelated files, programmers who needed to access the information would have to be aware of the interrelationships, know the structure of the files, and know the formats of all the records they would be working with.

In the worst case, suppose we had organized all the information into a single file containing many different record types. Programmers would have to be told how they could distinguish the records *they* required from all the other records. They would also have to know the general structure of the file, and how the records related to one another.

```
01  HOSPITAL.
    03  HOSPNAME            PIC   X(20).
    03  HOSP-ADDRESS        PIC   X(30).
    03  HOSP-PHONE          PIC   X(10).
    03  ADMIN               PIC   X(20).

01  WARD.
    03  WARDNO              PIC   XX.
    03  TOT-ROOMS           PIC   XXX.
    03  TOT-BEDS            PIC   XXX.
    03  BEDAVAIL            PIC   XXX.
    03  WARDTYPE            PIC   X(20).

01  PATIENT.
    03  PATNAME             PIC   X(20).
    03  PAT-ADDRESS         PIC   X(30).
    03  PAT-PHONE           PIC   X(10).
    03  BEDIDENT            PIC   X(4).
    03  DATEADMT            PIC   X(6).
    03  PREV-STAY-FLAG      PIC   X.
    03  PREV-HOSP           PIC   X(20).
    03  PREV-DATE           PIC   X(4).
    03  PREV-REASON         PIC   X(30).

01  SYMPTOM.
    03  DIAGNOSE            PIC   X(20).
    03  SYMPDATE            PIC   X(6).
    03  PREV-TREAT-FLAG     PIC   X.
    03  TREAT-DESC          PIC   X(20).
    03  SYMP-DOCTOR         PIC   X(20).
    03  SYMP-DOCT-PHONE     PIC   X(10).

01  TREATMNT.
    03  TRTYPE              PIC   X(20).
    03  TRDATE              PIC   X(6).
    03  MEDICATION-TYPE     PIC   X(20).
    03  DIET-COMMENT        PIC   X(30).
    03  SURGERY-FLAG        PIC   X.
    03  SURGERY-DATE        PIC   X(6).
    03  SURGERY-COMMENT     PIC   X(30).

01  DOCTOR.
    03  DOCTNAME            PIC   X(20).
    03  DOCT-ADDRESS        PIC   X(30).
    03  DOCT-PHONE          PIC   X(10).
    03  SPECIALT            PIC   X(20).

01  FACILITY.
    03  FACTYPE             PIC   X(20).
    03  TOT-FACIL           PIC   XXX.
    03  FACAVAIL            PIC   XXX.
```

Figure 2.1. COBOL DATA DIVISION coding for HOSPITAL data base

IMS CONCEPTS AND TERMINOLOGY

The first concept we will introduce is that of *hierarchical structure*. All IMS data bases are made up of one or more *hierarchies*, or *inverted tree structures*. Notice in Figure 2.2 that the information we are storing about hospitals is already laid out in the form of a hierarchy. At the top of the outline is general information about *hospitals*. Under hospitals, at the second level of the outline, are two categories of information: information about *wards* and information about *special facilities*. Under wards, at the third level, is *patient* information. And finally, at the fourth level, under patient information, is specific *symptom*, *treatment*, and *doctor* information.

IMS Hierarchical Structure

As with any hierarchical structure, we can represent our hospital information in the form of a series of boxes arranged in the form of an inverted tree. The HOSPITAL data base tree structure is shown in Figure 2.2. (TREATMNT is not misspelled; most IMS names are limited to a maximum of eight characters.)

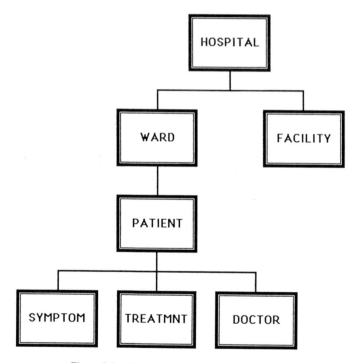

Figure 2.2. HOSPITAL data base hierarchy chart

Data Base Hierarchy Chart

Figure 2.2 is called a *data base hierarchy chart*. We will use the hierarchy chart in Figure 2.2 to define some terms. Each box in the chart represents a type of *segment*; in each box is the segment's name. A segment represents the smallest unit of information that IMS transfers to and from the data base. Within each segment is one or more data *fields*. Notice that each 01 level data name defines one of the *segments* in the HOSPITAL data base. Each 03 level data name defines a *field*.

In designing the data base, the data base designer attempts to group together fields that are normally required at the same time and by the same application. For example, if we need a patient's address, the chances are good that we will need the patient's phone number as well. At one extreme, each field can be defined in a segment by itself; at the other extreme, all fields can be grouped together in a single segment. In most cases, neither extreme makes for a good design.

There are many advantages to storing our hospital data base information in the form of multiple segments. For example, if a particular application requires only general information about hospitals, that application only needs to know the format of the HOSPITAL segment. It does not even have to know that the other segments exist, or what are their relationships to the HOSPITAL segment.

Segment Types and Segment Occurrences

We must now make a distinction between *segment types* and *segment occurrences*. In the HOSPITAL data base there are seven segment types. Each is represented by one of the boxes in the hierarchy chart. For each segment type, we can store as many segment occurrences as will fit in the available storage space. For example, if we are storing information about three hospitals, we will have three occurrences of the hospital segment type in our data base, as shown in Figure 2.3.

We sometime use the term *segment* alone to mean either segment *type* or segment *occurrence*. When we use the term *segment* by itself, it will generally be clear from the context which we mean. Notice that Figure 2.3 shows multiple segment occurrences at the HOSPITAL level, but not at any level below it. Including *all* segment occurrences would make the chart hopelessly complicated. We usually show multiple occurrences only for selected segment types in the chart. There are, of course, normally multiple segment occurrences for each segment type. For example, there is only one PATIENT segment type, but there is an occurrence of the PATIENT segment type for each patient, in each ward, in each hospital. Figure 2.4 shows examples of multiple segment occurrences of each segment type.

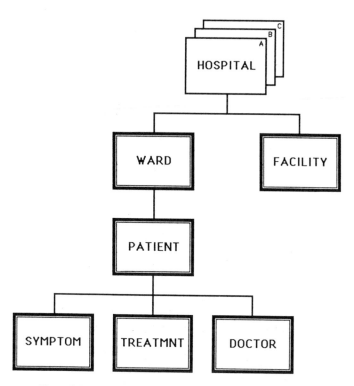

Figure 2.3. Three occurrences of the HOSPITAL segment type

We normally represent the structure of the data base in the form of a simple hierarchy chart showing segment types, as in Figure 2.2. The fact that multiple occurrences exist for each segment type is taken for granted.

Relationships between Segment Types

The terms *parent* and *child* are used to describe the relationships between segment types. Any segment type having one or more segment types directly *below* it is called a *parent*. Any segment type having a segment type directly *above* it is called a *child*. For example, the PATIENT segment type is a parent, and the SYMPTOM, TREATMNT, and DOCTOR segment types are its children. However, the PATIENT segment type is also a child of its parent, the WARD segment type. *Parent* and *child* are relative terms; whether a segment type is considered a parent or a child depends upon which portion of the data base we are viewing. A segment type that is a child of some other segment type is also known as a *dependent segment*. For example, the DOCTOR segment type is a *dependent* of the PATIENT segment type.

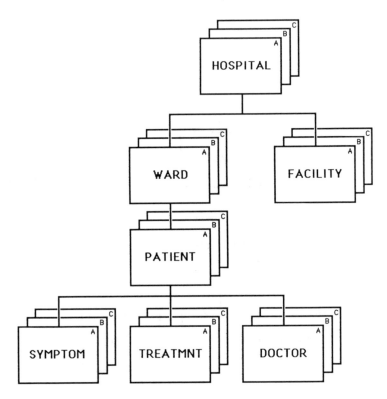

Figure 2.4. Segment occurrences

The concept of parent and child relationships can be extended to apply to individual segment occurrences as well as to segment types. A particular DOCTOR segment occurrence cannot exist unless there is a PATIENT segment occurrence above it in the data base. The converse is not true. It is valid to have a PATIENT segment occurrence that does not have SYMPTOM, TREATMNT, or DOCTOR segment occurrences below it.

The term *dependent* is often used to describe all those segment occurrences below a particular segment occurrence in the data base. For example, all the occurrences of SYMPTOM, TREATMNT, and DOCTOR below a particular PATIENT segment occurrence are know as that PATIENT segment occurrence's *dependents*. The concept of dependent segment occurrences extends more than one level in the hierarchy. For example, all occurrences of WARD, PATIENT, SYMPTOM, TREATMNT, DOCTOR and FACILITY segment types below a particular HOSPITAL segment occurrence are known as that HOSPITAL segment occurrence's *dependent* segments.

All occurrences of a particular segment type under a single parent segment

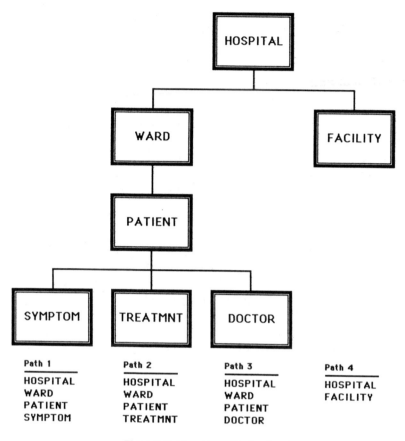

Figure 2.5. Four hierarchical paths

occurrence are called *twins*. For example, if a particular patient has five symptoms, there will be five occurrences of the SYMPTOM segment type under that PATIENT segment occurrence. Those five SYMPTOM segment occurrences are twins. However, if patient A has one symptom and patient B has another, those two SYMPTOM segment occurrences are not twins, because they have different segment occurrences as parents. The set of all twins dependent on a particular parent is often referred to as a *twin chain*.

In order to maintain the inverted tree structure required by IMS, no segment type can have more than one parent. Any IMS data base must have a single segment type at the top of the hierarchy. The segment type at the top of the inverted tree is only a parent; it is not a child of any other segment type. The segment type at the top has special significance and is called the *root segment type*. The root segment type is the segment type through which all dependent segments are accessed. For example, to locate a particular PATIENT segment occurrence, the proper HOSPITAL root segment occurrence must be located first.

Hierarchical Paths

Segment occurrences are normally retrieved along *hierarchical paths*. A path is an imaginary line that starts at the root segment type, passes through segment types at intermediate levels in the hierarchy, and ends at a segment type at the bottom of the inverted tree. The four paths in the HOSPITAL data base are shown in Figure 2.5. Hierarchical paths govern the types of retrieval that are allowed. We will discuss the various types of retrieval in later chapters.

Data Base Records

We now define the terms *data base record* and *data base*. A *data base record* consists of a single occurrence of the root segment type and all of its dependent segment occurrences. In our example, a single data base record consists of all the segment occurrences belonging to a particular hospital. Each data base record includes a single occurrence of the HOSPITAL segment type, and all of the segment occurrences below it. The *data base* is the collection of all the base records. In other words the HOSPITAL data base consists of all the HOSPITAL root segments and all of their dependents.

EXERCISES

1. Match each of the terms below with the statement that best describes it. Each term matches only one statement.

TERMS	STATEMENTS
A. Hierarchy chart	a. Collection of all root segment occurrences and all their dependents.
B. Dependent segments	
	b. Segment directly below some other segment.
C. Field	
	c. Individual data item.
D. Segment type	
E. Segment occurrence	d. Structure in which no segment can have more than one parent.
F. Parent	
	e. One occurrence of the root segment and all its dependents
G. Child	
H. Tree structure	f. All occurrences of a segment type under a single parent.
I. Twins	

TERMS	STATEMENTS
J. Root segment	g. Chart showing the relationships between segments.
K. Data base record	h. Segment type having no parent.
L. Data base	i. Segment directly above some other segment.
	j. Collection of related data items retrieved as a unit.
	k. All those segments below a particular segment occurrence.
	l. Generic term that describes collections of related data items.

2. Figure 2.6 shows a hierarchy chart for a data base. Answer the following questions about it.

a. What are the names of all the segment types in the data base?
b. What is the name of the root segment?
c. Identify the hierarchical paths in the data base by listing the segments along each path.
d. What is the name of segment F's parent?
e. What are the names of segment B's children?
f. How many levels are there in the hierarchy?
g. How many segment types are there in the data base?.

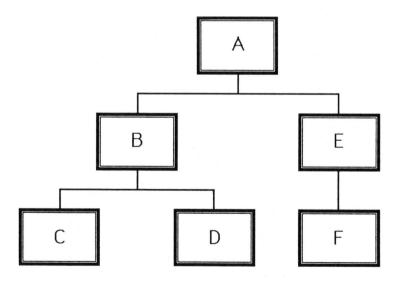

Figure 2.6. Exercise 2 hierarchy chart

3
IMS Data Base Definition

We begin this chapter by seeing how the various people in the installation view an IMS data base. After that, we see how the structure of a data base is defined. We then define a few more terms useful in describing data bases and in discussing IMS application programs. We also introduce the control blocks used by IMS and see how an application program runs in the IMS environment. At the end of this chapter, we describe some of the programming conventions that IMS application programs must observe.

THE DESIGNER'S VIEW OF THE DATA BASE

A data base is normally shared by a number of application programs. Therefore, the data must be organized so it serves the varied needs of all the applications that access it. However, the organization of the information stored in the data base often represents many compromises. Because the tasks involved in designing a data base require a variety of highly specialized skills, most installations that use data base systems have a *data base administration* group.

In general, the data base administration group is in charge of what goes into the data base, who can access it, and how it is organized. The data base administration function is normally performed by a group of people, but for simplicity we will refer to this group as though the function were performed by a single person. We call this person the *data base administrator* (DBA).

In some installations, a separate IMS systems programming group is in charge of installing and maintaining the IMS software. In other installations, the system programming tasks are performed by data base administration. For simplicity, we will assume these tasks are all performed by the data base administration group.

Factors in Designing Data Bases

When the DBA designs a data base, a number of factors must be considered, many of which are important to the application programming function. Some questions that programmers might ask about the data base include:

- What are the names of the segments that can be accessed?
- What are the formats of the various fields within those segments?
- What are the hierarchical relationships among the segments.
- What kind of processing can be performed on the segments?

There are a number of additional questions the DBA might ask that are of less concern to individual programmers, including:

- What are the hierarchical relationships that best fit the needs of the applications that will access the data base?
- Which physical access methods provide the best level of efficiency and storage economy for the data base?
- How often should the data base be reorganized?
- What kinds of data security should be built into the system?

The above lists are by no means complete, but they illustrate the kinds of decisions the DBA must make in designing a data base, and they illustrate the kinds of questions that must be answered for the application programmer.

So far, we have looked at the hierarchical structure of the HOSPITAL data base as it is viewed by the DBA. However, we have not yet provided all the information that the application program and IMS itself needs to know about the data base. For example, we do not yet have a way of asking IMS to search for information in the data base. For example, if we wanted to retrieve a particular occurrence of the HOSPITAL segment type, we do not yet have a method for asking for IMS to search for it based on a hospital name, address, phone number, or administrator's name.

Key and Search Fields

When we performed the DBA's role in designing the HOSPITAL data base, we had to decide not only what should be stored in each segment type, but also which of the fields within each segment would be known to IMS as *key fields* and *search fields*. For example, when we decided the HOSPITAL segment should contain the hospital's name, address, phone number, and administrator's

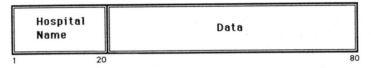

Hospital Name	Hospital Address	Hospital Phone	Administrator Name
1 20	21 50	51 60	61 80

Figure 3.1. The HOSPITAL segment to the program

Hospital Name	Data
1 20	80

Figure 3.2. The HOSPITAL segment to IMS

name, we also decided no application would ever need to ask IMS to search for a segment based on the address or phone number field. The only fields that IMS is interested in are the hospital name and administrator name fields. Figure 3.1 shows what the HOSPITAL segment looks like to an application program that retrieves it. But it looks like Figure 3.2 when IMS manipulates it.

IMS does not know the remaining fields contain an address and phone number; anything other than the hospital name and the administrator name are meaningless to IMS. When the DBA designs a data base, any data item, part of a data item, or combination of contiguous data items can be designated as a field on which IMS can search. The DBA assigns a one-to-eight character symbolic name to each field identified to IMS.

Key or Sequence Fields. One type of field that IMS works with is called a *key field* or *sequence field*. These terms mean the same thing and they are used interchangeably. A key or sequence field is a field that IMS uses to maintain segments in ascending sequence. In the HOSPITAL segment, we have designated hospital name as the key field, so IMS maintains HOSPITAL segments in ascending alphabetic sequence by hospital name. Only a single field within each segment can be designated as a key or sequence field. However, segments are generally *not required* to have a key or sequence field.

Sequence fields can be designated as unique or nonunique. If the HOSPITAL segment sequence field is designated as unique, IMS does not allow a program to place two HOSPITAL segments with the same hospital name into the data base.

Additional Search Fields. If the DBA determines it will be useful to perform a search for a segment based on the contents of some field, but the segments should not be sequenced on that field, the field can be designated as a *search field*. In the HOSPITAL segment, we have designated administrator name as an additional search field.

HOSPITAL DATA BASE KEY AND SEARCH FIELDS

Figure 3.3 shows another listing of the COBOL DATA DIVISION coding for the HOSPITAL data base segments. This time we have identified the key fields and search fields in each segment.

The HOSPITAL Segment

Normally, a root segment, such as the HOSPITAL segment is required to have a unique key field. We have chosen the hospital name field. We did not think it would be useful to search for a HOSPITAL segment based on a hospital's address or phone number, so we have not specified any additional search fields for the HOSPITAL segment. Figure 3.4 shows a diagram of the HOSPITAL segment as it is stored in the data base. Each key and search field is highlighted. We also underline key fields to distinguish them from search fields.

The WARD Segment

We will be able to search for a WARD segment based on the contents of up to three fields. (See Figure 3.5.) The key field, which we will require to be unique, is the ward number field. We also want to search for a WARD segment based on the number of beds available, and/or on the contents of a twenty-character description of the type of ward the segment describes. So we have designated those two fields as additional search fields.

The PATIENT Segment

We will also allow programs to search for PATIENT segments based on three different fields. (See Figure 3.6.) The unique key field for the PATIENT segment is the four-character bed identifier. It consists of a two-character room number and a two-character bed number. We did not use the patient's name for the key field, because we might have two patients with the same name, and we wanted to guarantee that this segment would have a unique key. We did want to allow programs to search for PATIENT segments based on a patient's name and also on the date the patient is admitted to the hospital, so we designated those fields as additional search fields.

```
01   HOSPITAL.
     03   HOSPNAME          PIC   X(20).    <-- unique key
     03   HOSP-ADDRESS      PIC   X(30).
     03   HOSP-PHONE        PIC   X(10).
     03   ADMIN             PIC   X(20).

01   WARD.
     03   WARDNO            PIC   XX.       <-- unique key
     03   TOT-ROOMS         PIC   XXX.
     03   TOT-BEDS          PIC   XXX.
     03   BEDAVAIL          PIC   XXX.      <-- search key
     03   WARDTYPE          PIC   X(20).    <-- search key

01   PATIENT.
     03   PATNAME           PIC   X(20).    <-- search key
     03   PAT-ADDRESS       PIC   X(30).
     03   PAT-PHONE         PIC   X(10).
     03   BEDIDENT          PIC   X(4).     <-- unique key
     03   DATEADMT          PIC   X(6).     <-- search key
     03   PREV-STAY-FLAG    PIC   X.
     03   PREV-HOSP         PIC   X(20).
     03   PREV-DATE         PIC   X(4).
     03   PREV-REASON       PIC   X(30).

01   SYMPTOM.
     03   DIAGNOSE          PIC   X(20).    <-- search key
     03   SYMPDATE          PIC   X(6).     <-- nonunique key
     03   PREV-TREAT-FLAG   PIC   X.
     03   TREAT-DESC        PIC   X(20).
     03   SYMP-DOCTOR       PIC   X(20).
     03   SYMP-DOCT-PHONE   PIC   X(10).

01   TREATMNT.
     03   TRTYPE            PIC   X(20).    <-- search key
     03   TRDATE            PIC   X(6).     <-- nonunique key
     03   MEDICATION-TYPE   PIC   X(20).
     03   DIET-COMMENT      PIC   X(30).
     03   SURGERY-FLAG      PIC   X.
     03   SURGERY-DATE      PIC   X(6).
     03   SURGERY-COMMENT   PIC   X(30).

01   DOCTOR.
     03   DOCTNAME          PIC   X(20).    <-- search key
     03   DOCT-ADDRESS      PIC   X(30).
     03   DOCT-PHONE        PIC   X(10).
     03   SPECIALT          PIC   X(20).    <-- search key

01   FACILITY.
     03   FACTYPE           PIC   X(20).    <-- search key
     03   TOT-FACIL         PIC   XXX.
     03   FACAVAIL          PIC   XXX.      <-- search key
```

Figure 3.3. HOSPITAL data base key and search fields

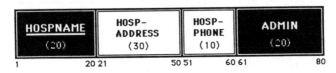

Figure 3.4. The HOSPITAL segment

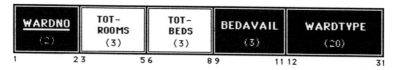

WARDNO (2)	TOT- ROOMS (3)	TOT- BEDS (3)	BEDAVAIL (3)	WARDTYPE (20)

Figure 3.5. The WARD segment

PATNAME (20)	PAT- ADDRESS (30)	PAT- PHONE (10)	BEDIDENT (4)	DATEADMT (6)	PREV- STAY- FLAG (1)	PREV- HOSP (20)	PREV- DATE (4)	PREV- REASON (30)

Figure 3.6. The PATIENT segment

The SYMPTOM and TREATMNT Segments

The SYMPTOM and TREATMNT segments are sequenced on the date on which the segments were stored in the data base. (See Figure 3.7.) The date fields were chosen as key fields because having the segments in date sequence provides useful historical information. For example, if the first SYMPTOM segment is stored in the data base at the time of a patient's admittance, and the last TREATMNT segment is entered at the time of the patient's release, we will be able to determine a patient's length of stay. We have designated a twenty-character description field in each segment as an additional search field as well. Notice in these two segments, the key fields are not unique. This is because many segments of each type might be stored in the data base under a single PATIENT segment in any given day.

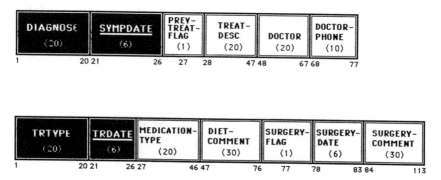

DIAGNOSE (20)	SYMPDATE (6)	PREV- TREAT- FLAG (1)	TREAT- DESC (20)	DOCTOR (20)	DOCTOR- PHONE (10)

TRTYPE (20)	TRDATE (6)	MEDICATION- TYPE (20)	DIET- COMMENT (30)	SURGERY- FLAG (1)	SURGERY- DATE (6)	SURGERY- COMMENT (30)

Figure 3.7. The SYMPTOM and TREATMNT segments

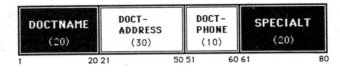

Figure 3.8. The DOCTOR segment

The DOCTOR Segment

The DOCTOR segment is straightforward. We have designated two fields as search fields, the doctor's name, and a description of the doctor's specialty. (See Figure 3.8.) The sequence of the DOCTOR segments is not important, so the DOCTOR segments do not have key fields.

The FACILITY Segment

The FACILITY segment is equally straightforward. We will allow a search based on a description of the facility or on the number of facilities of that type available. (See Figure 3.9.) Again, we did not feel the sequence of the segments to be important, so both will be search fields and there will be no key field.

In the HOSPITAL data base, each segment has at least one field defined as a key or search field. IMS does, however, allow the data base administrator to define a segment having no key or search fields. For example, a program might always need to access all occurrences of a particular segment type under one parent. In that case, key or search fields are not necessary.

DEFINING THE DATA BASE

Once segments have been defined, the hierarchical structure decided upon, and key and search fields chosen, the DBA communicates this information to IMS. To do this, a *control block* is created in a IMS library, called a *Data Base Description* (DBD). It describes the physical nature of a data base. A process called *DBD Generation* (DBDGEN) is used to create a DBD. The DBA creates a DBD by coding a series of DBDGEN control statements. We will go over the

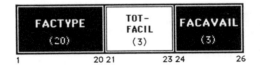

Figure 3.9. The FACILITY segment

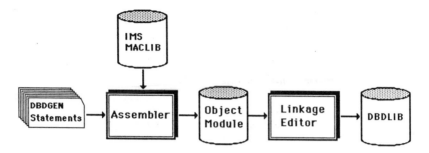

Figure 3.10. The DBDGEN process

coding for the HOSPITAL data base DBD later in this chapter; but remember, performing the DBDGEN for a data base is normally the job of the data base administrator; it is not normally done by the analyst or programmer.

The DBDGEN Process

Before we look at DBDGEN control statements, let us look at the DBDGEN process itself. (See Figure 3.10.) DBDGEN control statements consist of Assembler Language macro statements. The macros are supplied by IBM in a library named something like IMSVS.MACLIB. DBDGEN control statements are normally coded by the DBA and submitted to the system with JCL that invokes a cataloged procedure usually called DBDGEN. The DBDGEN procedure causes the DBDGEN control statement to be processed by the assembler, producing an *object module*. The object module is then passed to the linkage editor which, in turn, stores a load module in another IMS library, usually called something like IMS.DBDLIB or IMSVS.DBDLIB. We refer to this library as DBDLIB. The load module stored in DBDLIB by the DBDGEN procedure is the DBD itself, ready to be loaded into storage.

The DBD process is normally performed only once for a data base. All applications use the DBD in accessing the information in the data base. A new DBD is normally created only if the physical nature of the data base changes.

HOSPITAL Data Base DBDGEN

Figure 3.11 is a listing of the DBDGEN control statements that describe the HOSPITAL data base. PRINT NOGEN is an Assembler Language control statement that causes the assembler to suppress the listing of the machine instructions generated by each DBDGEN statement. These generated statements are not normally of interest to us.

```
            PRINT NOGEN
            DBD       NAME=HOSPDBD,ACCESS=(HISAM,ISAM)
            DATASET   DD1=PRIME,OVFLW=OVERFLOW,DEVICE=3350
  *
            SEGM      NAME=HOSPITAL,PARENT=0,BYTES=80
             FIELD     NAME=(HOSPNAME,SEQ,U),BYTES=20,START=1,TYPE=C
             FIELD     NAME=ADMIN,BYTES=20,START=61,TYPE=C
  *
            SEGM      NAME=WARD,PARENT=HOSPITAL,BYTES=31
             FIELD     NAME=(WARDNO,SEQ,U),BYTES=2,START=1,TYPE=C
             FIELD     NAME=BEDAVAIL,BYTES=3,START=9,TYPE=C
             FIELD     NAME=WARDTYPE,BYTES=20,START=12,TYPE=C
  *
            SEGM      NAME=PATIENT,PARENT=WARD,BYTES=125
             FIELD     NAME=(BEDIDENT,SEQ,U),BYTES=4,START=61,TYPE=C
             FIELD     NAME=PATNAME,BYTES=20,START=1,TYPE=C
             FIELD     NAME=DATEADMT,BYTES=6,START=65,TYPE=C
  *
            SEGM      NAME=SYMPTOM,PARENT=PATIENT,BYTES=77
             FIELD     NAME=(SYMPDATE,SEQ),BYTES=6,START=21,TYPE=C
             FIELD     NAME=DIAGNOSE,BYTES=20,START=1,TYPE=C
  *
            SEGM      NAME=TREATMNT,PARENT=PATIENT,BYTES=113
             FIELD     NAME=(TRDATE,SEQ),BYTES=6,START=21,TYPE=C
             FIELD     NAME=TRTYPE,BYTES=20,START=1,TYPE=C
  *
            SEGM      NAME=DOCTOR,PARENT=PATIENT,BYTES=80
             FIELD     NAME=DOCTNAME,BYTES=20,START=1,TYPE=C
             FIELD     NAME=SPECIALT,BYTES=20,START=61,TYPE=C
  *
            SEGM      NAME=FACILITY,PARENT=HOSPITAL,BYTES=26
             FIELD     NAME=FACTYPE,BYTES=20,START=1,TYPE=C
             FIELD     NAME=FACAVAIL,BYTES=3,START=24,TYPE=C
  *
            DBDGEN
            FINISH
            END
```

Figure 3.11. HOSPITAL data base DBD

DBD Statement. The second statement is the DBD statement. It communicates general information about the physical nature of the data base. In this case, it gives the DBD a name, HOSPDBD, and it tells which of the IMS access methods will be used to manipulate the data. There are several access methods the DBA can choose from, each having its own unique characteristics. IMS access methods are discussed in Chapter 12. Here we are using an IMS access method called *Hierarchical Indexed Sequential Access Method* (HISAM).

DATASET Statement. The DATASET statement gives information about the physical data sets used to implement the data base. A HISAM data base requires two data sets. In the example, the DD names we chose for these two data sets are PRIME and OVERFLW. DD statements with these names must be included in the execution JCL for any programs that access this data base. The DEVICE operand tells IMS what kind of device will be used to store the segments, in this case an IBM 3350 direct access storage device.

Defining the Hierarchical Structure. Following the DBD and DATASET statements are a series of SEGM and FIELD statements. Each SEGM statement names and describes one of the segment types that make up the HOSPITAL data base. Following each SEGM statement are one or more FIELD statements that name and describe sequence fields or search fields chosen for the segment.

SEGM Statements. In each SEGM statement, the NAME operand gives a name to the segment and the PARENT operand identifies its parent. The operand PARENT=0, or the absence of the PARENT operand, identifies the root segment. The PARENT operands define the hierarchical structure of the data base. As an exercise, try to construct a hierarchy chart by using the PARENT operands in the SEGM statements.

The SEGM statements are coded in *hierarchical sequence*. The concept of hierarchical sequence is explained in detail in Chapter 5, where we see how IMS reads sequentially through a data base. For now, notice that when we compare the sequence of the SEGM statements to the HOSPITAL data base hierarchy chart, hierarchical sequence of the segment types is *top to bottom, left to right*.

The only other operand in the SEGM statements is the BYTES operand. It gives the length of the segment in bytes.

FIELD Statements. In FIELD statements, NAME operands contain from one to three positional subparameters. The first subparameter gives a name to the key or search field. If it is the only subparameter coded, the field is a *search field*. If the characters SEQ are coded in the second position, the field is a *key* or *sequence field*. Only one of these is allowed per SEGM statement. If a U is coded in the third position, the field is a *unique* sequence field.

The START operand tells the starting byte location of the key or search field, relative to the beginning of the segment. The BYTES operand gives its length in bytes. TYPE=C says the field consists of character (alphanumeric) data.

Refer again to the DATA DIVISION coding in Figure 3.3. Notice that the names of the segments, key fields, and search fields in the SEGM and FIELD statements correspond to the data names used in the COBOL coding. This is not a requirement, however, since IMS has no knowledge of the data names used in the application program. All communication between the program and IMS is done by means of parameter lists. Using the same names, however, is a useful convention, which can help solve the communication problems that occur when many people are using the same data base or working on the same project.

DBDGEN Control Statements. The last three statements in Figure 3.11 are used for control purposes. The DBDGEN statement signifies the end of the SEGM and FIELD statements for the DBD. The FINISH statement causes the assembler to set a non-zero condition code if errors are caught during the assembly. The END statement signals end-of-data to the assembler. These three statements are normally used at the end of a DBDGEN.

LOGICAL AND APPLICATION DATA STRUCTURES

Individual application programs need not have access to *all* the segments defined in a DBD. We use the term *logical data structure* to define the group of segments that one or more application programs can access. The logical data structure defines a program's *view* of the data base. Suppose a program does nothing but retrieve PATIENT segments. Figure 3.12 shows the portion of the HOSPITAL data base the program is required to know about.

The program retrieves only PATIENT segments, but the hierarchical structure must include the HOSPITAL and WARD segments, because the PATIENT segments are dependent on them. We will use this retrieval program as an example throughout the rest of this chapter and into the first part of the next chapter. Chapter 4 presents the specifications of this program and includes a complete listing of it.

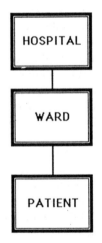

Figure 3.12. Retrieval program logical data structure

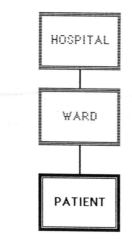

Figure 3.13. Key sensitivity

Figure 3.13 shows another way of representing our retrieval program's view of the data base. The DBA can let a program access the HOSPITAL and WARD segments to locate a dependent PATIENT segment and at the same time prevent the program from accessing the data stored in the HOSPITAL and WARD segments. Now let us see how the DBA defines a program's logical data structure.

Defining a Logical Data Structure

The DBA defines a logical data structure by creating a control block called a *program specification block* or *PSB*. This is done with a process called *PSB generations* (PSBGEN), which is similar to the DBDGEN process.

The PSBGEN Process

PSBGEN statements are processed by the assembler and the linkage editor to store a load module, or PSB, in a library usually called PSBLIB. (See Figure 3.14.) Each PSB consists of one or more control blocks called *Program Communication Blocks* (PCBs). Each PCB within a PSB defines one logical data structure. All the PCBs within a single PSB are collectively known as an *application data structure*.

IMS allows a PSB to define more than one logical data structure because a program is allowed to access to more than one data base. A program is also allowed to concurrently access different parts of the same data base. IMS allows the DBA to define any number of logical data structures in a single PSB.

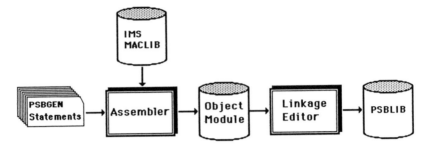

Figure 3.14. The PSBGEN process

```
PCB       TYPE=DB,NAME=HOSPDBD
SENSEG    NAME=HOSPITAL,PARENT=0,PROCOPT=K
SENSEG    NAME=WARD,PARENT=HOSPITAL,PROCOPT=K
SENSEG    NAME=PATIENT,PARENT=WARD,PROCOPT=G
PSBGEN    LANG=COBOL,PSBNAME=PATGET
END
```

Figure 3.15. Retrieval program PSB

PSBGEN for the Retrieval Program

Figure 3.15 shows the PSB coding for our PATIENT segment retrieval program. In this example, the PSB defines an application data structure containing one logical data structure.

PCB Statement. The first statement in the PSBGEN is the PCB statement. It begins the coding for one program communication block, or PCB. It specifies the type of PCB defined, in this case a data base PCB. We will see later that there are other types of PCBs, such as logical terminal PCBs. The PCB statement also gives the name of the DBD that defines the segments named in the PCB. A PSB can only identify segments that have already been defined in the DBD. In the example, the segments are defined in HOSPDBD, the DBD for the HOSPITAL data base.

SENSEG Statements. Following the PCB statement is a series of SENSEG statements. SENSEG statements identify the segments in the HOSPITAL data base that this application is *sensitive* to. The first operand in each SENSEG statement is the NAME operand. The name coded here must be the same as the name coded in the NAME operand in a SEGM statement in a DBD that defines the data base.

The PARENT operands identify the hierarchical structure of the logical data structure. The PARENT operands work in a similar manner to the PARENT parameters in the DBDGEN. One difference is that the hierarchical structure cannot be chosen arbitrarily. The PSB can only specify hierarchical relationships that have already been defined in the associated DBD.

The PROCOPT operands are optional. A PROCOPT parameter specifies *processing options* that define the type of processing that can be performed on a segment. PROCOPT=K means the segment is *key sensitive*. Key sensitive means the application can use the segment to gain access to segments below it in the hierarchy, but the application cannot access the data within the segment. If a sensitive segment is not key sensitive, it is *data sensitive*. PROCOPT=G means the segment is data sensitive and the application can *retrieve* the segment. With PROCOPT=G, the application cannot delete the segment or replace it. We discuss the other possible PROCOPT values in later chapters.

PSBGEN Statement. The PSBGEN statement ends the PSBGEN and is followed by the END assembler control statement. The PSBGEN statement identifies the language in which programs using this PSB must be coded and names the PSB. If more than one data base PCB is defined in a single PSB, there will be two or more PCB statements, each followed by a group of SENSEG statements for the segments making up each logical data structure. All the PCB and SENSEG statements are followed by a single PSBGEN statement.

Field-Level Sensitivity

In the above PSB example, the program is sensitive to all the fields defined in each of the segments named in SENSEG statements. For example, if the application program retrieves a WARD segment occurrence, it will appear in the application program's I/O area just as it is stored in the data base. (See Figure 3.5.) The DBA can alternatively use the *field-level sensitivity* feature to define a PCB that gives the program access only to selected fields in one or more segment types.

Figure 3.16 shows an example of a PCB that specifies field-level sensitivity

```
PCB      TYPE=DB,NAME=HOSPDBD
SENSEG   NAME=HOSPITAL,PARENT=0,PROCOPT=K
SENSEG   NAME=WARD,PARENT=HOSPITAL,PROCOPT=K
    SENFLD   NAME=WARDNO,START=1
    SENFLD   NAME=WARDTYPE,START=3
    SENFLD   NAME=BEDAVAIL,START=23
SENSEG   NAME=PATIENT,PARENT=WARD,PROCOPT=G
PSBGEN   LANG=COBOL,PSBNAME=SAMPFLD
END
```

Figure 3.16. PSB for field-level sensitivity

Figure 3.17. WARD segment sensitive fields

for three fields in the WARD segment. The SENFLD statements following the SENSEG statement name the specific fields from the WARD segment that should be passed to the application program. The START parameters in each SENFLD statement specify where in the I/O area each field should be placed. If the application program retrieves a WARD segment using this PCB, the retrieved WARD information will appear in the program's I/O area as shown in Figure 3.17.

SENFLD statements can be used to create a view of a particular segment that is quite different from the way the segment's data is actually stored in the data base. This is often useful where a segment's physical format must be changed and where existing application programs must continue to be used. The field-level sensitivity feature provides an example of how IMS allows programs to be independent of the physical format of the data it accesses.

The START parameters in SENFLD statements can specify that fields be placed anywhere in the I/O area, even allowing fields to overlap (not generally recommended) and allowing gaps between fields. When gaps are specified, IMS automatically fills the gaps with blanks when moving segment data to the I/O area.

One restriction with field-level sensitivity is that the fields specified in SENFLD statements are limited to those fields that are identified in DBD FIELD statements. For example, in the WARD example above, SENFLD statements cannot be included for the TOT-ROOMS and TOT-BEDS fields. Unless FIELD statements for these fields are added to the DBD, these fields can be made available to the program only by omitting the SENFLD statements and making the program sensitive to the entire WARD segment.

CONTROL BLOCK RELATIONSHIPS

We next use our PATIENT segment retrieval program to see how the DBD, the PSB and PCBs, and the application program work together to access the data in the data base. The DBD and PSB help the program communicate with IMS. We begin our investigation of how application programs communicate with IMS by seeing how our retrieval program gets into execution. Figure 3.18 shows the JCL for a job step to execute the retrieval program.

```
//RETRIEVE  EXEC  PGM=DFSRRC00,PARM='DLI,PATGET'
//STEPLIB   DD    DSN=IMSVS.RESLIB,DISP=SHR
//          DD    DSN=IMSVS.PGMLIB,DISP=SHR
//IMS       DD    DSN=IMSVS.PSBLIB,DISP=SHR
//          DD    DSN=IMSVS.DBDLIB,DISP=SHR
//SYSUDUMP  DD    SYSOUT=A
//PRIME     DD    DSN=IMS.VSAM.PRIME,DISP=OLD
//OVERFLW   DD    DSN=IMS.VSAM.OVERFLOW,DISP=OLD
//INPUT     DD    *
                  ---
            input transactions
                  ---
```

Figure 3.18. Retrieval program JCL

IMS Program Execution

As in any job step, the EXEC statement specifies the name of the program to execute. When we execute an IMS batch program, we specify in the EXEC statement the name of an IMS load module called the *region controller*. A convention, required for data communications programs and optional for batch programs, is that the load module name of the application program should be the same as the PSB's load module name. The PARM parameter of the EXEC statement specifies the name of the PSB, thus implying the load module name of our retrieval program. If a batch application program load module name is different from the PSB name, IMS allows both names to be specified in the PARM parameter.

From the NAME operand in the PCB statement in the PSB, the system locates and loads into memory the appropriate DBD. The DBD defines the DD names of the DD statements that describe the data base.

The PRIME and OVERFLW DD statements describe the data sets that contain the HOSPITAL data base. The INPUT DD statement identifies the input data set; the OUTPUT DD statement defines the output report. The STEPLIB and IMS DD statements define the various system libraries used by IMS. The SYSUDUMP data set defines a data set used to contain a storage dump produced if the program abends.

IMS Programming Conventions

To enable a program to communicate correctly with IMS, we must follow certain programming conventions. An application program is treated as a subroutine of IMS, and standard subroutine linkages and parameter lists hook IMS to application programs. IMS passes control to an application program by issuing an ATTACH macro. In the ATTACH, IMS passes a parameter list containing a list of PCB addresses. Each PCB consists of a series of data items used for communicating with IMS. For example, one of the fields within the PCB is

```
LINKAGE SECTION.
01  PCB-MASK.
    03  DBDNAME              PIC X(8).
    03  LEVEL-NUMBER         PIC XX.
    03  STATUS-CODE          PIC XX.
    03  PROC-OPTIONS         PIC XXXX.
    03  JCB-ADDRESS          PIC XXXX.
    03  SEGMENT-NAME         PIC X(8).
    03  KEY-LENGTH           PIC S(95)    COMP.
    03  NUMBER-SEGS          PIC S(95)    COMP.
    03  KEY-FEEDBACK.
        05  HOSPNAME-KEY     PIC X(20).
        05  WARD-NO-KEY      PIC XX.
        05  BEDIDENT-KEY     PIC XXXX.
        .
        .
        .
PROCEDURE DIVISION.
    ENTRY  'DLITCBL'  USING  PCB-MASK.
        .
        .
        .
```

Figure 3.19. COBOL entry linkage coding

used to determine whether a retrieval was successful. We will examine the PCB fields in detail in Chapter 5.

IMS Entry Linkage. In our PATIENT segment retrieval program, we must establish the proper linkage between the program and the PCBs passed to us by IMS. Figure 3.19 shows the coding, in COBOL, that performs this linkage. The ENTRY statement shown in Figure 3.19 assigns a standard IMS name to the entry point of the program. The entry point of a COBOL IMS program must be DLITCBL. The ENTRY statement also gives the program access to the PCB through the USING clause. The data names in the LINKAGE SECTION describe the data areas in the PCB. These data names make up a data structure called the *PCB mask*. The PCB mask is defined in the LINKAGE SECTION because the PCB itself resides in storage owned by IMS. It does not reside in any of the application program's data areas. As we discussed above, IMS passes the *address* of the PCB in a standard operating system parameter list.

Figure 3.20 shows the relationships that exist between IMS and our PATIENT segment retrieval program. Each programming language has linkage statements that let the programmer accomplish this same function. Appendices F and G include examples of PL/I and Assembler Language entry linkage statements.

Requesting IMS Services. So far, we have seen that the application program as a whole is treated as a subroutine of the IMS region controller. However, *other* IMS modules are treated as subroutines of the application program. Once

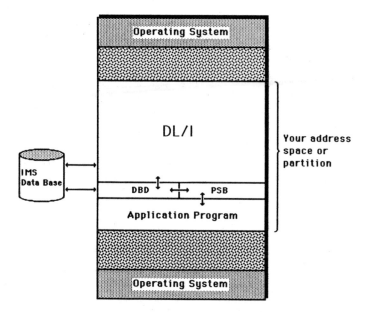

Figure 3.20. DL/I and the application program

the program has received control from IMS, it can request IMS services. Our PATIENT segment retrieval program, for example, asks IMS to retrieve selected segments. These retrievals are requested by making calls to IMS. The parameter list referenced by a IMS call points to information that specifies the type of retrieval we are making. In Chapter 4, we look at IMS CALL statement parameter lists for data base retrievals.

EXERCISES

1. Match each of the terms below with the statement that best describes it. Each term matches one of the statements.

TERMS	STATEMENTS
A. Physical data base	a. Segment the application program is allowed to access.
B. Key field	
C. Application data structure	b. Collection of all segments the application program is allowed to access.
D. DBD	
E. Search field	c. Group of segments and the hierarchical relationships between them as they reside on a physical storage device.

TERMS	STATEMENTS
F. PSB	d. Data item within a segment, known to IMS, on which a set of segments is sequenced.
G. Key sensitive	
H. Logical data structure	e. Segment that can be used only to gain access to segments below it in the hierarchy. The program cannot access the segment's data.
I. Sensitive segment	
J. PCB	f. Control block that describes one logical data structure.
	g. Set of control blocks that describes the program's application data structure.
	h. One set of segments and their hierarchical relationships.
	i. Field on which IMS can search for a segment, but on which segments are not sequenced.
	j. Control block that defines an IMS data base.

2. The listing in Figure 3.21 shows the DBD statements for a physical data base. Answer the following questions about the listing in Figure 3.21:

   a. What are the names and lengths of the segments described in the DBD?
   b. What are the names, lengths, and starting locations of the key fields? Indicate which of the key fields are unique.
   c. What are the names, lengths, and starting locations of the search fields?
   d. What is the name of the DBD?
   e. Sketch a hierarchy chart showing the hierarchical relationships in this physical data base.

```
PRINT    NOGEN
DBD      NAME=PAYROLL,ACCESS=HISAM
DATASET  DD1=KSDS,OVFLW=ESDS,DEVICE=3350
SEGM     NAME=EMPLOYEE,PARENT=0,BYTES=100
FIELD    NAME=(EMPNO,SEQ,U),BYTES=8,START=1,TYPE=C
FIELD    NAME=EMPNAME,BYTES=25,START=30
SEGM     NAME=TASK,PARENT=EMPLOYEE,BYTES=42
FIELD    NAME=(TASKNO,SEQ,U),BYTES=6,START=1,TYPE=C
FIELD    NAME=TASKNAME,BYTES=25,START=7
SEGM     NAME=TIME,PARENT=TASK,BYTES=20
FIELD    NAME=(DATE,SEQ),BYTES=6,START=15,TYPE=C
SEGM     NAME=PERSONNL,PARENT=EMPLOYEE,BYTES=56
DBDGEN
FINISH
END
```

Figure 3.21. Exercise 2 DBD listing

3. The listing in Figure 3.22 shows the PDS statements for an application program. Answer the following questions about the listing in Figure 3.22:

a. What are the names of the segments the application program using this PSB is sensitive to?

b. Sketch a hierarchy chart showing the application data structure represented by this PSB.

c. How many PCBs are in this application data structure?

d. What is the name of this PSB?

e. What is the name of the DBD that defines the segments named in this logical data structure?

f. In which segments can an application program access data using this PSB?

```
PRINT    NOGEN
PCB      TYPE=DB,NAME=PAYROLL
SENSEG   NAME=EMPLOYEE,PARENT=0,PROCOPT=K
SENSEG   NAME=TASK,PARENT=EMPLOYEE,PROCOPT=G
SENSEG   NAME=TIME,PARENT=TASK,PROCOPT=G
PSBGEN   LANG=COBOL,PSBNAME=HOURCALC
END
```

Figure 3.22. Exercise 3 PSB listing

Part II
Data Base
Programming

4
Random Retrieval

This chapter begins by presenting a complete listing of the PATIENT segment retrieval program introduced in Chapter 3. We use this program to point out some differences between an IMS application program and a traditional file-oriented program. We also discuss the basic rules for communicating with IMS when retrieving segments. In addition to presenting the basic rules, we show the format of IMS calls, discuss how to write segment search arguments to qualify IMS calls, and show how to use the Get-Unique call to retrieve randomly. Finally, we present examples of simple status code logic for random retrieval calls.

THE RETRIEVAL PROGRAM

Figure 4.1 is the COBOL listing of the complete retrieval program introduced in Chapter 3. Following the complete listing are discussions of each of the program's parts, with special emphasis on those parts unique to IMS. Those readers who write programs in languages other than COBOL will find Appendices F and G helpful. They contain listings of an equivalent PATIENT segment retrieval program in PL/I and in Assembler Language.

Entry Coding and the PCB

Notice that the entry coding and the PCB mask coding correspond to that discussed in Chapter 3. The entry point name is DLITCBL, and the program expects to be passed a single parameter, the address of the PCB. We are using the PSB from Chapter 3, so the program is key sensitive to the HOSPITAL and WARD segments and data sensitive to the PATIENT segment. Remember, however, the PROCOPT = parameter for the PATIENT segment says the program can only *retrieve* PATIENT segments; it cannot *replace* or *delete* them.

Notice the two COPY statements in the retrieval program; they copy pre-

```
000100 ID DIVISION.
000200 PROGRAM-ID. CHAP4C.
000300 AUTHOR.       JOE LEBEN.
000400 DATE-COMPILED.
000500 REMARKS: THIS IS A SIMPLE LIST PROGRAM.  IT DOES VERY
000600          LITTLE ERROR CHECKING.  IT READS AN INPUT
000700          DATA SET WHOSE RECORDS HAVE THE FOLLOWING FORMAT:
000900
001000          COLUMNS  1 - 20  HOSPITAL NAME
001100                  21 - 22  WARD NUMBER
001200                  23 - 42  PATIENT NAME
001210                  43 - 80  SPACES
001300
001400          FOR EACH RECORD READ, THE PROGRAM ISSUES A DL/I CALL
001500          FOR THE PATIENT SEGMENT IDENTIFIED IN THAT RECORD.
001600          IT THEN PRINTS OUT THAT PATIENT SEGMENT.
001700
001800 ENVIRONMENT DIVISION.
002200 INPUT-OUTPUT SECTION.
002300
002400 FILE-CONTROL.
002500     SELECT  INPUT-FILE   ASSIGN TO UT-S-INPUT.
002600     SELECT  OUTPUT-FILE  ASSIGN TO UT-S-OUTPUT.
002700
002800 DATA DIVISION.
002900 FILE SECTION.
003000
003100 FD  INPUT-FILE
003200     LABEL RECORDS ARE STANDARD
003300     RECORDING MODE IS F
003400     BLOCK CONTAINS 0 RECORDS
003500     DATA RECORD IS INPUT-DATA.
003600
003700 01  INPUT-DATA.
003800     03  HOSPNAME-INPUT     PIC X(20).
003900     03  WARD-NO-INPUT      PIC X(2).
004000     03  PATNAME-INPUT      PIC X(20).
004010     03  FILLER             PIC X(38).
004100
004200 FD  OUTPUT-FILE
004300     LABEL RECORDS ARE STANDARD
004400     RECORDING MODE IS F
004500     BLOCK CONTAINS 0 RECORDS
004600     DATA RECORD IS PRINT-LINE.
004700
004800 01  PRINT-LINE.
004900     03  CARR-CNTRL         PIC X.
005000     03  PRINT-INFO         PIC X(125).
005100     03  FILLER             PIC X(7).
005200
```

Figure 4.1. PATIENT segment retrieval program (page 1 of 3)

defined COBOL coding from a source library. Figure 4.2 shows what is copied in as a result of the COPY statements. IMS does not require the use of COPY statements for segment descriptions or PCB masks, but their use represents good programming practice.

```
005300 WORKING-STORAGE SECTION.
005400
005500 77  TOP-PAGE                  PIC X         VALUE '1'.
005600 77  SINGLE-SPACE              PIC X         VALUE ' '.
005700 77  GET-UNIQUE                PIC X(4)      VALUE 'GU  '.
005800 77  LINE-COUNT                PIC S99       VALUE 50    COMP-3.
005900
006000 01  HOSPITAL-SSA.
006100     03  FILLER       PIC X(19)  VALUE 'HOSPITAL(HOSPNAME ='.
006200     03  HOSPNAME-SSA PIC X(20).
006300     03  FILLER       PIC X.     VALUE ')'.
006400
006500 01  WARD-SSA.
006600     03  FILLER       PIC X(19)  VALUE 'WARD     (WARDNO   ='.
006700     03  WARDNO-SSA   PIC X(2).
006800     03  FILLER       PIC X      VALUE ')'.
006900
007000 01  PATIENT-SSA.
007100     03  FILLER       PIC X(19)  VALUE 'PATIENT (PATNAME  ='.
007200     03  PATNAME-SSA  PIC X(20).
007300     03  FILLER       PIC X      VALUE ')'.
007400
007500 01  I-O-AREA COPY PATIENT.
007600
007700 LINKAGE SECTION.
007710
007800 01  PCB-MASK COPY MASKC.
007900
```

Figure 4.1. PATIENT segment retrieval program (page 2 of 3)

File Description Coding

One of the differences between IMS programs and traditional file-oriented programs is the absence of much of the conventional file description. Our retrieval program has file description coding only for an input file and an output report file. There is no file description coding for the data base, because we do not access the data base with standard data management coding. Access to the data base is made through calls to IMS, rather than with READ statements.

The Input Records

The data description coding shows that each input record supplies the information required to locate a particular occurrence of the PATIENT segment type. Each input record contains the name of the hospital, the number of the ward, and the name of the patient. (We assume for this simple example that no two patients in a given ward and hospital have the same name.)

The WORKING-STORAGE SECTION

Much of the coding in the WORKING-STORAGE SECTION is unique to IMS programs. The coding there defines *function codes* and *Segment Search Argu-*

```
008000 PROCEDURE DIVISION.
008010
008100 ENTRY-LINKAGE.
008200
008300     ENTRY 'DLITCBL' USING PCB-MASK.
008400
008500 PROGRAM-START.
008510
008600     OPEN INPUT   INPUT-FILE.
008700     OPEN OUTPUT  OUTPUT-FILE.
008800
008900 READ-INPUT.
008910
009000     READ INPUT-FILE  AT END GO TO  END-OF-JOB.
009100     MOVE HOSPNAME-INPUT TO HOSPNAME-SSA.
009200     MOVE WARDNO-INPUT   TO WARDNO-SSA.
009300     MOVE PATNAME-INPUT  TO PATNAME-SSA.
009400
009500     CALL  'CBLTDLI'  USING  GET-UNIQUE
009600                             PCB-MASK
009700                             I-O-AREA
009800                             HOSPITAL-SSA
009900                             WARD-SSA
010000                             PATIENT-SSA.
010100
010200     IF  STATUS-CODE  NOT EQUAL  SPACE
010300
010400         MOVE PCB-MASK TO I-O-AREA
010420         PERFORM PRINT-ROUTINE
010500         GO TO READ-INPUT.
010600
010800     PERFORM PRINT-ROUTINE.
010900     GO TO READ-INPUT.
011000
011500 PRINT-ROUTINE.
011510
011600     IF LINE-COUNT = 50
011700
011800         MOVE ZERO TO LINE-COUNT
011900         MOVE '        P A T I E N T  L I S T' TO PRINT-INFO
012000         WRITE PRINT-LINE AFTER POSITIONING TOP-PAGE
012100         MOVE SPACE TO PRINT-LINE
012200         WRITE PRINT-LINE AFTER POSITIONING SINGLE-SPACE.
012300
012400     MOVE I-O-AREA TO PRINT-INFO.
012500     WRITE PRINT-LINE AFTER POSITIONING SINGLE-SPACE.
012600     ADD 1 TO LINE-COUNT.
012700
012800 END-OF-JOB.
012810
012900     CLOSE INPUT-FILE.
013000     CLOSE OUTPUT-FILE.
013100     GOBACK.
```

Figure 4.1. PATIENT segment retrieval program (page 3 of 3)

```
000010 01  HOSPITAL.
000020     03   HOSPNAME          PIC  X(20).
000030     03   HOSP-ADDRESS      PIC  X(30).
000040     03   HOSP-PHONE        PIC  X(10).
000050     03   ADMIN             PIC  X(20).

000010 01  WARD.
000020     03   WARDNO            PIC  XX.
000030     03   TOT-ROOMS         PIC  XXX.
000040     03   TOT-BEDS          PIC  XXX.
000050     03   BEDAVAIL          PIC  XXX.
000060     03   WARDTYPE          PIC  X(20).

000010 01  PATIENT.
000020     03   PATNAME           PIC  X(20).
000030     03   PAT-ADDRESS       PIC  X(30).
000040     03   PAT-PHONE         PIC  X(10).
000050     03   BEDIDENT          PIC  X(4).
000060     03   DATEADMT          PIC  X(6).
000070     03   PREV-STAY-FLAG    PIC  X.
000080     03   PREV-HOSP         PIC  X(20).
000090     03   PREV-DATE         PIC  X(4).
000100     03   PREV-REASON       PIC  X(30).

000010 01  SYMPTOM.
000020     03   DIAGNOSE          PIC  X(20).
000030     03   SYMPDATE          PIC  X(6).
000040     03   PREV-TREAT-FLAG   PIC  X.
000050     03   TREAT-DESC        PIC  X(20).
000060     03   SYMP-DOCTOR       PIC  X(20).
000070     03   SYMP-DOCT-PHONE   PIC  X(10).

000010 01  TREATMNT.
000020     03   TRTYPE            PIC  X(20).
000030     03   TRDATE            PIC  X(6).
000040     03   MEDICATION-TYPE   PIC  X(20).
000050     03   DIET-COMMENT      PIC  X(30).
000060     03   SURGERY-FLAG      PIC  X.
000070     03   SURGERY-DATE      PIC  X(6).
000080     03   SURGERY-COMMENT   PIC  X(30).

000010 01  DOCTOR.
000020     03   DOCTNAME          PIC  X(20).
000030     03   DOCT-ADDRESS      PIC  X(30).
000040     03   DOCT-PHONE        PIC  X(10).
000050     03   SPECIALT          PIC  X(20).

000010 01  FACILITY.
000020     03   FACTYPE           PIC  X(20).
000030     03   TOT-FACIL         PIC  XXX.
000040     03   FACAVAIL          PIC  XXX.
```

Figure 4.2. Segment description COPY statements

ments (SSAs) used for data base segment retrieval. A function code and an SSA list describe to IMS a particular type of segment retrieval.

The PROCEDURE DIVISION

The PROCEDURE DIVISION coding at the beginning of the program is an example of the type of coding IMS programs use to retrieve segments randomly. The program reads an input record, stores the information contained in the record into data areas used as SSAs, and then executes a call to IMS. After the retrieval call, the program checks a field in the PCB to see if the retrieval was successful. After printing a line on the report, it repeats the process and reads another input record. The rest of the PROCEDURE DIVISION is similar to that of a traditional program.

Notice that execution of the program terminates with a GOBACK statement. GOBACK is used instead of STOP RUN because all IMS programs are subroutines of IMS. If an IMS program terminates with a STOP-RUN, it will not properly return control to IMS.

We next see how the call to IMS works, and what the various entries in the parameter list mean.

THE IMS CALL

The CALL statement parameter list and the data items identified in the parameter list make up the DL/I interface language. Standard CALL statements and parameter lists make DL/I language independent, so IMS programs can be written in COBOL, PL/I, or Assembler Language. (Each language has a few individual rules. We discuss COBOL rules here; Appendices F and G discuss Assembler Language and PL/I conventions.)

The Parameter List

The parameter list names data items in the application program that supply information about the call. We will next look at the parameter list and see what each item means. Some sample coding from a COBOL program is shown in Figure 4.3.

Function Code. The first parameter names a four-byte *function code* that describes the type of service we are requesting. In the retrieval program, the function code is Get-Unique (GU). The function code of GU directs IMS to perform a random segment retrieval. Following is a list of available function codes for retrieving and manipulating data base segments.

- GU   —Get-Unique
- GN   —Get-Next
- GNP —Get-Next-Within-Parent
- GHU —Get-Hold-Unique
- GHN —Get-Hold-Next
- GHNP—Get-Hold-Next-Within-Parent
- DLET—Delete
- REPL —Replace
- ISRT —Insert

```
DATA DIVISION.
WORKING-STORAGE SECTION.

01  PATIENT-SEG  COPY  PATIENT.
        .
        .

77  GET-UNIQUE      PIC X(4)    VALUE 'GU '.
        .
        .

01  HOSPITAL-SSA.
    03  FILLER     PIC X(19)  VALUE 'HOSPITAL(HOSPNAME ='.
    03  HOSPNAME   PIC X(20).
    03  FILLER     PIC X      VALUE ')'.

01  WARD-SSA.
    03  FILLER     PIC X(19)  VALUE 'WARD     (WARDNO   ='.
    03  WARDNO     PIC XX.
    03  FILLER     PIC X      VALUE ')'.

01  PATIENT-SSA.
    03  FILLER     PIC X(19)  VALUE 'PATIENT (PATNAME   ='.
    03  PATNAME    PIC X(20).
    03  FILLER     PIC X      VALUE ')'.
        .
        .

LINKAGE SECTION.

01  PCB-MASK       COPY HOSPPCB.

PROCEDURE DIVISION.
        .
        .

    CALL  'CBLTDLI'  USING  GET-UNIQUE
                            PCB-MASK
                            PATIENT-SEG
                            HOSPITAL-SSA
                            WARD-SSA
                            PATIENT-SSA.
```

Figure 4.3. Retrieval program coding

PCB Mask. The second parameter identifies the PCB referenced in the call. The PCB mask parameter is included in the call parameter list as well as in the entry coding, because many IMS programs use more than one PCB. The PCB mask parameter is required even if the program accesses only one PCB.

I/O Area. The third parameter gives the address of the data area into which IMS places the retrieved segment. We know we are going to retrieve a PATIENT segment, so we have coded the name of a data area that describes the PATIENT segment. Some programs retrieve segments of various types using the same retrieval call, in which case an I/O area must be provided that is large enough to contain the largest segment type. After the program has determined which segment has been retrieved, it could move the segment to an area describing it. Another option is to use the REDEFINES clause to separately describe the I/O area for each segment type.

Segment Search Arguments. The first three parameters—the function code, PCB address, and I/O area address—are required with all retrieval calls. We can optionally specify from one to fifteen SSAs to further describe a retrieval. In the retrieval program, we are using three SSAs.

Discussions of IMS calls are easier to follow when we look at SSAs as they appear in memory, rather than in the form of COBOL coding. Figure 4.4 shows the input record just read by the READ statement. Following is what the SSAs look like after the input record in Figure 4.4 is read, and just before the call is executed:

```
GU      HOSPITAL(HOSPNAME = RIVEREDGE             )
^^^^    ^^^^^^^^^^^^^^^^^^^^^^^^^^^^^^^^^^^^^^^^^^^^^

        WARD      (WARDNO   =02)
        ^^^^^^^^^^^^^^^^^^^^^^^^^

        PATIENT (PATNAME  =BROWN                 )
        ^^^^^^^^^^^^^^^^^^^^^^^^^^^^^^^^^^^^^^^^^^^^
```

In showing IMS calls and the SSAs they reference, we generally use the above format. To the left of the sequence of SSAs referenced by the call we will usually put the four-byte function code issued by the call. The small "caret" symbols below each SSA are provided to help point out where blanks must be supplied.

Later in this chapter we discuss the rules for setting up SSAs. But first, we

Figure 4.4. Retrieval program input record

will look at the information in the three above SSAs. The first SSA starts with a segment name, HOSPITAL. Following the segment name is a left parenthesis following by the name of the key field for the HOSPITAL segment. Next is an equal sign followed by the name of a hospital. Notice that the HOSPITAL SSA uniquely identifies a particular occurrence of the HOSPITAL segment.

The second SSA identifies a unique occurrence of the WARD segment under the *Riveredge* HOSPITAL segment, and the third SSA identifies the particular PATIENT segment occurrence to be retrieved. Together the above three SSAs give IMS the information needed to efficiently find the required segment occurrence.

USING SSAS

The SSAs we have been looking at are examples of *fully-qualified* SSAs. They are called fully-qualified because they give complete information about a segment occurrence. We will next look at the specific format of a fully-qualified SSA.

Fully-Qualified SSAs

Figure 4.5 repeats the fully-qualified SSAs for the retrieval program we looked at earlier. The first field in each SSA is eight characters long, and identifies the segment type each SSA describes. If the segment name is less than eight characters in length, the name must be padded to the right with blanks.

The ninth position in the SSA identifies the SSA type. A left parenthesis in the ninth position indicates a qualified SSA; a blank indicates an unqualified SSA. We will look at unqualified SSAs shortly. An asterisk in position 9 tells IMS the SSA includes one or more command codes. Command codes are one-character codes in the SSA that request special options. (We discuss command codes in Chapter 8.)

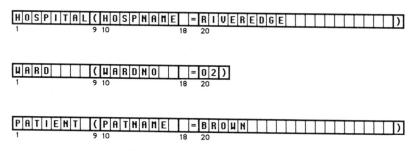

Figure 4.5. Retrieval program SSAs

Following the left parenthesis in each of our sample qualified SSAs is the name of either the key field or one of the search fields defined for that segment type. If the key or search field name is less than eight characters in length, the name must be padded to the right with blanks.

Following the key or search field name, beginning in position 18, is a two-position relational operator. The relational operator tells IMS what kind of comparison to make when it performs the search. Following are the valid relational operators and their meanings.

OPERATOR	MEANING
= or EQ	equal
> or GT	greater than
< or LT	less than
> = or GE	greater than or equal to
< = or LE	less than or equal to
¬= or NE	not equal to

If the relational operator consists of a single character, such as the equal sign, the operator can be coded in either position 18 or position 19. The other position must be blank. For example, the following two SSAs are equivalent:

```
HOSPITAL(HOSPNAME =RIVEREDGE            )
HOSPITAL(HOSPNAME= RIVEREDGE            )
```

Following the relational operator is a field that contains the value against which IMS is to compare when it searches for the segment. For example, each of the above two HOSPITAL SSAs tell IMS to search for a HOSPITAL segment whose HOSPNAME key field contains *Riveredge*. The length of the comparison-value field must correspond to the length of the key or search field in the data base. For example, the key fields in the HOSPITAL and PATIENTS segments are each twenty bytes in length, so the comparison-value fields in the HOSPITAL and PATIENTS SSAs must be twenty positions in length. The key field for the WARD segment is two bytes in length, so the comparison-value field in the WARD SSA must be two positions in length. These lengths can be determined by looking at the segment description coding or in the DBDGEN for the HOSPITAL data base.

Following the comparison-value field is a right parenthesis. It marks the end of the SSA. All qualified SSAs must be coded following this rather rigid format. IMS returns an error code if the correct format is not followed.

```
HOSPITAL
```

Unqualified SSAs

In addition to qualified SSAs, we can also use *unqualified* ones. Following is an unqualified SSA for the HOSPITAL segment:

Notice the ninth position contains a blank, rather than a left parenthesis, identifying the SSA as unqualified. We use unqualified SSAs when we do not want to indicate a particular occurrence of a segment, for example, when we will accept any occurrence of a particular segment type.

Unqualified SSAs are treated differently depending on the function code used. Later in this chapter we discuss the use of unqualified SSAs with Get-Unique calls; in later chapters we discuss the use of unqualified SSAs with other function codes.

Calls without SSAs

We can also issue calls that use no SSAs. Again, the way IMS handles calls without SSAs depends on the function code. We will next take a more detailed look at IMS calls with the GU function code to see how the various combinations of SSA types work with random retrievals. We will use a diagram showing actual segment occurrences within the HOSPITAL data base.

RANDOM RETRIEVALS

Figure 4.6 shows segments from the HOSPITAL data base in an indented form simulating the way in which segments are retrieved sequentially from the data base. The indentations show the hierarchical levels of the segment types. Since our retrieval program is only interested in HOSPITAL, WARD, and PATIENT segments, these are the only segment types shown. In the examples coming up, assume these are the only segments in the data base that our retrieval program can access.

Each box in the diagram represents a segment occurrence. The first line of each box identifies the segment type, and the second line shows the values of key and search fields. To make it easy to read, we have left out all the other information in each segment, and we are showing only the first ten positions of each twenty-position key or search field. We have also numbered each segment in the upper left-hand corner. We will use these numbers to refer to segment occurrences, but the numbers are *not* stored in the data base.

Key and search fields are in the same order as they are coded in the data descriptions for each segment. So, in segment 3, *Moriarty* is the value stored

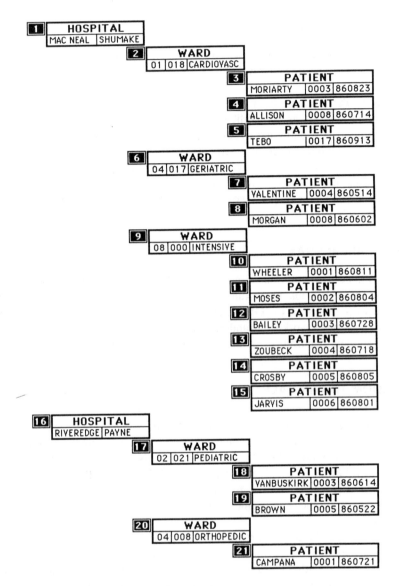

Figure 4.6. HOSPITAL data base segment occurrences

in that PATIENT segment's PATNAME search field, *0003* is the value in the BEDIDENT key field, and *082377* is the value in the DATEADMT search field. Notice the PATIENT segments under each WARD segment are sequenced on the BEDIDENT key field.

SSA Combinations

We will use the segment occurrence chart to show which segments are retrieved from the data base when different combinations of SSAs are used with Get-Unique calls. Suppose, for these examples, that our PSB specifies that we are data sensitive to all three segment types, allowing us to retrieve any of the segments shown in the chart. We begin with examples of fully-qualified SSAs.

Fully-Qualified Calls. We normally use sets of fully-qualified SSAs when we know exactly which segment we want and we have all the information available that IMS needs to find it directly. To fully qualify a call for a particular PATIENT segment occurrence, we must supply a fully-qualified SSA for the PATIENT segment, and one for each level above it. The SSAs must be coded in hierarchical sequence, starting with the one for the root segment. The call in the retrieval program is an example of a fully-qualified call.

In any retrieval call, except in a special case involving SSAs using the D command code, only the segment identified in the last SSA in the list is retrieved. (Chapter 8 discusses command codes.) The other SSAs above the final SSA are used only to supply information that IMS needs to locate a particular segment occurrence.

Suppose we wanted to make a fully-qualified call for a particular WARD segment occurrence. It is at the second level of the hierarchy, so two SSAs are required, as in the following example:

```
GU      HOSPITAL(HOSPNAME =MAC NEAL           )

        WARD     (WARDTYPE =INTENSIVE          )
```

The GU function code used with the above SSAs causes segment 9 to be retrieved from the data base. Notice the second SSA specifies a search field rather than the key field for the WARD segment. Any search field or the key field can be referenced in an SSA.

To make a fully-qualified call for a HOSPITAL segment, we need only one SSA, as in the following example:

```
GU      HOSPITAL(HOSPNAME =RIVEREDGE          )
```

Calls using Unqualified SSAs. An unqualified SSA with the GU function code indicates to IMS that we are interested in the *first occurrence* of that segment type. For example, suppose we issue the following Get-Unique call:

```
GU      HOSPITAL
```

The above call retrieves the first occurrence of the root segment—segment 1, the *Mac Neal* HOSPITAL segment occurrence.

Now suppose we issue the following Get-Unique call:

```
GU      HOSPITAL
^^^^    ^^^^^^^^^^

        WARD
        ^^^^^^^^^^

        PATIENT
        ^^^^^^^^^^
```

The above call retrieves the first occurrence of the PATIENT segment, under the first occurrence of the WARD segment, under the first occurrence of the HOSPITAL segment—segment 3, the *Moriarty* PATIENT segment.

Combinations of Qualified and Unqualified SSAs. In making Get-Unique calls, we can use any combination of qualified and unqualified SSAs. The way IMS handles these depends on the level at which the unqualified SSAs are coded. Suppose we issue the following Get-Unique call:

```
GU      HOSPITAL(HOSPNAME =RIVEREDGE                )
^^^^    ^^^^^^^^^^^^^^^^^^^^^^^^^^^^^^^^^^^^^^^^^^^^^^

        WARD     (WARDNO  =02)
        ^^^^^^^^^^^^^^^^^^^^^^^

        PATIENT
        ^^^^^^^^^^
```

Since there are fully-qualified SSAs at levels one and two, IMS uses the information in those SSAs to locate segment 17. It then retrieves the first occurrence of the PATIENT segment under segment 17—segment 18, the *Vanbuskirk* PATIENT segment.

Now let us suppose we issue the following call:

```
GU      HOSPITAL
^^^^    ^^^^^^^^^^

        WARD
        ^^^^^^^^^^

        PATIENT (PATNAME  =CAMPANA                 )
        ^^^^^^^^^^^^^^^^^^^^^^^^^^^^^^^^^^^^^^^^^^^^^^
```

The two unqualified SSAs in the above example tell IMS to locate segment 2, and search from there. IMS then searches all the way through the data base until it reaches segment 21, the PATIENT segment for *Campana*. Using unqualified SSAs is not the most efficient way to retrieve the *Campana* segment. IMS allows unqualified SSAs, however, and it might be the only way to locate the *Campana* segment if we did not know which hospital and ward Campana is in.

Notice IMS does not limit its search to only those PATIENT segment occurrences under the first occurrence of the WARD segment. Supplying unqualified SSAs at high levels, and qualified SSAs at lower levels simply tells IMS where to begin the search.

Missing Hierarchical Levels. It is possible to make retrieval calls without supplying an SSA for each level in the hierarchy above the segment we are retrieving. For example, suppose we issue the following Get-Unique call:

```
GU      PATIENT (PATNAME  =WHEELER                )
```

The above call retrieves segment 10, the *Wheeler* PATIENT segment. A normal fully-qualified call requires an SSA for each level down to the segment being retrieved. But if any levels are skipped, IMS assumes an unqualified SSA for each skipped level. In other words, issuing the above Get-Unique call has the same effect as issuing the following call:

```
GU      HOSPITAL

        WARD

        PATIENT (PATNAME  =WHEELER                )
```

Calls with No SSAs. We can also issue a Get-Unique call that references no SSAs, in which case IMS assumes an unqualified SSA for the root segment. Therefore, a Get-Unique call with no SSAs always retrieves the first occurrence of the root segment.

Get-Unique Calls. The most common type of Get-Unique call in random retrieval programs is a fully-qualified call that supplies a fully-qualified SSA for each level in the hierarchy down to the segment being retrieved. It is the most efficient way to retrieve a segment randomly. For random retrievals, other combinations of SSAs should normally be used only for special purposes and only when absolutely necessary.

Status Code Logic

Following each retrieval call, we must determine whether the retrieval was successful by examining one of the fields in the PCB. There is a two-position field in the PCB called the *status code field*. The status code field tells us what happened as a result of the call. Only two values are normally of interest when making Get-Unique calls: *blanks* and *GE*. A status code of *blanks* indicates that the retrieval was successful; a status code of *GE* indicates that the segment could not be found.

Suppose we issue the following Get-Unique call:

```
GU      HOSPITAL(HOSPNAME =MAC NEAL                )
∧∧∧∧    ∧∧∧∧∧∧∧∧∧∧∧∧∧∧∧∧∧∧∧∧∧∧∧∧∧∧∧∧∧∧∧∧∧∧∧∧∧∧∧∧∧∧∧∧

        WARD
        ∧∧∧∧∧∧∧∧∧

        PATIENT (PATNAME  =SMITH               )
        ∧∧∧∧∧∧∧∧∧∧∧∧∧∧∧∧∧∧∧∧∧∧∧∧∧∧∧∧∧∧∧∧∧∧∧∧∧∧∧∧∧∧
```

IMS places GE in the status code field, because there is no PATIENT segment occurrence in the data base with the name *Smith*.

The following call also causes IMS to return a status code of GE:

```
GU      HOSPITAL(HOSPNAME =RIVEREDGE           )
∧∧∧∧    ∧∧∧∧∧∧∧∧∧∧∧∧∧∧∧∧∧∧∧∧∧∧∧∧∧∧∧∧∧∧∧∧∧∧∧∧∧∧∧∧∧∧∧∧

        WARD    (WARDNO   =04)
        ∧∧∧∧∧∧∧∧∧∧∧∧∧∧∧∧∧∧∧∧∧∧∧∧∧∧

        PATIENT (PATNAME  =MOSES               )
        ∧∧∧∧∧∧∧∧∧∧∧∧∧∧∧∧∧∧∧∧∧∧∧∧∧∧∧∧∧∧∧∧∧∧∧∧∧∧∧∧∧∧
```

There is a PATIENT segment with the name *Moses* in the data base, but the fully-qualified SSAs for the HOSPITAL and WARD segments caused IMS to look for it under the wrong HOSPITAL and WARD segments.

Other Function Codes

In this chapter, we have been discussing random retrievals. In Chapter 5, we discuss sequential retrievals that use the GN and GNP function codes. We will see that the same combinations of qualified and unqualified SSAs sometimes produce different results with these calls.

VARIABLE-LENGTH SEGMENTS

Variable-length segments save space within the data base for segment types whose occurrences have varying space requirements. In the HOSPITAL data base, some segments have description fields, such as PREV-REASON, DIET-COMMENT, and SURGERY-COMMENT. We have arbitrarily limited description fields to thirty positions. In many segment occurrences, these fields contain blanks; in others, the thirty characters might not be enough to hold the required information. Segment types containing these fields would be likely candidates for variable-length segments in an actual implementation of the HOSPITAL data base.

Variable-Length Segment Format

Figure 4.7 shows what a variable-length segment occurrence looks like in the I/O area. Each segment starts with a two-byte length field. The length field

Figure 4.7. Variable-length segment format

gives the length, in bytes, of the segment, including the two-byte length field. The length is expressed as a binary number.

In retrieving a variable-length segment, the application program uses the first two bytes of the segment in determining how much of the I/O area contains useable information.

EXERCISES

1. Figure 4.8 shows an IMS CALL statement and its parameter list. Below is a list of five statements describing the five indicated parts of the CALL statement. Match each part with the statement that best describes it.

    a. Address of an SSA
    b. Entry point in IMS used by COBOL calls
    c. Address of I/O area
    d. Name of PCB mask in the program
    e. Address of function code

Figure 4.8. CALL statement for Exercise 1.

2. Following are Get-Unique calls and the SSAs they reference. Indicate the segment in Figure 4.6 that would be retrieved, if any, and the status code IMS would return.

    a. GU   PATIENT

    b. GU   HOSPITAL

             WARD

             PATIENT (PATNAME   =WHEELER   )

c. GU   HOSPITAL(HOSPNAME =RIVEREDGE   )
            ^^^

            WARD
            ^^^^^^^^^^

            PATIENT (BEDIDENT =0017)
            ^^^^^^^^^^^^^^^^^^^^^^^^^

d. GU   PATIENT (PATNAME =CAMPANA   )
            ^^

3. Using the same notation for SSAs used in this chapter, show the SSAs required to retrieve the following segments from the data base using Get-Unique calls.

   a. The PATIENT segment for the patient whose name is *Wheeler*. The patient is in an *Intensive* ward in the *Mac Neal* hospital.
   b. A WARD segment for a ward that has more than 100 beds available. You do not care which hospital it is in.
   c. A DOCTOR segment for the doctor whose name is *Rogers*. He is the doctor for the patient whose name is *Bailey*. You do not know which hospital or ward the patient is in.
   d. The FACILITY segment under the *Mac Neal* HOSPITAL segment for the *Cobalt* facility type.

4. What are the meanings of the blank and GE status codes when received after Get-Unique calls?

5
Sequential Retrieval

In this chapter, we discuss two retrieval calls: the *Get-Next* (GN) call and the *Get-Next-Within-Parent* (GNP) call. These calls are used to retrieve a series of segments in sequential order. We show how to use Get-Next and Get-Next-Within-Parent calls with all combinations of SSAs, including no SSAs, unqualified SSAs, and qualified SSAs. We see how IMS handles sequential retrieval with an IMS data base, and discuss the help IMS provides in determining which segment types are retrieved as an application program moves up and down in level within the data base. We then introduce the concept of parentage within the data base, which allows a program to limit the range of retrieval of a series of sequential retrieval calls. Finally, we examine the use of boolean operators in SSAs. This chapter ends with a coding problem that consists of writing a complete IMS application program in COBOL, PL/I, or Assembler Language.

SEQUENTIAL RETRIEVAL CONCEPTS

We begin this chapter by seeing how IMS handles sequential retrievals. We also examine the program logic that is required in writing sequential retrieval programs. In the examples in this chapter, we assume that Figure 5.1 shows all the segments in the HOSPITAL data base that application programs can access.

IMS Processing Sequence

In Chapter 3, we introduced the concept of hierarchical sequence. Hierarchical sequence proceeds first from top to bottom, next from left to right, and finally, from front to back. The numbers in the upper right-hand corners of the boxes in Figure 5.1 show the hierarchical sequence of the segment occurrences in our sample data base.

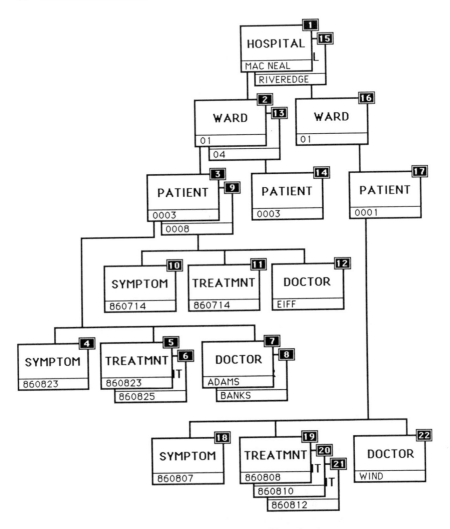

Figure 5.1. HOSPITAL data base hierarchy chart

Reading Sequentially through the Data Base

A common technique for sequentially processing all the segment occurrences
in a data base is to issue a series of Get-Next calls without SSAs. If a program
that reads the HOSPITAL data base repeatedly executes a single Get-Next call
with no SSAs, it will retrieve all the segment occurrences in the sequence shown
in Figure 5.2.

Notice that as we read sequentially through the data base with an unqualified

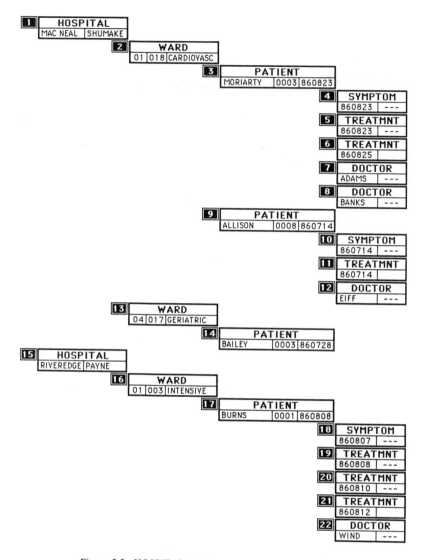

Figure 5.2. HOSPITAL data base segment occurrence chart

sequential retrieval call, we retrieve different segment types at different levels within the data base. The first call retrieves a segment at the first, or root, level, specifically the *Mac Neal* HOSPITAL segment. The next call moves down to the second level, the third call retrieves a segment at the third level, and the fourth call gets a segment at the fourth level. The fifth, sixth, seventh, and eighth calls stay at the fourth level, but retrieve different segment types. Finally, the ninth call moves back up from the fourth to the third level.

Notice that it is possible to move up more than one level in one retrieval call. After we retrieve segment twelve, the last DOCTOR segment stored under the *0008* PATIENT segment, we jump up to segment 13, the *04* WARD segment, thus moving from level 4 to level 2 in a single call.

Sequential Retrieval Logic

When a program uses unqualified calls to sequentially retrieve segments of more than one type, the program must have logic that allows it to determine which segment type is retrieved after each call execution. In this chapter, we describe the fields in the PCB that can be used in implementing program logic that helps in navigating through the data base when using unqualified calls.

GET-NEXT RETRIEVAL CALLS

The concept of *position within the data base* is important when issuing sequential retrieval calls. The results of each new sequential retrieval call is dependent on the position within the data base established by the previous call. A common way of establishing an *initial* position in the data base is to issue a Get-Unique call for a particular segment. After a Get-Unique call is issued, IMS remembers the position of that segment, and any sequential retrieval that follows is made relative to that location in the data base. In a retrieval program, a new position is established after each Get-Unique, Get-Next, and Get-Next-Within-Parent call. We will next see how sequential retrievals are handled with Get-Next calls using no SSAs.

Get-Next Calls without SSAs

The Get-Next call with no SSAs implements a simple form of sequential retrieval. Figure 5.3 shows the COBOL coding for a Get-Next call with no SSAs.

The Get-Next call without SSAs is an unqualified call, which provides no information as to which particular segment should be retrieved. When a program issues a Get-Next call with no SSAs, IMS retrieves the next segment in hierarchical sequence, relative to current position in the data base.

If the program's first call is a Get-Next call without SSAs, IMS retrieves the first segment in the data base, which is always the first occurrence of the root segment. Issuing a Get-Next call without SSAs as the first call gives the

```
77  FUNCTION-CODE      PIC X(4)  VALUE 'GN  '.
       .
       .

    CALL  'CBLTDLI'  USING  FUNCTION-CODE
                           PCB-MASK
                           I-O-AREA.
```

Figure 5.3. Get-Next with no SSAs

same result as issuing a Get-Unique call without SSAs; each is a common method of establishing a position on the first segment in the data base.

Get-Next Calls with Unqualified SSAs

Get-Next calls *without* SSAs allow a program to sequentially retrieve segment occurrences of all types. By using Get-Next calls with *unqualified* SSAs we can restrict retrieval to only occurrences of a particular segment type. The following call provides an example:

```
GN      PATIENT
```

If a program issues the above call at the beginning of the program's execution, IMS retrieves the first PATIENT segment—segment 3 in Figure 5.2, the PATIENT segment whose bed identifier is *0003*. The next time the program issues the call, IMS scans through the data base until it finds the next occurrence of the PATIENT segment—in this case segment 9, the PATIENT segment for patient *0008* in ward *01* under the *Mac Neal* HOSPITAL segment.

IMS then scans ahead to segment 14, the PATIENT segment for patient *0003* in ward *04* under the *Mac Neal* HOSPITAL segment. Segment 17 is retrieved next. Finally, the next execution of the call returns a status code of GE, indicating that there are no more PATIENT segments.

Get-Next calls with unqualified SSAs are useful for retrieving, in hierarchical sequence, occurrences of a particular segment type. Notice, however, that using Get-Next calls with only an unqualified SSA for the PATIENT segment does not restrict the retrieval of PATIENT segment occurrences to those for patients in a particular hospital. With a sequence of Get-Next calls with an unqualified SSA, IMS retrieves all the PATIENT segments, no matter what segments they are dependent on.

Get-Next Calls with Qualified SSAs

On first glance, the use of a Get-Next call with qualified SSAs does not seem to lend itself to sequential retrieval. For example, look at the following call:

```
GN      HOSPITAL(HOSPNAME =RIVEREDGE              )
~~~~    ~~~~~~~~~~~~~~~~~~~~~~~~~~~~~~~~~~~~~~~~~~~~~

        WARD    (WARDNO   =01)
        ~~~~~~~~~~~~~~~~~~~~~~~~

        PATIENT (BEDIDENT =0001)
        ~~~~~~~~~~~~~~~~~~~~~~~~~
```

In the above call, we are asking IMS to retrieve a particular occurrence of the PATIENT segment. If we look at the above call out of context, it produces the same result as an equivalent Get-Unique call. The main reason for using a Get-Next call instead of a Get-Unique call is to perform *skip-sequential processing*.

Skip-Sequential Processing

When a program performs skip-sequential processing, it processes *selected* segment occurrences in hierarchical sequence. For example, a program might retrieve only PATIENT segments for patients in certain beds, in a particular ward, and in a particular hospital. If we know the key values for the PATIENT segments that we want, and can present them to the program in key sequence, we might use coding similar to that shown in Figure 5.4. The program executes a processing loop that reads a key value from an input file, stores the key value into an SSA, and issues a Get-Next call using that SSA.

The program logic for the above call sequence is similar to the program logic for executing a series of Get-Unique calls. The only difference between the two is that when issuing a sequence of Get-Next calls, the program must present the key values to IMS in key sequence. If the program attempts to back up in the data base when issuing Get-Next calls, by presenting a key value that is lower than the one used in the previous call, IMS returns a status code of GE, as if the segment did not exist. When executing Get-Unique calls, IMS backs up in the data base if necessary and locates the requested segment.

```
01  PATIENT-SSA.
        03  FILLER          PIC X(19)   VALUE 'PATIENT (BEDIDENT ='.
        03  BEDIDENT-SSA    PIC X(4).
    03  FILLER      PIC X       VALUE ')'.
    .
    .

    MOVE INPUT-BEDIDENT TO BEDIDENT-SSA.
    CALL 'CBLTDLI' USING  FUNCTION-CODE
                          PCB-MASK
                          I-O-AREA
                          HOSPITAL-SSA
                          WARD-SSA
                          PATIENT-SSA.
```

Figure 5.4. Skip-Sequential processing with Get-Next

A reason for using a sequence of Get-Next calls instead of a sequence of Get-Unique calls is that a series of Get-Next calls is generally more efficient. When executing a sequence of Get-Next calls, IMS uses current position in performing the search for each new segment. When executing a sequence of Get-Unique calls, IMS normally goes back to the beginning of the data base before performing each search.

Using Search Fields

Skip-sequential processing can normally only be performed using the key field of a segment, not other search fields. As an example to illustrate the reason for this, suppose a program reads a series of patient names from an input file. If we sort the input file by patient name, we will not be able to use a sequence of Get-Next calls to retrieve segments in patient name sequence. Suppose the program begins by issuing the following call:

```
GN      HOSPITAL(HOSPNAME =MAC NEAL          )
^^^^    ^^^^^^^^^^^^^^^^^^^^^^^^^^^^^^^^^^^^^^^^^^
        WARD    (WARDNO   =01)
        ^^^^^^^^^^^^^^^^^^^^^^^^
        PATIENT (PATNAME  =ALLISON           )
        ^^^^^^^^^^^^^^^^^^^^^^^^^^^^^^^^^^^^^^^^^^
```

IMS begins by retrieving segment 9 in the data base. Notice, in Figure 5.2, that segment 9 has a bed identifier of *0008*. Suppose the program next issues the following Get-Next call:

```
GN      HOSPITAL(HOSPNAME =MAC NEAL          )
^^^^    ^^^^^^^^^^^^^^^^^^^^^^^^^^^^^^^^^^^^^^^^^^
        WARD    (WARDNO   =01)
        ^^^^^^^^^^^^^^^^^^^^^^^^
        PATIENT (PATNAME  =MORIARTY          )
        ^^^^^^^^^^^^^^^^^^^^^^^^^^^^^^^^^^^^^^^^^^
```

On first glance, the above call appears to be valid, because we are presenting search field values to IMS in alphabetical sequence. However, notice in Figure 5.2 that the bed identifier for the *Moriarty* PATIENT segment is *0003*. The above call, in effect, asks IMS to back up in the data base. Since this is not allowed with Get-Next calls, IMS returns a status code of GE, and it appears to the program as if the *Moriarty* segment does not exist. Skip-sequential processing requires the program to process segment in *key* sequence, and not necessarily in sequence according to some other search field.

Status Codes with Get-Next Calls

When the program issues Get-Next calls with qualified SSAs, IMS returns similar status codes to those for Get-Unique calls. The two most common status codes are blanks, for a successful retrieval call, and GE, for a segment-not-found condition.

When using Get-Next calls without SSAs, there are three more status codes that the program might need to test for:

- GA — Moved up in level
- GK — New segment type encountered at same level
- GB — End of data base encountered

In scanning through the data base sequentially, a program normally tests for the GB status code to find out when the end of the data base has been reached. If the program issues another call after the GB status code has been returned, IMS goes back to the beginning of the data base.

When a program issues unqualified Get-Next calls, it can test for the GA and GK status codes to help determine which segment type has been retrieved. Figure 5.5 shows how a program can use the GA and GK status codes with a series of Get-Next calls with no SSAs. It shows the status codes that IMS issues after each Get-Next call execution for the segment occurrences in Figure 5.2.

Segment Number	Segment Level	Segment Type	Status Code
1	1	HOSPITAL	blanks
2	2	WARD	blanks
3	3	PATIENT	blanks
4	4	SYMPTOM	blanks
5	4	TREATMNT	GK
6	4	TREATMNT	blanks
7	4	DOCTOR	GK
8	4	DOCTOR	blanks
9	3	PATIENT	GA
10	4	SYMPTOM	blanks
11	4	TREATMNT	GK
12	4	DOCTOR	GK
13	2	WARD	GA
14	3	PATIENT	blanks
15	1	HOSPITAL	GA
16	2	WARD	blanks
17	3	PATIENT	blanks
18	4	SYMPTOM	blanks
19	4	TREATMNT	GK
20	4	TREATMNT	blanks
21	4	TREATMNT	blanks
22	4	DOCTOR	GK
--	-	-------	GB

Figure 5.5. Reading sequentially through the data base

Notice that each successive Get-Next call that retrieves a segment of the same type, or retrieves a segment lower in the hierarchy than the previous one, returns a status code of blanks. When a call retrieves a segment at a higher level, IMS returns a status code of GA. If the call retrieves a segment of a different type, but at the same level, IMS returns a status code of GK. The program can use these status codes to help navigate in the data base when issuing a series of unqualified Get-Next calls.

The GA and GK status codes do not always provide the information needed to determine the segment type that has been retrieved. For example, there is no status code that tells when the program has moved *down* in level. And when we receive the GA status code, we do not know *how many* levels up we have moved since the previous call. Later in this chapter, we will look at some of the other fields in the PCB and see how they can be used when positive segment-type identification is required.

GET-NEXT-WITHIN-PARENT CALLS

The Get-Next-Within-Parent (GNP) function code, works in a similar manner to Get-Next; it is used to perform sequential retrieval within the data base. However, Get-Next-Within-Parent calls can be used to limit sequential retrieval to a particular range of segment occurrences within the data base. To understand how Get-Next-Within-Parent works, we must discuss the concept of *parentage*.

Setting Parentage

Whenever a Get-Next or Get-Unique call is issued, IMS not only establishes a *position* on some segment occurrence, it also establishes *parentage* on that occurrence. This means that the segment retrieved by the Get-Next or Get-Unique call is treated as the parent segment for any Get-Next-Within-Parent calls that follow. Get-Next-Within-Parent calls only retrieve segments that are dependent on the segment on which parentage is currently established. This allows the program to limit the area of search within the data base. We will next look at examples of Get-Next-Within-Parent calls to see how parentage works.

GNP Calls Without SSAS

A Get-Next-Within-Parent call with no SSAs is similar to a Get-Next call with no SSAs. The difference is in the range of segments that sequences of the two types of call have access to. A series of Get-Next calls without SSAs reads segments from current position to the end of the data base. A series of Get-Next-Within-Parent calls using no SSAs reads only those segments that are dependent on the segment on which parentage is currently established. Let us use the segments in Figure 5.2 to see how this works.

Suppose that a program issues a Get-Unique call for the *Mac Neal* HOSPITAL segment. This establishes parentage on segment 1. If the program then issues a series of Get-Next-Within-Parent calls without SSAs, the first one retrieves segment 2, the first WARD segment. If we continue issuing Get-Next-Within-Parent calls without SSAs, the calls scan through the data base and retrieve, in hierarchical sequence, all the segments that are dependent on the *Mac Neal* HOSPITAL segment. The last segment that the Get-Next-Within-Parent call retrieves is segment 14. If the program issues another Get-Next-Within-Parent call with no SSAs, IMS returns a status code of GE. In this case the GE status code means that there are no more segments dependent on the current parent segment.

The lower in level that parentage is established, the fewer segments an unqualified Get-Next-Within-Parent call has access to. For example, let us suppose a program issues the following Get-Unique call:

```
GN      HOSPITAL(HOSPNAME =MAC NEAL             )

        WARD    (WARDNO   =01)

        PATIENT (BEDIDENT =0003)
```

The above call establishes parentage on segment 3, the PATIENT segment for patient *0003*. If we followed the above call with a series of Get-Next-Within-Parent calls without SSAs, those calls would retrieve only segments 4,5,6,7, and 8. Once the program retrieves segment 8, the next Get-Next-Within-Parent call returns a status code of GE, indicating that there are no more segments dependent on segment 3.

Get-Next-Within-Parent Using SSAs

We can use unqualified and qualified SSAs with the GNP function code in the same manner as for Get-Next calls. Unqualified SSAs cause the Get-Next-Within-Parent call to sequentially retrieve only segments of a particular segment type. We can also use qualified SSAs with GNP to fully qualify calls when performing skip-sequential processing.

Skip-sequential processing can often be simplified with GNP calls. Skip-sequential processing with Get-Next requires SSAs at all levels in the hierarchy. With GNP, we can first establish parentage on a particular segment occurrence and then perform a series of Get-Next-Within-Parent calls using an SSA for a particular segment type. An example will make this more clear. Suppose we would like to retrieve a set of PATIENT segments that are dependent on ward

01. We can do this by issuing a series of Get-Next calls that has the following format:

```
GN      HOSPITAL(HOSPNAME =RIVEREDGE              )
^^^^    ^^^^^^^^^^^^^^^^^^^^^^^^^^^^^^^^^^^^^^^^^^^^

        WARD    (WARDNO  =01)
        ^^^^^^^^^^^^^^^^^^^^^^^^

        PATIENT (BEDIDENT =    )
        ^^^^^^^^^^^^^^^^^^^^^^^^^^
```

Notice that in the above example we have to use qualified SSAs for all segments above the segment we are retrieving in order to appropriately limit the search. We could obtain the same result by first issuing a Get-Unique call for ward *01*, as shown in the following example:

```
GU      HOSPITAL(HOSPNAME =MAC NEAL              )
^^^^    ^^^^^^^^^^^^^^^^^^^^^^^^^^^^^^^^^^^^^^^^^^^^

        WARD    (WARDNO  =01)
        ^^^^^^^^^^^^^^^^^^^^^^^^
```

The above call establishes parentage at ward *01*. We could next issue a series of GNP calls with a single SSA for the PATIENT segment:

```
GNP     PATIENT (BEDIDENT =    )
^^^^    ^^^^^^^^^^^^^^^^^^^^^^^^^^
```

By using the GNP function code instead of GN we automatically limit the area of search to only those segments dependent on ward *01*. A Get-Next call with that single SSA causes IMS to read through all the PATIENT segments in the data base, rather than stopping at the end of the ward *01* segments.

EXAMINING FIELDS IN THE PCB

Up to this point the only field in the PCB that we have examined is the status code field. In performing sequential retrievals, it is often necessary to examine other PCB fields to determine which segment type the program has retrieved. A number of fields in the PCB provide information about the results of retrieval calls.

PCB Linkage

Remember that the PCB is a control block that is loaded into memory by IMS before the application program is executed. The data names in the PCB mask refer to fields in the PCB itself. This is done in COBOL by defining PCB fields in the LINKAGE SECTION of the program. Similar techniques are used in Assembler Language and PL/I programs. (See Appendices F and G.)

Figure 5.6 shows an example of the COBOL coding that establishes the

.
.

```
LINKAGE SECTION.
01  PCB-MASK.
    03  DBDNAME              PIC X(8).
    03  LEVEL-NUMBER         PIC XX.
    03  STATUS-CODE          PIC XX.
    03  PROC-OPTIONS         PIC XXXX.
    03  JCB-ADDRESS          PIC XXXX.
    03  SEGMENT-NAME         PIC X(8).
    03  KEY-LENGTH           PIC S(95)  COMP.
    03  NUMBER-SEGS          PIC S(95)  COMP.
    03  KEY-FEEDBACK.
        05  HOSPNAME-KEY     PIC X(20).
        05  WARD-NO-KEY      PIC XX.
        05  BEDIDENT-KEY     PIC XXXX.
        .
        .

PROCEDURE DIVISION.
    ENTRY  'DLITCBL'  USING  PCB-MASK.
    .
    .
```

Figure 5.6. COBOL entry linkage coding

linkage between the application program and IMS. The name of the PCB mask appears in the ENTRY statement of the program as well as in the LINKAGE SECTION. All the data names in the PCB mask below the 01 level name refer to the actual data areas of the PCB. We will next see how each PCB field is used.

PCB Fields

The first field in the PCB is an eight-position field that contains the name of the DBD referenced by this PCB.

The next field contains a two-position, right-justified, decimal number, which indicates the level of the segment that has just been retrieved. With the HOSPITAL data base, this field contains 1 after a HOSPITAL segment is retrieved, 2 after a WARD or FACILITY segment is retrieved, 3 after a PATIENT segment is retrieved, and 4 after a SYMPTOM, TREATMENT, or DOCTOR segment is retrieved.

The next field in the PCB is the status code field. We have already discussed its use.

The next field is four positions in length and contains the processing options coded in the PCB statement. The codes in this field can be used by a general-purpose program in determining what types of calls are valid.

Next is a four-position field that is described in much of the IBM documentation as "reserved for DL/I." This field is actually a four-byte virtual-storage address field that points to an internal operating system control block called the *Job Control Block* (JCB). The JCB is useful in debugging, and its use is described in Appendix B.

The next field is eight positions long and contains the eight-position name of the segment just retrieved.

Key-Feedback Area. The next three fields describe the keys of all the segments retrieved by the previous call. The key-length field is a fullword binary number that gives the length, in bytes, of the *concatenated key*. The concatenated key area contains the key values of all the segments along the retrieval path strung together one after the other. The number-of-segments field is another fullword binary number that gives the number of key fields that are stored in the concatenated key area. Some examples will illustrate how a program can use the key-feedback fields.

Let us see what these last three PCB fields would look like after some segments have been retrieved. Following is a Get-Next call to retrieve a PATIENT segment:

```
GN       HOSPITAL(HOSPNAME =RIVEREDGE           )
         ^^^^^^^^^^^^^^^^^^^^^^^^^^^^^^^^^^^^^^^^^^^^
         WARD    (WARDNO   =01)
         ^^^^^^^^^^^^^^^^^^^^^^^^^
         PATIENT (PATNAME  =BURNS               )
         ^^^^^^^^^^^^^^^^^^^^^^^^^^^^^^^^^^^^^^^^^^^^
```

Notice that we are searching for the PATIENT segment on one of the search fields, the PATNAME field. Figure 5.7 shows what the key-length, number-of-segments, and key-feedback fields look like after this segment is retrieved. (As we said earlier, the key-length and number-of-segments fields are actually each fullword binary numbers, but we are showing them in decimal for clarity.)

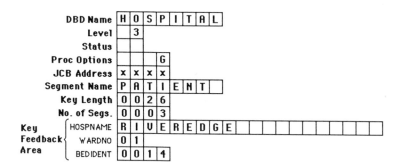

Figure 5.7. PCB after successful PATIENT retrieval

The key-length field says that the key feedback area contains twenty-six bytes: the key field for the HOSPITAL segment is twenty bytes in length, the key field for the WARD segment is two bytes in length, and the key field for the PATIENT segment is four bytes in length. The number-of-segments field says that there are three concatenated keys in the key feedback area, and the key feedback area contains the key values for the three segments along the retrieval path.

Notice that the concatenated key area contains the key field of the PATIENT segment, even though it was retrieved using a search field. If a segment along the retrieval path has no key field, that level of the hierarchy is skipped in the concatenated key. For example, the DOCTOR segment in the HOSPITAL data base contains no key field, only two search fields are defined. If we retrieve a DOCTOR segment using one of those search fields, the concatenated key area contains the key fields for the HOSPITAL, WARD, and PATIENT segments, but does not contain the search field value for the DOCTOR segment.

Describing the Concatenated-Key Area. The concatenated-key area is the only variable portion of the PCB. The rest of the fields are fixed in format. Data descriptions for the concatenated-key area can be coded from the information contained in the PCB and DBD coding. The SENSEG statements in the PCB and the FIELD statements for key fields in the DBD provide the information needed to describe the concatenated key for each retrieval path the program is expected to handle. The concatenated key coding in Figure 5.6 shows that the concatenated key data areas correspond to the hierarchical structure of the segments the program has access to.

PCB Fields for Unsuccessful Calls

The fields in the PCB are useful even after unsuccessful retrieval calls. Suppose a program issues the following Get-Unique call:

```
GN      HOSPITAL(HOSPNAME =MAC NEAL              )

        WARD    (WARDNO   =04)

        PATIENT (PATNAME  =BAILEY                )
```

If IMS returns a status code of GE as a result of the above call, indicating that the segment was not found, the program might need to know whether it is only the PATIENT segment that is missing, or whether the WARD segment or even the HOSPITAL segment could not be found. To provide that information, IMS stores information in the PCB that corresponds to the highest level in the data base at which the search *was* satisfied.

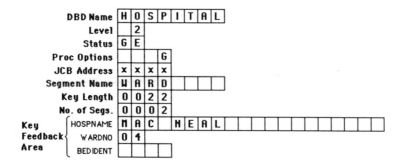

Figure 5.8. PCB for missing PATIENT segment

For example, suppose there is a *Mac Neal* HOSPITAL segment, there is a WARD segment, but that the PATIENT segment for *Bailey* is not in that ward. Figure 5.8 shows what the PCB fields would look like after the above call. Notice that the status code field contains GE, indicating that the segment was not found, but other parts of the PCB look as if the program attempted to retrieve the ward *01* segment. The PCB information indicates that the WARD segment level is the highest level at which the call was satisfied.

Figure 5.9 shows what the PCB fields look like if the WARD segment cannot be found.

Using the PCB Fields

The PCB normally provides more than enough information to determine the results of any call. Under normal circumstances, the program should make use of as little of the information as possible. This is to make the program as independent as possible of the physical structure of the data base. The more PCB

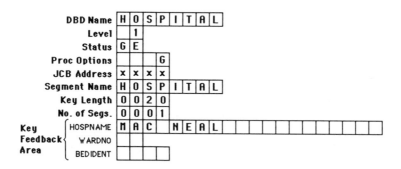

Figure 5.9. PCB for missing WARD segment

information a program uses, the more likely it is that the program will require modification if the physical structure of the data base changes.

BOOLEAN OPERATORS IN SSAS

It is sometimes necessary to perform a search for a segment based on more than one field in a segment. A good example of this would be retrieving a TREATMNT segment from the HOSPITAL data base. The key field is treatment date and another search field within the segment is treatment type. There may be many TREATMNT segments with the same treatment date and at the same time there might be many TREATMNT segments with the same treatment type given on different dates.

Suppose a program needs to search for a TREATMNT segment whose treatment type is *morphine* and whose treatment date is *080387*. The program could issue the following Get-Unique call:

```
GN     TREATMNT(TRTYPE   =MORPHINE          &TRDATE   =080387)
```

Notice that the SSA specifies two qualification statements connected by a *boolean operator*.

In this case the boolean operator is an ampersand, which specifies a logical AND operation. The SSA causes IMS to retrieve a TREATMNT segment whose treatment type is *morphine* and whose treatment date is *080377*.

Boolean Operators

Following is a list of the boolean operators that can be used in coding boolean qualification statements:

- * or &   — AND
- + or | — OR
- #   — Independent-AND

Either the asterisk (*) or the ampersand (&) can be used to indicate a logical AND; either the plus (+) sign or the vertical bar (|) can be used to indicate a logical OR. The independent-AND operator, indicated by the pound sign (#), is described in Chapter 13, where we discuss the secondary indexing feature of IMS/VS.

Complex Boolean Statements

We will next see how IMS evaluates a more complex group of qualification statements, as in the following example:

```
GU      SEGMENT (A      =1*B        =2+C        =3*D        =4)
^^^^    ^^^^^^^^^^^^^^^^^^^^^^^^^^^^^^^^^^^^^^^^^^^^^^^^^^^^^^^^
```

Any group of qualification statements connected by AND operators is called a *set* of qualification statements. In order for the entire expression to be satisfied, any one set of qualification statements needs to be satisfied. In order for a set to be satisfied, all the qualification statements within that set must be satisfied. For example, in the above example, the qualification statements would be considered satisfied if either field A equals 1 AND field B equals 2, OR field C equals 3 AND field D equals 4. The normal logic rules of AND and OR apply in boolean SSA statements.

CODING PROBLEM

Following are the specifications for an IMS application program. Code a complete program to satisfy the specifications using COBOL, PL/I, or Assembler Language.

The Previous Hospital Stay Inquiry Program

The purpose of the program is to retrieve segments from the HOSPITAL data base and print out lists of those patients in a particular hospital who are presently in wards whose WARDTYPE SEARCH field equals *quarantine*, and who have had a previous hospital stay within one year of their present admittance date. The results are provided in the form of Previous Stay reports.

Program Input. The program reads an input file whose records have the following format:

Columns 1–2	Constant—OR
Columns 3–22	Left-justified hospital name
Columns 23-80	Blanks

The records can be presented in any sequence. Each record contains the name of a hospital for which the Previous Stay report should be prepared.

Program Output. The program should print a separate report for each input record. The report is called the Previous Stay report. The Previous Stay report should print out the hospital's name, address, and phone number at the top of the report. Following the hospital information, the report should print header information for each *quarantine* ward in the hospital, listing the information in each *quarantine* WARD segment.

```
                    P R E V I O U S   S T A Y   R E P O R T
PAGE    1

HOSPITAL NAME            HOSPITAL ADDRESS                 HOSP PHONE

MAC NEAL                 1234 MAIN STREET, CHICAGO IL     3125554376

WARD NO    TOT ROOMS     TOT BEDS     BEDS AVAIL     WARD TYPE

  01          34           112          018          QUARANTINE

PATIENT NAME          BED    ADMIT DATE  PREV DATE  PREVIOUS HOSPITAL    PREVIOUS REASON

O'HARA               0050    062377      1176       MAC NEAL             BUBONIC PLAGUE
OZIER                0051    052177      1176       ST JOSEPH            BUBONIC PLAGUE
PARELLA              0056    052777      1076       MAC NEAL             BUBONIC PLAGUE
WRIGHT               0057    052677      1176       MAC NEAL             BUBONIC PLAGUE
YANCEY               0058    052977      0976       RIVEREDGE            BUBONIC PLAGUE
ERIN                 0059    051277      1176       MAC NEAL             BUBONIC PLAGUE
KAPP                 0060    061777      1076       MAC NEAL             BUBONIC PLAGUE
CLAPPER              0070    071877      1176       MAC NEAL             BUBONIC PLAGUE
LEBEN                0071    080177      1076       ST JOSEPH            BUBONIC PLAGUE
CAROL                0072    080177      1176       MAC NEAL             BUBONIC PLAGUE
JOE                  0074    071777      1076       RIVEREDGE            BUBONIC PLAGUE
KATIE                0077    080177      1176       MAC NEAL             BUBONIC PLAGUE
PAT                  0078    072677      1076       ST JOSEPH            BUBONIC PLAGUE
LANOU                0079    072677      1076       MAC NEAL             BUBONIC PLAGUE
ELLGLASS             0080    072277      1176       MAC NEAL             BUBONIC PLAGUE
CARLSON              0082    072177      1176       MAC NEAL             BUBONIC PLAGUE
BUHL                 0090    072477      1076       MAC NEAL             BUBONIC PLAGUE
```

Figure 5.10. Sample page of Previous Stay report

Following each set of ward header information should be a single line for each patient in the ward that had a previous hospital stay in the last year. Each line should contain a patient's name, bed identifier, date admitted, name of the hospital at which the patient previously stayed, the date of the previous stay, and the reason for the previous stay.

Figure 5.10 shows a sample page from this report. Print a single page with a line such as the following line if a HOSPITAL segment is not found.

```
HOSPITAL MAC NEAL            NOT FOUND
```

Follow the hospital header information with the following line if the hospital does not have any quarantine wards:

```
NO QUARANTINE WARDS
```

Follow the ward header information with the following line if there are no patients in that ward with a previous stay in the last year:

```
NO PATIENTS WITH PREVIOUS STAY
```

HOSPITAL Data Base Information

Figure 5.11 shows the coding for the PSB that the program uses. Notice that the program is sensitive only to HOSPITAL, WARD, and PATIENT segments.

```
         PRINT   NOGEN
         PCB     TYPE=DB,DBNAME=HOSPDBD,PROCOPT=G,KEYLEN=26
    *
         SENSEG  NAME=HOSPITAL,PARENT=0
         SENSEG  NAME=WARD,PARENT=HOSPITAL
         SENSEG  NAME=PATIENT,PARENT=WARD
    *
         PSBGEN  LANG=COBOL,PSBNAME=CHAP5C
         END
```

Figure 5.11. Chapter 5 coding problem PSB

Figure 5.11 shows the COBOL coding for the three segments the program is sensitive to. Assume that this coding, or PL/I or Assembler Language versions, is stored in a source statement library. The PREV-STAY-FLAG in the PATIENT segment contains "0" if the patient has had no previous hospital stay, and "1" if the patient has had a previous hospital stay.

Appendix D summarizes in one place all the information about the HOSPITAL data base needed for the coding problems in this book.

6
Loading and Inserting Segments

In this chapter we examine the Insert (ISRT) function code. Insert calls are used both to load a data base from scratch and to insert segments into an existing data base. Insert calls are used in a similar manner for both purposes, but the program logic and SSAs are somewhat different. We look at both uses of the Insert call in this chapter and examine a complete load program for the HOS-PITAL data base. We also see how IMS processes Insert calls and examine alternatives for load and insert status code logic.

THE INSERT CALL

We begin this chapter by examining a call statement and SSA for inserting a segment occurrence into the HOSPITAL data base. Figure 6.1 shows the COBOL coding for inserting a new PATIENT segment. Notice that only a single SSA is specified—an unqualified SSA for the PATIENT segment. The rest of the entries in the parameter list are the same as those for any other call. When the program issues this call, the I/O area must contain an image of the PATIENT segment occurrence that is to be inserted into the data base.

The call sequence in Figure 6.1 can be used for both loading a new data base or for inserting a segment into an existing data base. Notice, however, that the single unqualified SSA does not give IMS any information as to where in the data base to insert this particular PATIENT segment. As with other IMS calls, unless the call is fully qualified, IMS uses current position in determining where to insert or load the segment.

```
77  FUNCTION      PIC X(4)  VALUE 'ISRT'.
77  SSA-AREA      PIC X(9)  VALUE 'PATIENT '.
        .
        .

    CALL  'CBLTDLI'  USING  FUNCTION
                            PCB-MASK
                            IOAREA
                            SSA-AREA.
```

Figure 6.1. An Insert call

Using Qualified SSAs with Insert Calls

When loading a data base or inserting a segment into an existing data base, the program can include qualified SSAs for all higher levels, as in the following example:

```
ISRT    HOSPITAL(HOSPNAME =MAC NEAL              )
^^^^    ^^^^^^^^^^^^^^^^^^^^^^^^^^^^^^^^^^^^^^^^^^^^^

        WARD    (WARDNO   =04)
        ^^^^^^^^^^^^^^^^^^^^^^^

        PATIENT
        ^^^^^^^^^^
```

Notice that we have included qualified SSAs for both the HOSPITAL and WARD segments but the PATIENT segment is referenced with an unqualified SSA. A segment being loaded or inserted must always be identified with an unqualified SSA. IMS extracts further identification for that segment from the I/O area; it is not valid to code a qualification statement in the final SSA, the one that describes the segment being loaded.

A program designed to load a data base normally uses Insert calls that reference a single unqualified SSA. The reason for this will become more clear when we examine a load program. Programs designed to insert segments into an existing data base generally use sets of qualified SSAs to completely describe the paths along which new segments are to be inserted. This ensures that segments are not inserted in the wrong place.

Insert Call Processing Options

IMS knows whether the program is going to load a data base from scratch or insert segments into an existing data base from the processing options specified in the PCB. Following is a list of the processing options that apply for Insert calls:

- L —Load mode
- LS—Load mode, ascending sequence
- A —Get, Insert, Delete, Replace
- AS—Get, Insert, Delete, Replace, ascending sequence
- I —Insert mode
- IS —Insert mode, ascending sequence

PROCOPT=L allows the program to issue Insert calls in the load mode to load a data base from scratch. PROCOPT=LS allows the program to issue Insert calls in the load mode, and indicates that segments must be loaded in ascending sequence. PROCOPT=A allows the program to issue Get, Insert, Replace, and Delete calls. PROCOPT=AS allows the program to issue Get, Insert, Replace and Delete calls, and indicates that new segments must be inserted in ascending sequence. With A and AS, Insert calls can only be used to insert segments into an existing data base. PROCOPT=I indicates that only Insert calls in the insert mode can be issued. And PROCOPT=IS indicates that only Insert calls in the insert mode are allowed, and that segments must be inserted in ascending sequence.

A load program must reference a PCB that has an L coded in the PROCOPT parameter; a program that inserts segments into an existing data base must reference a PCB that has a PROCOPT of A or I.

DATA BASE LOADING

A load program is generally more straightforward than a program written to process Insert calls in the insert mode, so we will next examine a load program. Figure 6.2 shows a complete program to load the HOSPITAL data base. We will use this program to illustrate a few key concepts about using Insert calls in the load mode.

Notice that there is a single Insert call in the sample load program. It is used to insert segments of all types. Segment images are read from an input data set, and the program determines what type of segment is being loaded. It then moves the proper unqualified SSA to the SSA area referred to by the CALL statement parameter list. The Insert call is issued, and some simple status code logic is executed. This process continues until the input data set is completely processed.

Data Base Loading Options

For most applications, segment images must be presented to the load program in *hierarchical sequence*. In other words, root segments usually must be pre-

```
000100 ID DIVISION.
000200 PROGRAM-ID.  CHAP6C.
000300 AUTHOR.  JOE LEBEN.
000400 DATE-COMPILED.
000500 REMARKS:  LOADING THE HOSPITAL DATA BASE.  CAUTION:  THIS PROGRAM
000600           ASSUMES THE INPUT DATA SET CONTAINS SEGMENT IMAGES
000700           IN HIERARCHICAL SEQUENCE.  EACH SEGMENT IMAGE IS
000800           CONTAINED IN TWO 80-BYTE RECORDS.  RECORD FORMAT IS:
000900
001000           COLUMNS  1 -  8  SEGMENT NAME
001010                    9       BLANK
001100                   10 - 72  FIRST OR SECOND HALF OF SEGMENT
001200                   73 - 80  SEQUENCE NUMBER
001300
001800 ENVIRONMENT DIVISION.
002200 INPUT-OUTPUT SECTION.
002400 FILE-CONTROL.
002500     SELECT  INPUT-FILE    ASSIGN TO UT-S-INPUT.
002600     SELECT  OUTPUT-FILE   ASSIGN TO UT-S-OUTPUT.
002700
002800 DATA DIVISION.
002900 FILE SECTION.
003000
003100 FD  INPUT-FILE    LABEL RECORDS ARE STANDARD
003300                   RECORDING MODE IS F
003400                   BLOCK CONTAINS 0 RECORDS
003500                   DATA RECORD IS SEGMENT-INFO.
003700 01  SEGMENT-INFO.
003800     03  SEG-NAME     PIC X(8).
003900     03  FILLER       PIC X.
004000     03  INPUT-DATA   PIC X(63).
004010     03  FILLER       PIC X(8).
004100
004200 FD  OUTPUT-FILE    LABEL RECORDS ARE STANDARD
004400                    RECORDING MODE IS F
004500                    BLOCK CONTAINS 0 RECORDS
004600                    DATA RECORD IS PRINT-LINE.
004800 01  PRINT-LINE.
004900     03  CARR-CNTRL      PIC X.
005000     03  PRINT-INFO      PIC X(80).
005100     03  FILLER          PIC X(52).
005200
005300 WORKING-STORAGE SECTION.
005400
005500 77  INSERT-FUNCTION       PIC X(4)      VALUE 'ISRT'.
005800 77  LINE-COUNT            PIC S99       VALUE 50    COMP-3.
005900
006000 01  UNQUAL-SSA.
006200     03  SSA-SEG-NAME  PIC X(8).
006300     03  FILLER        PIC X.      VALUE SPACE.
006400
006500 01  I-O-AREA.
006600     03  FIRST-HALF    PIC X(63).
006700     03  SECOND-HALF   PIC X(63).
006800
007700 LINKAGE SECTION.
007710
007800 01  PCB-MASK COPY MASKC.
```

Figure 6.2. HOSPITAL data base load program (page 1 of 2)

```
007900
008000 PROCEDURE DIVISION.
008010
008100 ENTRY-LINKAGE.
008200
008300     ENTRY  'DLITCBL'  USING  PCB-MASK.
008400
008500 PROGRAM-START.
008510
008600     OPEN INPUT   INPUT-FILE.
008700     OPEN OUTPUT  OUTPUT-FILE.
008800
008900 READ-INPUT.
008910
009000     READ INPUT-FILE  AT END GO TO  END-OF-JOB.
009100     MOVE INPUT-DATA TO FIRST-HALF.
009200     PERFORM PRINT-ROUTINE.
009300     READ INPUT-FILE  AT END GO TO  END-OF-JOB.
009400     MOVE INPUT-DATA TO SECOND-HALF.
009500     PERFORM PRINT-ROUTINE.
009600     MOVE SEG-NAME TO SSA-SEG-NAME.
009700
009800 LOAD-ROUTINE.
009810
009900     CALL  'CBLTDLI'  USING  INSERT-FUNCTION
010000                             PCB-MASK
010100                             I-O-AREA
010200                             UNQUAL-SSA.
010300
010400     IF STATUS CODE IS NOT EQUAL TO ' '
010420
010440         DISPLAY 'BAD STATUS -- ' STATUS-CODE
010460         GO TO END-OF-JOB.
010480
010500     GO TO READ-INPUT.
010600
010800 PRINT-ROUTINE.
011510
011600     IF LINE-COUNT = 50
011700
011800         MOVE ZERO TO LINE-COUNT
011900         MOVE SPACE TO PRINT-LINE
012000         WRITE PRINT-LINE AFTER ADVANCING 1 LINES.
012010
012100     MOVE SEGMENT-INFO TO PRINT-INFO.
012200     WRITE PRINT-LINE AFTER ADVANCING 1 LINES.
012300
012800 END-OF-JOB.
012810
012900     CLOSE INPUT-FILE.
013000     CLOSE OUTPUT-FILE.
013100     GOBACK.
```

Figure 6.2. HOSPITAL data base load program (page 2 of 2)

sented to the load program in root key sequence and all dependent segments are loaded in hierarchical sequence following each root.

When an Insert call in the insert mode is being used to insert segments into an existing data base, segments can normally be inserted in any sequence. Since it is sometimes difficult to sort segments into hierarchical sequence, a two-step load process is sometimes performed. An initial load program, using Insert calls in the load mode, processes all of the root segments and some of the dependent segments under each root, thus loading a skeleton data base. Following the initial load, a program using Insert calls in the insert mode is used to insert the remaining segments into the data base.

A program designed to load all of the segments in one pass will run faster than the two programs required with the two-step approach. So if it is possible to sort the segments into hierarchical sequence, the one-pass approach is usually best.

When using the two-step approach to data base loading, it is desirable to reorganize the data base immediately after the initial load. As we discuss in Chapter 12 on IMS access methods, inserting a large volume of segments into an existing data base can alter the physical structure of the data base so that access to segments becomes inefficient. Reorganizing the data base immediately after the load eliminates these inefficiencies.

SSAs for Load-Mode Insert Calls

Figure 6.3 shows the CALL statement and SSA area used in the sample load program. Notice that the SSA area for this program consists of one nine-byte data item. The appropriate unqualified SSA is moved into this area before each segment is inserted. As we stated earlier, it is not valid to qualify this SSA; IMS gets qualification information from the I/O area, which contains an image of the segment being inserted. Since segments are normally loaded in hierarchical sequence, IMS never has to stray from current position in loading each subsequent segment. For most load programs, additional SSAs that further qualify the Insert calls are not necessary.

It is valid, however, to include qualified SSAs to completely describe the path along which each segment is to be loaded. The only restriction here is that no qualification statement can be included in the final SSA—the one for the

```
01  UNQUAL-SSA.
    03  SEGNAME          PIC X(8).
    03  FILLER           PIC X     VALUE SPACE.
        .
        .

    CALL 'CBLTDLI' USING  INSERTION
                          PCB-MASK
                          I-O-AREA
                          UNQUAL-SSA.
```

Figure 6.3. Call and SSA for data base load

segment being loaded. And of course, no SSAs can be included at levels *below* the segment being loaded.

When high-level qualified SSAs are used in an Insert call, those SSAs function in the same manner as they do in a Get-Unique call—they cause IMS to locate the hierarchical path along which the segment is to be loaded. However, in a program designed to load segments in hierarchical sequence, high-level SSAs that describe a path other than the one pointed to by current position normally causes the call to be unsuccessful.

Load-mode Status Codes

The following four status codes are of particular interest to programs that issue ISRT calls in the load mode.

- LB—Segment already exists
- LC—Key values out of sequence
- LD—No parent for segment being loaded
- LE—Segment types out of sequence

There are many more status codes that IMS can return as a result of an Insert call in the load mode; however, most of them result from programming errors, and programs do not usually test for them. The *Application Programming Reference Manual* contains descriptions of all status codes.

IMS returns the LB status code when the program tries to load the same segment twice. The LC status code indicates that the segments being loaded are not in hierarchical sequence. The LD status code also indicates that something is wrong with the sequence of the segment images in the input data set. A dependent segment cannot be loaded until its parent has been loaded. The LE status code indicates that segment types are not being presented to the program in the right sequence.

Inserting Segments into an Existing Data Base

An Insert call to insert a segment into an existing data base looks essentially the same as the Insert call used to load a data base. Figure 6.4 shows the Insert call and SSA that could be used to insert a PATIENT segment into the data base. Notice that this call is identical to the one seen earlier for loading PATIENT segments.

Using Qualified SSAs for Segment Insertion

In general, when inserting a segment into an existing data base, it is necessary to describe to IMS exactly where each segment should be inserted. When seg-

```
77   FUNCTION      PIC X(4)  VALUE 'ISRT'.
77   SSA-AREA      PIC X(9)  VALUE 'PATIENT '.
       .
       .

     CALL  'CBLTDLI'  USING  FUNCTION
                             PCB-MASK
                             IOAREA
                             SSA-AREA.
```

Figure 6.4. Insert-mode Insert call

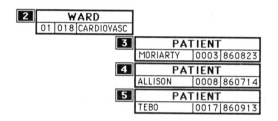

Figure 6.5. PATIENT segments before Insert

ments are loaded in hierarchical sequence, each new segment is loaded relative to current position. When segments are being inserted into an existing data base, unless a retrieval call has been made that correctly establishes current position, the Insert call must supply qualified SSAs that describe the path along which the insertion is to be made.

Figure 6.5 shows the segments in a portion of the HOSPITAL data base. Suppose we are adding a PATIENT segment for a patient in ward *01* in the *Mac Neal* hospital. Following is a call that inserts the new PATIENT segment occurrence in the proper place:

```
ISRT   HOSPITAL(HOSPNAME =MAC NEAL            )
^^^^   ^^^^^^^^^^^^^^^^^^^^^^^^^^^^^^^^^^^^^^^^^

       WARD    (WARDNO   =01)
       ^^^^^^^^^^^^^^^^^^^^^^^

       PATIENT
       ^^^^^^^^^
```

The partial contents of the I/O area for the above call are as follows:

```
FREDERICKS              ... 0011 ... 101177
^^^^^^^^^^^^^^^^^^^^^^^      ^^^^     ^^^^^^
```

After the above Insert call is executed, the PATIENT segments dependent on the ward *01* segment look like those shown in Figure 6.6.

Since the PATIENT segment has a unique key field, IMS uses the key of the new PATIENT segment to determine where in the twin chain to insert the

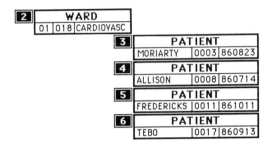

Figure 6.6. PATIENT segments after Insert

new segment. IMS maintains twin chains in key sequence wherever a key field has been specified for a segment type.

Notice that the SSAs in the above call completely describe the path along which to insert the new PATIENT segment. Another way to handle the insertion is to perform a retrieval call to establish a position within the data base. For example, the following Get-Unique call retrieves the ward *01* segment and establishes a position within the data base at that point.

```
GU    HOSPITAL(HOSPNAME =MAC NEAL               )

      WARD    (WARDNO   =01)
```

We could then follow the above Get-Unique call with an Insert call referring to a single unqualified SSA for the PATIENT segment, as follows:

```
ISRT   PATIENT
```

The above two-call sequence accomplishes the same insertion. The program must either establish the proper position within the data base before issuing the Insert call, or it must fully qualify the Insert call to describe the path along which the insertion is to be made.

DBD Insert Rules

When the DBA defines a segment type that does not have a key field, or has a non-unique key field, the SEGM statement must contain information that tells IMS where to insert new occurrences of that segment type. The RULES parameter of the SEGM statement is used for this purpose. The following is a possible SEGM statement for the DOCTOR segment:

```
SEGM  NAME=DOCTOR,PARENT=PATIENT,BYTES=20,RULES=(,HERE)
```

The three available options for coding the second subparameter of the RULES operand are FIRST, LAST, and HERE. This subparameter, called the *insert rule*, tells IMS where in the twin chain to insert a new segment when a segment does not have a unique key field. The insert rule FIRST indicates that new segments are inserted at the beginning of the twin chain. The insert rule LAST indicates that new segments are inserted at the end of the twin chain. LAST is the default if no RULES operand is coded. The insert rule HERE indicates that current position is used to determine where in the twin chain new segments are inserted. A new segment is inserted immediately *before* the segment on which current position is established.

Segments with No Key Field. Figure 6.7 shows a portion of the data base containing DOCTOR segments. Since the DOCTOR segment has two search fields, but no key field, the insert rule helps to determine where new DOCTOR segments are inserted. Suppose a program issues the following Insert call: ·

```
ISRT    HOSPITAL(HOSPNAME =MAC NEAL              )
~~~~    ~~~~~~~~~~~~~~~~~~~~~~~~~~~~~~~~~~~~~~~~~~~~~~

        WARD    (WARDNO   =01)
        ~~~~~~~~~~~~~~~~~~~~~~~~~

        PATIENT (BEDIDENT =0003)
        ~~~~~~~~~~~~~~~~~~~~~~~~~~

        DOCTOR
        ~~~~~~~~~~
```

The SSAs in the above call establish position on the appropriate PATIENT segment occurrence. The insert rule then tells IMS where in the DOCTOR segment twin chain to place the new segment. The insert rules of FIRST or LAST clearly tell IMS where to place the new segment. If the insert rule is HERE and the program issued the above call, the new segment is placed at the beginning of the twin chain. This is because we have not yet established a position within the DOCTOR segments. With the insert rule HERE, a new segment is placed at the beginning of the twin chain if no position has been established within that twin chain.

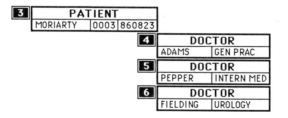

Figure 6.7. Some DOCTOR segments

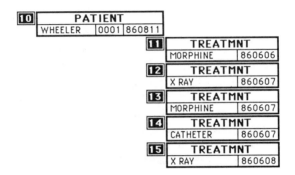

Figure 6.8. Some TREATMNT segments

Segments with Non-Unique Key Fields. An insert rule may also be specified for a segment that has a non-unique key field. In this case IMS can use the key field to find the approximate position within the twin chain to insert the segment. The insert rule is then used to determine where to put the new segment relative to all the segments having the same key field value. For example, Figure 6.8 shows a TREATMNT segment twin chain. If we insert a new TREATMNT segment with the key value *060776* into the data base, IMS uses the insert rule to determine where to insert the new segment relative to the other TREATMNT segments having the same key value.

The insert rule FIRST tells IMS to insert the segments at the beginning of all of those segments having the same key value. The insert rule LAST tells IMS to put the new segment after all of those segments having the same key value. And the insert rule HERE indicates that new segments will be inserted into the twin chain relative to current position. If the program has not established position on a segment having the appropriate key field value, IMS inserts the new segment at the beginning of the set of segments having the same key value.

Insert-Mode Status Codes

Following are the two status codes that are common to Insert calls in the insert mode:

- II —Segment already exists
- IX—Insert rule violation

The II status code is self-explanatory. It is never valid to insert a segment that already exists in the data base. IMS returns the IX status code if the program tries to insert a segment into the wrong place in the data base. Suppose the program issues the following Insert call:

```
ISRT    HOSPITAL(HOSPNAME =MAC NEAL              )
^^^^    ^^^^^^^^^^^^^^^^^^^^^^^^^^^^^^^^^^^^^^^^^^^
        FACILITY(FACTYPE  =PUMP-OXYGENATOR    )
        ^^^^^^^^^^^^^^^^^^^^^^^^^^^^^^^^^^^^^^^^^^
        PATIENT
        ^^^^^^^^^^
```

IMS returns an IX status code as a result of the above call, because the PATIENT segment is dependent on the WARD segment, not the FACILITY segment.

Loading and Inserting Variable-Length Segments

With variable-length segments, the length field that is part of the segment must be properly formatted in the I/O area before a new segment is inserted. For example, if the program inserts a segment, either into an existing data base or when loading a new data base, it must calculate the length of the new segment and insert the proper value into the first two bytes of the I/O area before issuing the Insert call.

In working with the segment length field, the program must have access to the maximum and minimum values specified in the SEGM statement for the segment in the DBD. The following is an example of a SEGM statement for a variable-length TREATMNT segment:

```
SEGM  NAME=TREATMNT,PARENT=PATIENT,BYTES=(160,90)
```

The first subparameter of BYTES indicates the maximum size of the TREATMNT segment, including the two-byte length field; the second subparameter of BYTES indicates the minimum size. The length field that the program places in a new segment occurrence must be between these two values for an Insert call to be valid.

EXERCISES

1. Match each processing option below with the statement that best describes it.

OPTIONS	STATEMENTS
A. L	a. Insert segments in the load mode.
B. LS	b. Get, replace, delete, and insert segments in the insert mode, in hierarchical sequence only.
C. A	
D. AS	c. Insert segments in the insert mode in hierarchical sequence only.

10	PATIENT		
	WHEELER	0001	860811

11	TREATMNT	
	MORPHINE	860606

12	TREATMNT	
	X RAY	860607

13	TREATMNT	
	MORPHINE	860607

14	TREATMNT	
	CATHETER	860607

15	TREATMNT	
	X RAY	860608

16	DOCTOR	
	GIRGIS	SURGERY

17	DOCTOR	
	BAAB	RADIOLOGY

18	DOCTOR	
	CUSICK	UROLOGY

Figure 6.9. Segments for Exercise 4

OPTIONS	STATEMENTS
E. I	d. Insert segments in the load mode in hierarchical sequence only.
F. IS	
	e. Get, replace, delete, and insert segments in the insert mode.
	f. Insert segments in the insert mode.

2. Write the function code and SSAs to load a PATIENT segment in a new data base. Assume that position is established correctly and that the PATIENT segment is already in the I/O area.

3. Write the function code and SSAs needed to insert a DOCTOR segment into an existing HOSPITAL data base. Insert the new DOCTOR segment under the *Valentine* PATIENT segment, under ward *04*, and under the *Mac Neal* HOSPITAL segment. Assume that position is not established and that the new DOCTOR segment is already in the I/O area.

4. Figure 6.9 shows the segments that are stored in a portion of the hospital data base. Current position within the data base is described by referencing the numbers in the upper left hand corner of each segment. Following are two Insert calls, with the key and search search field values that are stored in the I/O area for each call:

```
a.   ISRT   TREATMNT
     ^^^^   ^^^^^^^^^

            BRAIN SCAN          ... 060776
            ^^^^^^^^^^^^^^^^^^^^    ^^^^^^
```

b.   ISRT   DOCTOR
     ～～～   ～～～～～～～～～

           MELLIN   ... NEUROLOGIST
           ～～～～～～～～～～～～～～～～～～ ～～～～～～～～～～～～～～～～～～

For each of the above calls, indicate after which existing segment in the data base each new segment would be inserted. Assume that before each call, current position is established on segment 10. If a segment insertion depends on the insert rule in the DBD, indicate after which existing segment the new segment would be inserted for each of the three insert rules: FIRST, LAST, and HERE.

7
Deleting and Updating Segments

In this chapter we discuss the rules for using Get-Hold, Delete, and Replace calls updating the data base. We see that in order to delete or replace a segment, a sequence of two calls is used. The *Get-Hold* function code is used to retrieve a segment to be deleted or replaced. The Get-Hold retrieval call is then followed by either a Delete or Replace call. In addition to discussing the above calls, we examine PCBs and status code logic to support them. At the conclusion of this chapter is a coding problem for a data base update program.

GET-HOLD CALLS

Following are the function codes for the three Get-Hold retrieval calls that can be issued in preparation for replacing or deleting a segment occurrence:

- GHU —Get-Hold-Unique
- GHN —Get-Hold-Next
- GHNP—Get-Hold-Next-Within-Parent

The above function codes perform similar functions as the three retrieval calls we have already examined. The Get-Hold-Unique call corresponds to the Get-Unique call, the Get-Hold-Next call corresponds to the Get-Next call, and the Get-Hold-Next-Within-Parent call corresponds to the Get-Next-Within-Parent call. Everything that we have discussed concerning the Get-Unique, Get-Next, and Get-Next-Within-Parent function codes also applies to the three Get-Hold calls. The Get-Hold calls cause IMS to perform additional functions as well. When a program issues a Get-Hold call, IMS saves information about the segment's location so the segment can later be deleted or replaced. Get-Hold calls also cause IMS to write information on the *system log data sets* that are used to restore the data base should recovery ever be necessary.

The same types of SSAs are used with Get-Hold calls as are used with non-hold Get calls. The status codes that IMS returns are also identical. Again, the only difference between Get-Hold calls and Get calls is that with Get-Hold calls the program is allowed to follow the call with a Delete or Replace call. Following a non-hold Get call with a Delete or Replace is not allowed.

DELETE AND REPLACE RULES

Following are the function codes for the Delete and Replace calls:

- DLET—Delete function code
- REPL—Replace function code

There are four general rules that concern both deleting and replacing segments. We will discuss these rules before examining Delete and Replace calls in detail.

Get-Hold Call Requirement

We have already introduced the first rule above. Before issuing a Delete or Replace call, the program must first issue a Get-Hold call to retrieve the desired segment. The Get-Hold call brings the segment occurrence into the I/O area and causes IMS to save information about that segment. The program can then examine the segment image in the I/O area and decide whether the segment occurrence should be deleted or replaced. To delete the segment, the program issues a call with the DLET function code. The retrieved segment is then deleted from the data base. To replace the segment, the program makes any desired modifications to the segment image in the I/O area and then issues a call with the REPL function code. IMS then causes the segment image in the I/O area to be written back into the data base, thus replacing the original segment occurrence.

No Intervening Calls

The second general rule specifies that between the time that the program issues the Get-Hold call and the time that it issues the Delete or Replace call, no other calls are allowed that reference the same PCB. If the program issues a call other than a Delete or Replace, that call nullifies the effect of the Get-Hold call, and the program is then not allowed to issue a Delete or Replace call until another Get-Hold call is issued.

No SSAs

The third rule states that the program does not normally include SSAs when issuing a call with the DLET or REPL function code. The only exception to this rule is a Delete or Replace call following a Get-Hold that specifies one or more SSAs using the D command code. The D command code causes more than one segment to be brought into the I/O area with a single call. We introduce the D command code later in this chapter, and we discuss it in detail in Chapter 8, the chapter on command codes.

No Key Field Modification

The fourth rule concerns modifying the key field. As we stated earlier, the program can perform any desired processing (except for issuing IMS calls using the same PCB) between the time it issues the Get-Hold call, and the time it issues the Delete or Replace call. However, the program is not allowed to modify the key field of the segment image in the I/O area. The Delete or Replace call fails if the program modifies the key field.

DELETE CALLS

As we introduced earlier, deleting segments is a two-step process. The program first retrieves the segment to be deleted. This can be done with any sequence of retrieval calls; however, the last retrieval call—the one that is used to actually retrieve the segment to be deleted—must be of the Get-Hold variety. The following is a call sequence that deletes a PATIENT segment from the data base:

```
GHU    HOSPITAL(HOSPNAME =MAC NEAL            )

       WARD    (WARDNO   =01)

       PATIENT (BEDIDENT =0008)


DLET
```

Notice that in above example, we know exactly which PATIENT segment we want to delete, so we simply issue a single Get-Hold-Unique call to bring that segment into the I/O area. We then issue a call using the DLET function code. Notice that the Delete call does not include an SSA.

If, after the program issues the Get-Hold-Unique call, the program determines that the segment should not be deleted, the program can perform any desired processing, including issuing other calls. Issuing a Get-Hold retrieval call does not require the program to issue a Delete or Replace call.

Delete Calls with SSAs

As we will see later in Chapter 8 on command codes, a retrieval call can include D command codes in the SSAs for a retrieval call. A call that references SSAs with D command codes is called a *path call* and causes more than one segment to be brought into the I/O area. When a path call is followed by a Delete call, the program is allowed to reference a single SSA that includes the N command code. This SSA tells IMS which segment to delete. If no SSA is referenced by a Delete call that follows a path call, the last segment in the I/O area is deleted.

Automatic Deletion of Dependent Segments

When a program issues a Delete call for a segment that has other segments dependent on it, *all of its dependent segments* are automatically deleted along with it.

Figure 7.1 shows the segments stored in the HOSPITAL data base. If we retrieve the ward number *08* segment from the data base with a Get-Hold call and follow that with a Delete call, we delete not only that WARD segment but also segments 10 through 15. Those are all of the PATIENT segments dependent on the ward number *08* segment.

Deleting root segments from the data base can cause a great many dependent segments to be automatically deleted. Suppose we retrieve the *Mac Neal* HOSPITAL segment with a Get-Hold call, and follow that call with a Delete. That call deletes the *Mac Neal* HOSPITAL segment and all of the segment occurrences dependent on it, thus deleting segments 1 through 15. We have deleted three quarters of the data base with a single Delete call.

REPLACE CALLS

As with Delete calls, the first requirement when replacing a segment is to issue a Get-Hold call for it. Again, the program can use any desired call sequence to retrieve the segment to be replaced; however, the final call—the one that actually brings the segment to be replaced into the I/O area—must be a Get-Hold call. Once the segment is in the I/O area, the program can make any desired changes other than modifying the key field. The following is a call sequence to replace a WARD segment:

```
GHU     HOSPITAL(HOSPNAME =MAC NEAL                )
~~~~    ~~~~~~~~~~~~~~~~~~~~~~~~~~~~~~~~~~~~~~~~~~~~~~~~~~~
        WARD    (WARDNO   =04)
        ~~~~~~~~~~~~~~~~~~~~~~~~~~~~~

REPL
~~~~
```

After retrieving the desired WARD segment with the Get-Hold call and making the desired changes to the segment image in the I/O area, the program then issues a call using the REPL function code. No SSAs are normally referenced by a Replace call. The Replace call causes the segment image in the I/O area to be written into the data base, replacing the original version of the segment occurrence.

Replace Calls Following a Get-Hold Path Call

When a program uses a Get-Hold path call to bring more than one segment into the I/O area, the Get-Hold path call can be followed by a Replace call that references one or more SSAs. When multiple segments are retrieved using a Get-Hold path call and a Replace call is issued with no SSAs, *all* the retrieved segments are replaced. The Replace call can reference SSAs that include the N command code to indicate which segments are not to be replaced.

DELETE AND REPLACE STATUS CODES

The status codes that can be returned as a result of the three Get-Hold calls are the same ones that are returned for Get-Unique, Get-Next, and Get-Next-Within-Parent calls. Thus, the status code logic used with Get-Hold calls is the same as for non-hold Get calls.

Following are four status codes that are of particular interest to programs that issue Delete or Replace calls:

- DJ —No previous Get-Hold call
- DA—Key field modified
- DX—Delete rule violation
- RX—Replace rule violation

DJ indicates that the program has issued either a Delete or a Replace call, but neglected to precede it with a Get-Hold call. The DA status code is returned if the key field of the segment image in the I/O area is changed before the program issues the Delete or Replace call. The DX and RX status codes generally apply only to data bases that use logical relationships (discussed in Chapters 14 and 15).

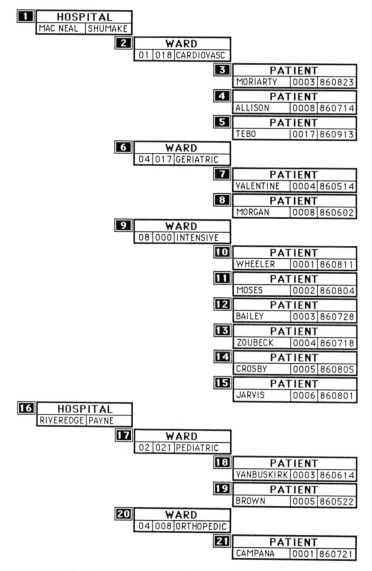

Figure 7.1. HOSPITAL data base segment occurrences

Replacing Variable-Length Segments

When replacing a variable-length segment, the program must modify the segment's two-byte length field if the length of the segment is changed. The program must be aware of the minimum and maximum length values that are specified in the DBD SEGM statement for the variable-length segment; the program cannot make the segment smaller or larger than the limits set there.

CODING PROBLEM

This coding problem presents the specifications of a complete program that uses all of the calls we have discussed thus far, including the following:

- Get-Hold Calls
- Replace Calls
- Insert Calls
- Delete Calls

The purpose of the program is to prepare a Recovery Room Schedule report having two parts. The first part lists all patients who are scheduled for surgery on a particular day. Assume that all of the patients will require the use of the recovery room. The second part of the report lists all patients who are released from the recovery room that day. Assume that all patients stay in the recovery room for a fixed period of time. The program should perform the following processing:

1. Read a parameter record from an input file. The record contains a date that tells the program which patients are to be released from the recovery room.
2. Look for all the patients in the *Columbus* hospital who are scheduled for surgery today. The SURGERY-FLAG field in the last TREATMNT segment occurrence for a patient must contain a ''1'' if the patient is scheduled for surgery. The SURGERY-DATE field indicates the day the patient is scheduled for surgery.
3. For each patient who is scheduled for surgery today, insert a copy of that patient's PATIENT segment, and the last TREATMNT and DOCTOR segments for that patient, under the *Columbus* hospital WARD segment whose WARD-TYPE is equal to *Recovery Room*. At the same time, write a line on the part of the recovery room report that lists patients that are scheduled for surgery on the date read from the parameter record.
4. After finding all the patients who are scheduled for surgery that day, the program should check all the patients who are currently in the *Recovery Room* ward to see which ones should be released. For each patient whose first TREATMNT segment has a treatment date equal to or less than the date read from the parameter record, delete that patient's PATIENT, TREATMNT, and DOCTOR segments. Delete the segments dependent on the recovery room WARD segment, not the original segments.
5. For each patient's segments that are deleted, the program should write a line on the second part of the recovery room report, the list of patients released from the recovery room.

Figure 7.2 is a listing of the PSB coding that this program references. Figure 7.3 is a sample listing of the Recovery Room Schedule Report. Assume that the segment description coding is stored in a sample library. The listings in Appendix D can be used to determine the data names to use.

```
        PRINT   NOGEN
        PCB     TYPE=DB,DBNAME=HOSPDBD,KEYLEN=26
  *
        SENSEG  NAME=HOSPITAL,PARENT=0,PROCOPT=G
        SENSEG  NAME=WARD,PARENT=HOSPITAL,PROCOPT=G
        SENSEG  NAME=PATIENT,PARENT=WARD,PROCOPT=A
        SENSEG  NAME=SYMPTOM,PARENT=PATIENT,PROCOPT=G
        SENSEG  NAME=TREATMNT,PARENT=PATIENT,PROCOPT=A
        SENSEG  NAME=DOCTOR,PARENT=PATIENT,PROCOPT=A
  *
        PSBGEN  LANG=COBOL,PSBNAME=CHAP7C
        END
```

Figure 7.2. PSB coding

R E C O V E R Y   R O O M   S C H E D U L E

DATE 06/30/77   PAGE   1

                        PATIENTS SCHEDULED FOR SURGERY

PATIENT NAME   PATIENT ADDRESS   PATIENT PHONE BED ID

CARLSON   1234 WAVERLY, CHICAGO, IL   312-555-1234   0002
BIDWELL   3344 MAIN STREET, CHICAGO, IL 312-555-4455   0004
EO SANG Y   3312 ROSE PLACE, CHICAGO, IL   312-555-1187   0006
OLSON   3256 BURLINGTON, CHICAGO, IL   312-555-5562   0010
WOLF   5562 ROSE PLACE, CHICAGO, IL   312-555-9935   0012

                PATIENTS TO BE RELEASED FROM RECOVERY ROOM

PATIENT NAME   PATIENT ADDRESS   PATIENT PHONE BED ID

PONIC   1276 COLFAX, CHICAGO, IL   312-555-5519   0005
O'HARA   1298 BURLINGTON, CHICAGO, IL   312-555-6620   0007
TEKCOM   9834 COLFAX, CHICAGO, IL   312-555-8892   0009
KASPER   7345 WAVERLY, CHICAGO, IL   312-555-9034   0013
POPEYE   8834 1ST STREET, CHICAGO, IL   312-555-8832   0015

Figure 7.3. Recovery room schedule report

8
Command Codes

SSA command codes allow the program to request a number of useful IMS functions that can be used to save programming and processing time. In this chapter, we examine situations that might come up in working with the HOSPITAL data base. We see how each situation might be handled without a command code, and then we see how a command code can simplify each task.

COMMAND CODE SSA FORMAT

Using a *command code* in an SSA causes IMS to modify the way the call is handled. There are ten command codes, and they can be used in combination to perform various functions that would be difficult, or impossible, with SSAs that do not use command codes.

Following is a summary of command functions:

- D—Put this segment into the I/O area (path call)
- N—Don't replace this segment
- C—Concatenated key in this SSA
- F—Locate first occurrence
- L—Locate last occurrence
- P—Establish parentage at this level
- Q—Enqueue this segment
- U—Maintain current position at this level
- V—Maintain current position here and higher
- ——Null command code

This chapter discusses each of the above command codes in detail. We will begin by examining the format of an SSA that uses command codes.

Command Codes in Qualified SSAs

Following is an example of a qualified SSA that uses the D command code:

```
WARD    *D(WARDNO  =04)
```

Notice that position 9 does not contain a left parenthesis; it contains an asterisk instead. The asterisk in position 9 indicates to IMS that one or more command codes follow the asterisk. In a qualified SSA, IMS treats all characters following the asterisk as command codes until it reaches a left parenthesis or blank. This allows multiple command codes to be used when required. Following is an example of a qualified SSA specifying three command codes:

```
PATIENT *DNP(PATNAME  =SMITH                    )
```

Command Codes in Unqualified SSAs

In an unqualified SSA, a blank tells IMS where the command codes end. Following is an unqualified SSA with two command codes:

```
WARD    *PD
```

We will next look at each of the ten command codes and see how they are used.

THE D AND N COMMAND CODES

The D and N command codes work together to allow the program to process multiple segments using a single call. The D command code directs IMS to perform a *path call*. When segments are retrieved with a path call, IMS places multiple segments into the I/O area. In retrievals that do not use the D command code, only the segment identified in the last SSA is placed into the I/O area.

An example will help show how path calls can be useful. Suppose we want to print hospital and ward information for a patient, and we also want to update the PATIENT segment. To do that, we have to retrieve the PATIENT segment and also the WARD and HOSPITAL segments above it. Figure 8.1 shows the segments in the data base that we are sensitive to. Suppose we need to retrieve segment 19. Following is the processing logic that we might use to perform the retrieval without using command codes.

1. Store HOSPITAL, WARD, and PATIENT identification in the appropriate SSAs.

2. Issue a Get-Unique call to retrieve a HOSPITAL segment:

```
GU      HOSPITAL(HOSPNAME =RIVEREDGE             )
```

3. Save the appropriate hospital information.

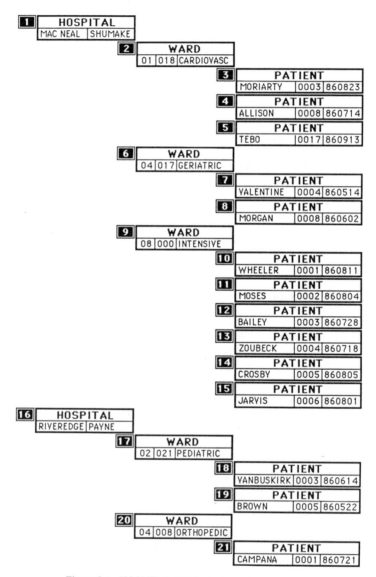

Figure 8.1. HOSPITAL data base segment occurrences

4. Issue a Get-Next call for a WARD segment:

```
GN     WARD    (WARDNO    =02)
```

5. Save the appropriate ward information.
6. Issue a Get-Hold-Next call to retrieve a PATIENT segment:

```
GHN    PATIENT (BEDIDENT =0005)
```

7. Print patient, ward, and hospital information.
8. Update information in the PATIENT segment
9. Issue a Replace call to update the PATIENT segment.

Now let us see how we can perform all of the above retrieval steps by using the D command code. The following Get-Hold-Unique call retrieves all three segments and stores them, one after another, in the I/O area:

```
GN     HOSPITAL*D(HOSPNAME =RIVEREDGE            )

       WARD    *D(WARDNO    =02)

       PATIENT (BEDIDENT =0005)
```

If command codes are not used in the above call, IMS places only the PA-TIENT segment into the I/O area. The D command codes in the higher-level SSAs cause IMS to store into the I/O area the segments referenced by those SSAs as well. The segments are placed in the I/O area in hierarchical sequence.

In issuing a path call, it is not necessary to retrieve *all* the segments in the hierarchical path. We can code the D command code in the SSAs only for the segments we want placed in the I/O area.

The PSB must specify a processing option of P for D command codes to be valid.

Replacing Segments after a Path Call

Whenever we make a Get-Hold Path call, IMS remembers how many segments it has stored in the I/O area. When we make a subsequent Replace call without SSAs, IMS replaces *all* of the segments in the I/O area. In order to replace only the PATIENT segment, the program issues a Replace call referencing SSAs that include N command codes for those segments that we do *not* want to re-place.

In a normal Replace call, SSAs are not used. SSAs with the N command code are an exception to this rule. Following is the call to replace only the PATIENT segment:

```
REPL    HOSPITAL*N(HOSPNAME =RIVEREDGE            )
        ^^^^   ^^^^^^^^^^^^^^^^^^^^^^^^^^^^^^^^^^^^^^^^^^^^^

        WARD    *N(WARDNO   =02)
        ^^^^^^^^^^^^^^^^^^^^^^^^^

        PATIENT
        ^^^^^^^^^^
```

If we wanted to use the same set of SSAs for both the retrieval path call and the Replace call, we could use both D and N command codes in combination in the first two SSAs, as shown in the following example:

```
HOSPITAL*DN(HOSPNAME =RIVEREDGE            )
^^^^^^^^^^^^^^^^^^^^^^^^^^^^^^^^^^^^^^^^^^^^^^

WARD    *DN(WARDNO   =02)
^^^^^^^^^^^^^^^^^^^^^^^^^

PATIENT (BEDIDENT =0005)
^^^^^^^^^^^^^^^^^^^^^^^^^
```

IMS ignores the N command codes in the above SSAs for the Get-Hold call and then ignores the D command codes for the Replace call. A qualification statement is not ordinarily coded for the segment being replaced, but IMS ignores it if it were present. This allows the same SSAs to be shared by the two calls.

THE C COMMAND CODE

The C command code can save programming and processing time in situations where a fully-qualified call would normally be used. It allows the use of a *concatenated key* in a single SSA rather than using a full set of fully-qualified SSAs. Suppose we wanted to retrieve DOCTOR segments from the HOSPITAL data base. Assume our program reads input records like the one in Figure 8.2. To retrieve a DOCTOR segment, the program performs logic similar to the following:

1. Move hospital name to HOSPITAL SSA.
2. Move ward number to WARD SSA.
3. Move patient key to PATIENT SSA.

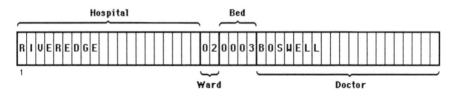

Figure 8.2. Retrieval program transaction

4. Move doctor name to DOCTOR SSA.
6. Issue the following Get-Unique call:

```
GU      HOSPITAL(HOSPNAME =RIVEREDGE             )
^^^^    ^^^^^^^^^^^^^^^^^^^^^^^^^^^^^^^^^^^^^^^^^^^^^^^^^
        WARD     (WARDNO   =02)
        ^^^^^^^^^^^^^^^^^^^^^^^^
        PATIENT (BEDIDENT =0003)
        ^^^^^^^^^^^^^^^^^^^^^^^^^
        DOCTOR  (DOCTNAME =BOSWELL            )
        ^^^^^^^^^^^^^^^^^^^^^^^^^^^^^^^^^^^^^^^^^^^^^^
```

Notice in the input record in Figure 8.2 that the information in the record consists of the entire concatenated key of a DOCTOR segment. To retrieve a DOCTOR segment, we could move the entire 46 positions of the input record to a single SSA with the C command code and use them in a Get-Unique call, as shown in the following example:

```
GU      DOCTOR  *C(RIVEREDGE         020003BOSWELL              )
^^^^    ^^^^^^^^^^^^^^^^^^^^^^^^^^^^^^^^^^^^^^^^^^^^^^^^^^^^^^^^^^^^^^^^
```

In using the C command code, the program must reference only one SSA naming the segment being retrieved. The entire concatenated key for that segment must be enclosed in parentheses, and no levels can be skipped in the concatenated key.

THE L AND F COMMAND CODES

The L and F command codes are used in unqualified SSAs for locating the *first* or *last* twin occurrence of a segment type. Let us see first how the L command code works.

The L Command Code

We will retrieve the last twin occurrence of the TREATMNT segment type in the structure shown in Figure 8.3. Without command codes, the required program logic looks something like the following:

1. Move key values to SSAs
2. Issue the following Get-Unique call:

```
GU      HOSPITAL(HOSPNAME =MAC NEAL          )
^^^^    ^^^^^^^^^^^^^^^^^^^^^^^^^^^^^^^^^^^^^^^^^^^^^^
        WARD     (WARDNO   =08)
        ^^^^^^^^^^^^^^^^^^^^^^^^
        PATIENT (BEDIDENT =0004)
        ^^^^^^^^^^^^^^^^^^^^^^^^^
```

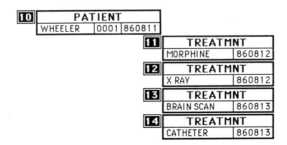

Figure 8.3. TREATMNT segment twin chain

3. Issue a sequence of Get-Next-Within-Parent calls until a GE status code is received:

```
GNP    TREATMNT
```

Coding the L command code in an unqualified SSA for the TREATMNT segment directs IMS to search for the last twin occurrence. Using a command code, we can accomplish the same retrieval as in the above call sequence with the following single call:

```
GU     HOSPITAL(HOSPNAME =MAC NEAL            )

       WARD    (WARDNO  =08)

       PATIENT (BEDIDENT =0004)

       TREATMNT*L
```

The F Command Code

The F command code is similar to the L command code; only instead of retrieving the last occurrence, it directs IMS to retrieve the first occurrence in a twin chain. A common use for the F command code is to back up in the data base when doing sequential retrievals.

The following is an example that illustrates when this might be useful. Suppose we would like to search through all the TREATMNT segments under a particular PATIENT segment occurrence for a treatment type of *morphine*. If we find one, we will print out *all* the TREATMNT segments for that patient.

Following is the logic to accomplish this without using command codes:

1. Issue a Get-Unique call for the desired TREATMNT segment:

```
GU     HOSPITAL(HOSPNAME =RIVEREDGE             )
^^^^   ^^^^^^^^^^^^^^^^^^^^^^^^^^^^^^^^^^^^^^^^^^^^
       WARD    (WARDNO   =04)
       ^^^^^^^^^^^^^^^^^^^^^^^
       PATIENT (BEDIDENT =0008)
       ^^^^^^^^^^^^^^^^^^^^^^^^^
       TREATMNT(TRTYPE    =MORPHINE            )
       ^^^^^^^^^^^^^^^^^^^^^^^^^^^^^^^^^^^^^^^^^^^
```

2. If a status code of GE is returned, exit from the procedure; if a status code of blanks is returned, issue the following Get-Unique call to establish parentage on the PATIENT segment:

```
GU     HOSPITAL(HOSPNAME =RIVEREDGE             )
^^^^   ^^^^^^^^^^^^^^^^^^^^^^^^^^^^^^^^^^^^^^^^^^^^
       WARD    (WARDNO   =04)
       ^^^^^^^^^^^^^^^^^^^^^^^
       PATIENT (BEDIDENT =0008)
       ^^^^^^^^^^^^^^^^^^^^^^^^^
```

3. Issue a sequence of Get-Next-Within-Parent calls until a GE status code is received, to retrieve the TREATMNT segments for printing:

```
GNP    TREATMNT
^^^^   ^^^^^^^^^
```

We could use the F command code to perform a more efficient search, as follows:

1. Issue a Get-Unique call for the desired TREATMNT segment:

```
GU     HOSPITAL(HOSPNAME =RIVEREDGE          )
^^^^   ^^^^^^^^^^^^^^^^^^^^^^^^^^^^^^^^^^^^^^^^^
       WARD    (WARDNO   =04)
       ^^^^^^^^^^^^^^^^^^^^^^^
       PATIENT (BEDIDENT =0008)
       ^^^^^^^^^^^^^^^^^^^^^^^^^
       TREATMNT(TRTYPE    =MORPHINE           )
       ^^^^^^^^^^^^^^^^^^^^^^^^^^^^^^^^^^^^^^^^^^
```

2. If a status code of GE is returned, exit from the procedure; if a status code of blanks is returned, issue the following Get-Next-Within-Parent call, using an F command code, to retrieve the first TREATMNT segment for printing:

```
GNP    TREATMNT*F
^^^^   ^^^^^^^^^^^
```

3. Issue a sequence of Get-Next-Within-Parent calls until a GE status code is received, to retrieve the TREATMNT segments for printing:

```
GNP    TREATMNT
^^^^   ^^^^^^^^^
```

The logic of the second example may not be simpler than the first; however, the unqualified SSA with the F command code generally produces a more efficient search than the fully-qualified SSA in the Get-Unique call. This is because the GNP call with the F command code takes advantage of current position, while Get-Unique calls usually begin the search at the beginning of the data base.

THE P COMMAND CODE

The P command code directs IMS to set parentage on a segment occurrence other than the one identified by the last SSA referenced by the call. The P command code is coded in the SSA for the segment at which parentage should be established. IMS still retrieves the segment identified by the last SSA, but sets parentage according to where the P command code is set.

Suppose we wanted to retrieve all the PATIENT segments under a particular WARD segment. Without the P command code, the program logic looks something like this:

1. Issue a Get-Unique call for the appropriate WARD segment:

```
GU      HOSPITAL(HOSPNAME =MAC NEAL                )

        WARD    (WARDNO   =08)
```

2. Issue a sequence of Get-Next-Within-Parent calls until receiving a GE status code, to retrieve the PATIENT segments for printing:

```
GNP     PATIENT
```

By using the P command code, we can save one call by retrieving a PATIENT segment in the first call, as in the following example:

1. Issue a Get-Unique call to retrieve the first PATIENT segment for printing. Use the P command code in the SSA for the WARD segment to establish parentage on that WARD segment:

```
GU      HOSPITAL(HOSPNAME =MAC NEAL                )

        WARD    *P(WARDNO   =08)

        PATIENT
```

2. Issue a sequence of Get-Next-Within-Parent calls until receiving a GE status code, to retrieve the remaining PATIENT segments for printing:

```
GNP    PATIENT
^^^^   ^^^^^^^^^
```

Notice that in the above example one call is saved each time the procedure is executed.

THE Q COMMAND CODE

The Q command code is used only when multiple applications concurrently access the same data base. It directs IMS to enqueue a segment occurrence to prevent other users from retrieving it using Get-Hold calls. The Q command code is followed by a one-character class identifier—one of the letters from A through J. The program can then issue a system service DEQ call referencing that same class identifier to dequeue the segment.

When the Q command code is set at the root segment level, no other users are allowed to gain access to any segment in that data base record. When it is set at a segment lower in the hierarchy, no users are able to retrieve the segment using a Get-Hold call for that segment occurrence, but they can retrieve it using non-Hold calls.

The Q command code is often used in message processing programs. These usually run in an environment where many programs execute concurrently and may access the same data bases. We will look at message processing programs in Part III.

THE U AND V COMMAND CODES

The U and V command codes provide control over moving forward in the data base when making unqualified Get-Next or Get-Next-Within-Parent calls. They let the program exercise control over calls that cannot be satisfied for a particular parent, but can be satisfied further in the data base under a different parent. The U and V command codes can be used to prevent a GN or GNP call from leaving the current position.

Suppose we would like to read sequentially through the HOSPITAL data base and prepare a report for one hospital, listing all the patients in each ward. A likely way to do that is to use GNP calls with unqualified SSAs. Following is one possible call sequence:

1. Issue a Get-Unique call to establish parentage on the desired HOSPITAL segment:

```
GU     HOSPITAL(HOSPNAME =MACNEAL             )
^^^^   ^^^^^^^^^^^^^^^^^^^^^^^^^^^^^^^^^^^^^^^^^^
```

2. Issue a sequence of Get-Next-Within-Parent calls until receiving a GE status code, to retrieve the WARD segments:

```
GNP    WARD
```

3. For each WARD segment retrieved in step 2, issue a sequence of Get-Next-Within-Parent calls to retrieve the PATIENT segments for that ward:

```
GNP    PATIENT
```

Unfortunately, the above call sequence will not work. The Get-Unique call in step 1 establishes parentage on the desired HOSPITAL segment, thus limiting the search to only those segments under that HOSPITAL segment. However, the Get-Next-Within-Parent call for each WARD segment does not establish parentage on that WARD segment for the following set of Get-Next-Within-Parent calls for PATIENT segments. After the first WARD segment is retrieved in step 2, the first set of Get-Next-Within-Parent calls in step 3 retrieves all the PATIENT segments under the *Mac Neal* HOSPITAL segment.

A way to solve this problem might be to use a qualified SSA for the WARD segment in the call for PATIENT segments, and fill in the key value each time a WARD segment is retrieved, as in the following call sequence:

1. Issue a Get-Unique call to establish parentage on the desired HOSPITAL segment:

```
GU     HOSPITAL(HOSPNAME =MACNEAL              )
```

2. Issue a sequence of Get-Next-Within-Parent calls, until receiving a GE status code to retrieve the WARD segments:

```
GNP    WARD
```

3. For each WARD segment retrieved in step 2, get the key value for the WARD from PCB and store it in the WARD SSA in the following call sequence. Then issue a sequence of Get-Next-Within-Parent calls, referencing those SSAs, to retrieve the PATIENT segments only for that ward:

```
GNP    WARD    (WARDNO  = )
       PATIENT
```

A simpler way to handle this situation is to use the U command code. Coding the U command code in an unqualified SSA has the same effect as using a qualified SSA at that level. Look at the following call sequence:

1. Issue a Get-Unique call to establish parentage on the desired HOSPITAL segment:

```
GU      HOSPITAL(HOSPNAME =MACNEAL              )
```

2. Issue a sequence of Get-Next-Within-Parent calls, until receiving a GE status code to retrieve the WARD segments:

```
GNP     WARD
```

3. For each WARD segment retrieved in step 2, issue a sequence of Get-Next-Within-Parent calls to retrieve the PATIENT segments only for that ward:

```
GNP     WARD    *U
        PATIENT
```

Using the U command code in the WARD SSA has the same effect as a qualified SSA for that particular segment occurrence.

The V command code is similar to the U command code. The difference is that the V command code causes IMS to act as though a U command code were set at that level, and at all levels above it. Suppose we are retrieving SYMPTOM segments sequentially. The two sets of SSAs in the following call sequences are functionally equivalent:

```
GNP     WARD    *U
        PATIENT *U
        SYMPTOM


GNP     PATIENT *V
        SYMPTOM
```

The V command code avoids the necessity for coding an SSA at each level when the function of the U command code is required at each level.

THE NULL COMMAND CODE

In some cases, it may be desirable to store a command code into an SSA while the program is executing. The following SSA reserves room for three command codes:

```
GN      HOSPITAL*---(HOSPNAME =RIVEREDGE           )
^^^^    ^^^^^^^^^^^^^^^^^^^^^^^^^^^^^^^^^^^^^^^^^^^^^^^^^

        WARD     (WARDNO   =01)
        ^^^^^^^^^^^^^^^^^^^^^^^^^

        PATIENT (BEDIDENT =0001)
        ^^^^^^^^^^^^^^^^^^^^^^^^^^
```

The HOSPITAL SSA above is treated as though no command codes were coded. The null command code (−) reserves one or more positions in an SSA into which the program can store command codes, should they be needed during execution. In this way, it is possible to use the same set of SSAs for more than one purpose. Keep in mind, however, that dynamically modifying SSAs makes debugging more difficult.

EXERCISES

1. Match each of the command codes below with the statement that best describes it. Each command code matches one statement.

CODES	STATEMENTS
A. D	a. Establishes parentage at other than the segment identified by the last SSA.
B. N	
	b. Used to bring more than one segment into the I/O area in a single call.
C. C	
D. F	c. Locates the last segment occurrence in a twin chain.
E. L	
F. P	d. Reserves room in an SSA for a command code.
G. Q	e. Causes a segment to be enqueued.
H. U	f. Indicates that the SSA contains a concatenated key rather than a qualification statement.
I. V	
	g. Can be used to back up in the data base even during sequential retrieval.
J. space	
	h. Can be used in place of a qualified SSA to maintain position in the data base.
	i. Used to specify which segments not to replace following a path call.
	j. Performs the function of the U command code in higher-level SSAs.

2. Write a set of SSAs to do the following:

   a. Bring the HOSPITAL segment for the *Mac Neal* hospital, the WARD segment for ward number *01*, and the PATIENT segment whose bed identifier is *0002* into the I/O area with a single Get-Hold-Unique call.

   b. Cause only the WARD segment to be replaced if the same set of SSAs is referenced in a Replace call.

   c. Reserve one extra position in the SSA for the WARD segment to allow the program to set a command code during program execution.

3. Write a single SSA to retrieve the WARD segment for ward number *08* in the *Riveredge* hospital. Use a concatenated key instead of a qualification statement.

4. Write a set of SSAs to do the following:

   a. Retrieve the last PATIENT segment in a ward whose ward type is *Recovery* in the *Mac Neal* hospital.

   b. The SSAs should also cause the following Get-Next-Within-Parent calls to treat the *Mac Neal* HOSPITAL segment as the parent segment.

9
Multiple Positioning
and Multiple PCBs

The multiple positioning feature and the use of multiple PCBs allow the program to maintain positions on more than one segment at a time in the same data base. Multiple PCBs also allow the program to access segments from more than one physical or logical data base. This chapter ends with a coding problem for a complete application program that uses multiple positioning and many of the other facilities, such as command codes, that we have discussed up to this point.

MULTIPLE POSITIONING

Before discussing the multiple positioning facility, we have to expand on the concept of position within the data base. Remember first that IMS maintains a position within the data base for the purpose of sequential retrieval. The result of any Get-Next call with either unqualified SSAs or no SSAs is partially determined by where position has been established within the data base at the time of the call.

When single positioning is in effect, IMS maintains a single position within the data base. When multiple positioning is in effect, IMS maintains a separate position for each dependent segment type at each level in the data base. First we will look at some examples of the effects of single and multiple positioning on sequential retrieval in the HOSPITAL data base. Then we will look at the coding in the PCB that specifies either single or multiple positioning.

SYMPTOM, TREATMNT, and DOCTOR Segments

The relationships between the SYMPTOM, TREATMNT, and DOCTOR segments in the data base illustrates the need for multiple positioning for some types of sequential retrievals. Let us suppose that a one-to-one relationship is

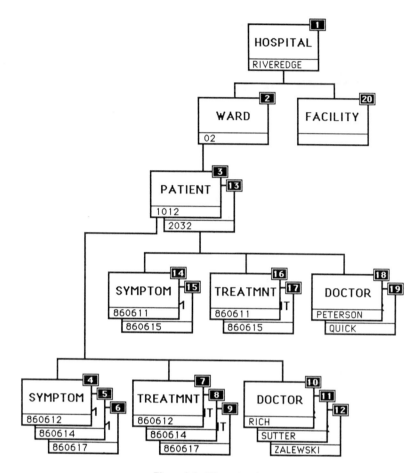

Figure 9.1. Hierarchy chart

required between SYMPTOM, TREATMNT, and DOCTOR segments. In other words, for each SYMPTOM segment there must be corresponding TREATMNT and DOCTOR segments.

The segments we reference in the following examples are shown in Figure 9.1 and Figure 9.2. Figure 9.1. shows the hierarchical structure, and Figure 9.2 shows the segments themselves.

If a one-to-one relationship between those segments exists, we might want to list, for a particular PATIENT segment, each set of SYMPTOM, TREATMNT, and DOCTOR segments under that PATIENT segment. If we do not care about the sequence of the segments, the following Get-Unique call followed by a series of Get-Next-Within-Parent calls accomplishes the retrieval:

```
GU     HOSPITAL(HOSPNAME =RIVEREDGE            )
^^^^   ^^^^^^^^^^^^^^^^^^^^^^^^^^^^^^^^^^^^^^^^^^

       WARD    (WARDNO   =02)
       ^^^^^^^^^^^^^^^^^^^^^^^

       PATIENT (BEDIDENT =1012)
       ^^^^^^^^^^^^^^^^^^^^^^^^^


GNP
^^^^
```

With the above call sequence, we first retrieve all the SYMPTOM segments, followed by all the TREATMNT segments, followed by all the DOCTOR segments.

If we want to maintain the one-to-one relationship between the segments, the above call sequence might not be appropriate, because we would have to retrieve all the SYMPTOM and TREATMNT segments before we could write the first line of the report. It would be better if we could retrieve a SYMPTOM segment, followed by its corresponding TREATMNT segment, followed by the corresponding DOCTOR segment.

On first glance, the following call sequence seems to satisfy our requirements:

```
GU     HOSPITAL(HOSPNAME =RIVEREDGE           )
^^^^   ^^^^^^^^^^^^^^^^^^^^^^^^^^^^^^^^^^^^^^^^^

       WARD    (WARDNO   =02)
       ^^^^^^^^^^^^^^^^^^^^^^^

       PATIENT (BEDIDENT =1012)
       ^^^^^^^^^^^^^^^^^^^^^^^^^


GNP    SYMPTOM
^^^^   ^^^^^^^^^

GNP    TREATMNT
^^^^   ^^^^^^^^^


GNP    DOCTOR
^^^^   ^^^^^^^^^
```

In the above call sequence, we repeat the set of Get-Next-Within-Parent calls, each time retrieving a set of SYMPTOM, TREATMNT, and DOCTOR segments, until we run out of segments under a PATIENT segment. If IMS is maintaining a single position within the data base, the call sequence works the first time through. We retrieve segments 4, 7, and 10—exactly what we want. But the second time through, we receive a GE status code indicating that there are no more SYMPTOM segments under that parent. The second time we issue the call sequence, current position is on segment 10, the first occurrence of the DOCTOR segment. To get the next SYMPTOM segment, IMS would have to

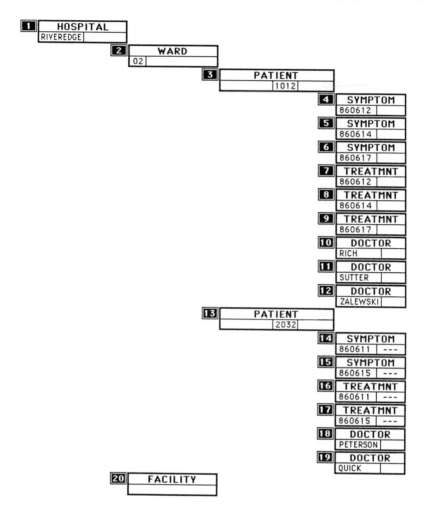

Figure 9.2. Indented structure chart

remember the position of the previous SYMPTOM segment retrieved as well as the positions of the previous TREATMNT and DOCTOR segments.

To further illustrate single positioning, let us see how single positioning works with the following call sequence:

```
GU      HOSPITAL(HOSPNAME =RIVEREDGE          )
^^^^    ^^^^^^^^^^^^^^^^^^^^^^^^^^^^^^^^^^^^^^^^^

        WARD    (WARDNO   =02)
        ^^^^^^^^^^^^^^^^^^^^^^^

        PATIENT (BEDIDENT =1012)
        ^^^^^^^^^^^^^^^^^^^^^^^^^
```

```
GN       SYMPTOM
```

```
GN       TREATMNT
```

```
GN       DOCTOR
```

This time the sequence of segments is 4, 7, 19, 14, 16, 18, followed by a GE status code. The above call sequence goes through the entire data base retrieving only the first occurrence of the SYMPTOM, TREATMNT, and DOCTOR segments under each PATIENT segment. There is no way to get past the first occurrence of those segment types.

With single positioning, it is often difficult to retrieve segments in the required sequence. The program must be unnecessarily complex to maintain the

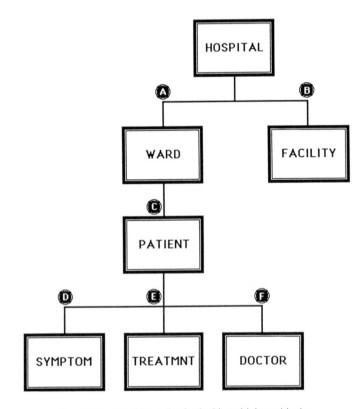

Figure 9.3. Positions maintained with multiple positioning

required relationships between segment types. We will next see how multiple positioning can simplify the program logic.

Retrieving with Multiple Positioning

With multiple positioning, IMS maintains a separate position within a data base record for each dependent segment type, at each level. Figure 9.3 shows the different points at which IMS maintains a position within the data base. The positions that we are interested in are the positions indicated by D, E, and F in the hierarchy chart.

Let us see how the following call sequence works with multiple positioning:

```
GU      HOSPITAL(HOSPNAME =RIVEREDGE                )
^^^^    ^^^^^^^^^^^^^^^^^^^^^^^^^^^^^^^^^^^^^^^^^^^^^^^

        WARD     (WARDNO    =02)
        ^^^^^^^^^^^^^^^^^^^^^^^^

        PATIENT (BEDIDENT =1012)
        ^^^^^^^^^^^^^^^^^^^^^^^^^


GNP     SYMPTOM
^^^^    ^^^^^^^^^^


GNP     TREATMNT
^^^^    ^^^^^^^^^^


GNP     DOCTOR
^^^^    ^^^^^^^^^^
```

The first time through, the above call sequence retrieves segments 4, 7 and 10, as in the single positioning example. IMS then establishes a separate position for SYMPTOM, TREATMNT, and DOCTOR segments. The next execution of the call sequence retrieves segments 5, 8, and 11. This is because current position for SYMPTOM segments was on segment 4 and current position for TREATMNT segments was on segment 7.

Specifying Single or Multiple Positioning

Coding in the PCB statement of the PSB specifies either single or multiple positioning for that PCB. Following is a PCB statement that specifies multiple positioning:

```
PCB  TYPE=DB,NAME=HOSPITAL,POS=M
```

The POS=M parameter specifies multiple positioning. Omitting the POS= parameter, or coding POS=S, specifies single positioning. It is necessary to know whether single or multiple positioning is in effect before coding a program. A program can operate quite differently depending on whether single or multiple positioning is in effect.

MULTIPLE PCBs

We mentioned earlier that it is possible for a PSB to include multiple PCB statements. Each PCB statement defines a separate PCB that the program has access to. In this section we will see how a program gains access to the various PCBs and how multiple PCBs can help simplify programming.

Applications for Multiple PCBs

A common application for multiple PCBs is to enable a program to access multiple data bases. A single PCB can refer to only one DBD. If a program requires access to two or more data bases, a separate PCB is required for each one.

Sometimes multiple PCBs are required even when working with a single data base. A program may require access to two different logical data structures, each describing different segments in the same data base. For example, Figure 9.4 shows two different HOSPITAL data base logical data structures that might possibly be useful in the same program. Each logical data structure is described by a different PCB statement followed by a separate set of SENSEG statements. Figure 9.5 shows a PSB that describes the two logical data structures in Figure 9.4.

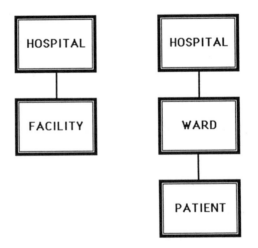

Figure 9.4. Two logical data structures

```
         PRINT   NOGEN
*
         PCB     TYPE=DB,DBNAME=HOSPITAL,PROCOPT=G
         SENSEG  NAME=HOSPITAL,PARENT=0
         SENSEG  NAME=FACILITY,PARENT=HOSPITAL
*
         PCB     TYPE=DB,DBNAME=HOSPITAL,PROCOPT=A
         SENSEG  NAME=HOSPITAL,PARENT=0
         SENSEG  NAME=WARD,PARENT=HOSPITAL
         SENSEG  NAME=PATIENT,PARENT=WARD
*
         PSBGEN  LANG=COBOL,PSBNAME=HOSP2PCB
         END
```

Figure 9.5. PSB with two PCBs

Accessing Multiple PCBs

In a COBOL program, the ENTRY statement normally includes a parameter for each PCB statement included in the PSB; other programming languages follow similar conventions. The parameters must be coded in the same order in which the PCBs appear in the PSB. Figure 9.6 shows COBOL coding to access the two PCBs in the PSB in Figure 9.5. Notice that each CALL statement identifies the appropriate set of PCB coding to indicate which PCB that CALL statement references.

```
LINKAGE SECTION.
01  PCB-MASK-ONE.
         .
         .

01  PCB-MASK-TWO.
         .
         .

PROCEDURE DIVISION.
    ENTRY  'DLITCBL'  USING  PCB-MASK-ONE
                             PCB-MASK-TWO.
         .
         .

    CALL  'CBLTDLI'  USING  FUNCTION
                            PCB-MASK-ONE
                            IOAREA
                            SSA-AREA-1.
         .
         .

    CALL  'CBLTDLI'  USING  FUNCTION
                            PCB-MASK-TWO
                            IOAREA
                            SSA-AREA-2.
```

Figure 9.6. COBOL coding for multiple PCBs

Multiple PCB Applications

Earlier in this chapter, when we discussed multiple positioning, we saw an example of parallel processing within one portion of a data base record. Multiple positioning allows the program to process different segment types in parallel, as long as those segment types have the same parent segment occurrence. Multiple PCBs allow the program to process segments in parallel, no matter where in the data base the segments are.

A Parallel Processing Example

Transferring a patient from one hospital to another provides an example of an application for parallel processing. To move a PATIENT segment occurrence from one place in the data base to another, we have to retrieve a PATIENT segment from one part of the data base and then reinsert it under a new HOSPITAL and WARD segment occurrence. We would then sequentially retrieve that patient's SYMPTOM, TREATMNT, and DOCTOR segments, and insert them under the new copy of the PATIENT segment. Finally, we could delete the original copy of the PATIENT segment and all of its dependents.

With a single PCB, as soon as the program inserts the PATIENT segment under a new WARD segment occurrence, the old position of the PATIENT segment is lost. The program is then unable to locate that segment's dependents without issuing a second retrieval call for the original PATIENT segment. And each time the program inserts one of the dependents under the new parent, position is lost again. The only practical way to handle the move, with a single PCB, is to retrieve the PATIENT segment, and all of its dependents, storing them in memory, before inserting them under the new WARD segment.

Figure 9.7 shows the coding we might use to accomplish the move using two PCBs. In this case, the PCBs describe the same logical data structure. The two PCBS allow the program to maintain two positions in different parts of the data base at the same time.

Other Types of PCBs

Multiple PCBS are also required when the program references PCBs that are other than standard data base PCBs. For example, in message processing programs, PCBs are used to describe logical terminals that the program communicates with. We will look at logical terminal PCBs in Chapters 10 and 11, which discuss message processing programs. Another type of PCB is used to describe a GSAM data base; GSAM data base PCBs are discussed in Appendix C.

```
CALL  'CBLTDLI'  USING  GET-UNIQUE
                        PCB1
                        IOAREA
                        HOSPSSA
                        WARDSSA
                        PATSSA.
      .
      .

CALL  'CBLTDLI'  USING  INSERT
                        PCB2
                        IOAREA
                        NEWHOSPSSA
                        NEWWARDSSA
                        PATSSA-UNQUAL.
      .
      .

CALL  'CBLTDLI'  USING  GNP
                        PCB1
                        IOAREA.
      .
      .

MOVE  PCB1-SEGTYPE TO UNQUAL-SSA.
      .
      .

CALL  'CBLTDLI'  USING  INSERT
                        PCB2
                        IOAREA
                        UNQUAL-SSA.
```

Figure 9.7. Moving a PATIENT segment and its dependents

CODING PROBLEM

The following coding problem presents the specifications for an IMS application program. Write the program in COBOL, PL/I, or Assembler Language.

The PATIENT History Program

The purpose of the PATIENT History Program is to print the history of each patient, by ward, for all the hospitals in the data base. Since the entire data base is to be processed, there is no input to the program other than the HOSPITAL data base. Figure 9.8 shows the PSB to use for this coding problem.

History Program Output

Figure 9.9 shows a sample page of the report the program should produce. The information relating to the doctors to be printed for each patient is obtained from two places. Information about the first doctor is obtained from the patient's *first* SYMPTOM segment (SYMP-DOCTOR and SYMP-DOCT-PHONE). The information about the second

```
PRINT    NOGEN
PCB      TYPE=DB,DBNAME=HOSPDBD,PROCOPT=G,POS=MULTIPLE,        *
         KEYLEN=32
SENSEG   NAME=HOSPITAL,PARENT=0
SENSEG   NAME=WARD,PARENT=HOSPITAL
SENSEG   NAME=PATIENT,PARENT=WARD
SENSEG   NAME=SYMPTOM,PARENT=PATIENT
SENSEG   NAME=TREATMNT,PARENT=PATIENT
SENSEG   NAME=DOCTOR,PARENT=PATIENT
PSBGEN   LANG=COBOL,PSBNAME=CHAP9C
END
```

Figure 9.8. Chapter 9 coding problem PSB

doctor is obtained from the patient's *last* DOCTOR segment (DOCTNAME, DOCT-PHONE, and SPECIALT). Print the information from the SYMPTOM and TREATMNT segments in ascending sequence by date.

Assume that path calls and multiple positioning can be used. Appendix D summarizes in one place information about the HOSPITAL data base.

```
                      P A T I E N T   H I S T O R Y

DATE  06/30/77

HOSPITAL NAME  MAC NEAL                                    PAGE    1

WARD TYPE      INTENSIVE

PATIENT NAME        PATIENT ADDRESS          PHONE        BED ID   ADMIT DATE

BINKIS             1234 ROSE PLACE, CHICAGO, IL   312-555-1234   003    06/29/77

PREVIOUS HOSPITAL   PREVIOUS DATE   PREVIOUS REASON

RIVEREDGE          05/23/77        GALL BLADDER

PREVIOUS DOCTOR     PHONE           DIAGNOSIS        TREATMENT DESCRIPTION   DATE

GRILL              312-555-1144    UNKNOWN              NONE              06/24/77

MEDICATION TYPE     DIET COMMENT                    SURGERY DATE   SURGERY COMMENT

NONE               NONE                                NONE

DOCTOR NAME         DOCTOR ADDRESS               DOCTOR PHONE   SPECIALTY

AHAB               1134 BURLINGTON, CHICAGO, IL   312-555-6667   GENERAL PRACTICE
```

Figure 9.9. Patient history chart

Part III
Data Communications
Programming

10
IMS-DC Concepts

In Part I and Part II, we discussed techniques for accessing *data base segments* using IMS calls. In Part III, we discuss the other major part of the IMS software—the *data communications portion*. Since there is no data communications support provided in DL/I VSE systems (CICS is often used to supply data communications services in the DL/I VSE environment), these chapters apply only to IMS/VS installations. We begin with a brief overview of the differences between the IMS batch environment and the data base/data communications environment. We then look at the various resources that are under the control of IMS. After that we see how data flows through the IMS data communications system, and how that data is processed by IMS and by application programs.

THE IMS DB/DC ENVIRONMENT

An IMS application program that requests the services solely of DL/I, the interface to IMS data bases, uses only a portion of the IMS software. A full implementation of IMS uses both DL/I and the data communications interface. This type of system is called an *IMS data base/data communications* (IMS DB/DC) system. We will begin this chapter by reviewing the IMS batch environment. We will then discuss the main differences between the batch environment and the DB/DC environment.

The Batch Environment

In the batch environment, an individual set of JCL is supplied for the execution of each IMS batch program. Figure 10.1 shows an application program operating in batch mode. Depending on the operating system used, an application program occupies one of the operating system's *partitions*, *regions*, or *address spaces*. Most of the IBM IMS documentation is written to be independent of any particular operating system and uses the term *region* in a generic fashion

Main or Virtual Storage

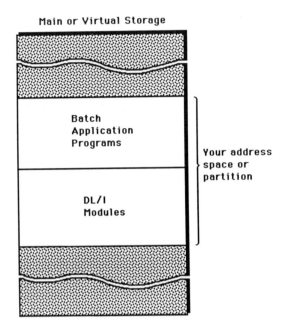

Figure 10.1.   Executing a DL/I batch application program

to refer to the areas of main or virtual storage that programs occupy; this book uses the same convention.

Notice that in the batch environment, the region assigned to an application program contains a copy of IMS. Everything the program needs for execution is contained within its own region, and the program is independent of any other job in the system. An IMS application program, in combination with IMS modules, competes for system resources in the same manner as any other operating system job.

In the batch environment, application programmers and designers need not be concerned with the IMS system definition process. The IMS system definition is performed once for all users, and data bases and application programs can be added at any time without having to modify the IMS system definition.

DB/DC Differences

In the DB/DC environment, application programs can be automatically scheduled by IMS as a result of data coming into the system from remote terminals. The data communication portion of the DB/DC system handles information in the form of *messages* that flow between remote terminals and application programs.

A typical IMS DB/DC system handles a great number of application programs, and the resources under the control of IMS have a more system-wide orientation. For this reason, the IMS system definition for a DB/DC system must include information about the various application programs that will be under the control of IMS. Let us begin by looking at the types of resources that are under the control of IMS in the DB/DC environment and how those resources are defined to IMS.

The Resources That IMS-DC Controls

In the DB/DC environment, programs and data bases cannot be added to the system at will as they can be when operating in the batch mode. All programs and data bases that run under the control of the IMS DB/DC system must be defined in the IMS system definition. There are two main categories of system resources that are defined to IMS during IMS system definition: *application resources* and *data communications resources*. Let us look at each resource individually.

Application Resources

These are the system resources that are related to application programs which operate in the IMS DB/DC system. Specifically, these resources consist of application programs, transaction codes, and data bases.

Application Programs. There are two types of application programs in the IMS DB/DC environment. These are *message processing programs* (MP programs), and *batch message processing programs* (BMP programs). The scheduling of MP programs is entirely under the control of IMS. A message processing program is automatically loaded by IMS when a message to be processed by that program is received. A batch message processing program is manually scheduled by the system operator. A typical BMP program is used to process information that has been received from remote terminals, but has been held by IMS in a *message queue*. More about message queues later in this chapter.

MP programs and BMP programs are identified to IMS during IMS system definition in APPLCTN system definition macros. The following is an APPLCTN macro for an MP program named PROGRAM1:

```
APPLCTN  PSB=PROGRAM1
```

The following APPLCTN macro is for a BMP program named BMPPGM1:

```
APPLCTN  PSB=BMPPGM1,PGMTYPE=BATCH
```

There must be an APPLCTN macro for each MP and BMP program that is allowed to execute in the system. An APPLCTN macro names the program's PSB. The load module name of an MP or BMP program must be the same as the PSB name.

Transaction Codes. Messages can be sent to MP and BMP programs either from remote terminals, or from other programs. A message that has an MP or BMP program as a destination, whether it originates at a terminal or in a program, is called a *transaction*. Each type of transaction allowed in the IMS DB/DC system is identified by a unique one- to eight-character transaction code. These transaction codes are defined to IMS during IMS system definition with TRANSACT macros. Following is an example of a TRANSACT macro for transaction code TRANS1:

```
TRANSACT  CODE=TRANS1
```

A TRANSACT macro names a transaction code, and follows the APPLCTN macro for the program that processes it. This indicates to IMS which MP or BMP program processes each type of transaction. One, and only one, program can be assigned to process a given transaction, but a given program can process more than one type of transaction.

Message Queues. As transactions arrive from remote terminals or are generated within programs, they are processed by IMS and stored in *message queues*. There is a separate message queue maintained for each valid transaction code. For transactions that are processed by MP programs, IMS automatically schedules the appropriate MP program when messages having those transaction codes are received. Because the queues often contain more transactions than can be processed at one time, a priority scheme is used in determining which transaction to select first from the queues. Later in this chapter we discuss this priority scheme.

Transactions that are processed by BMP programs remain in message queues until the appropriate BMP program is manually scheduled by the operator. The BMP program then reads the transactions from its message queue.

IMS Data Bases. Programs that run in the DB/DC environment cannot indiscriminately access any IMS data base. DBD names for the data bases that MP and BMP programs access must be defined to IMS in DATABASE system definition macros. Following is an example of a DATABASE macro for the DBD whose name is HOSPITAL:

```
DATABASE  HOSPITAL
```

System definition macros do not indicate which data bases are processed by which programs. DATABASE macros simply identify all the data bases that all MP and BMP programs access.

Defining Application Resources to IMS-DC. Assume our system supports four transaction codes: TRANS1, TRANS2, TRANS3, and TRANS4. Transactions with transaction codes TRANS1 and TRANS2 are both processed by an MP program named PROGRAM1. Transactions having transaction code TRANS3 are processed by an MP program named PROGRAM2. Transactions with transaction code TRANS4 are processed by a BMP program named BMPPGM1. The MP and BMP programs in the system require access to three data bases. Their DBD names are DBD1, DBD2, and DBD3. Figure 10.2 shows the IMS system definition macros that might be used to define these application resources to IMS.

Data Communications Resources

A second category of resource that must be defined during IMS system definition includes all the data communications hardware in the communications network. Data communications hardware used by IMS/DC is often managed by sophisticated software subsystems called *teleprocessing access methods* (TP access methods). The specific system definition statements used to define data communications resources vary depending on the TP access method used. In this chapter, we will look at a very simple data communications network under the control of a simple TP access method. In the real world, communication networks are often much more complex than the examples we are using.

The most important of the physical resources under the control of IMS/DC are communications lines that handle data communications, often telephone lines, and remote terminals.

Communications Lines. In an IMS DB/DC network, a single communications line can handle one or more remote terminals of a particular type. A line can

```
DATABASE    DBD1
DATABASE    DBD2
DATABASE    DBD3
APPLCTN     PSB=PROGRAM1
  TRANSACT    CODE=TRANS1
  TRANSACT    CODE=TRANS2
APPLCTN     PSB=PROGRAM2
  TRANSACT    CODE=TRANS3
APPLCTN     PSB=BMPPGM1
  TRANSACT    CODE=TRANS4
```

Figure 10.2. IMS system definition macros

be switched or non-switched. Users gain access to a switched line by dialing a phone number. A non-switched line is dedicated to the use of a set of terminals, and the terminals remain connected at all times. Lines that connect terminals of a similar type can be grouped together into *line groups*. Each line group is identified in the IMS DB/DC JCL by a DD statement.

The LINEGRP and LINE system definition macros are used to define the network of communication lines to IMS. We will look at examples of these macros after we define the rest of the communications resources.

Physical Terminals. One or more physical terminals can be connected to each communication line through one or more levels of controllers. In a switched line network, each terminal can be connected to any one of several lines. In a non-switched network, a terminal is always connected to the same line.

Different physical terminal types require different combinations of IMS system definition macros. A common type of network uses remote 3277 display terminals. In this type of network, a CTLUNIT macro is used to define each 3271 control unit followed by a set of TERMINAL macros to define the 3277 display terminals connected to each control unit.

Logical Terminals. MP and BMP programs do not communicate directly with physical terminals. Instead, messages that are destined for remote terminals include a one- to eight-character logical terminal name. As with transactions, logical terminal messages are held in the message queues. There is one message queue for each valid logical terminal name defined in the system. NAME system definition macros are used to define logical terminal names to IMS. During IMS system definition, each TERMINAL macro that defines a particular physical terminal can be followed by one or more NAME macros which assign one or more logical terminal names to each physical terminal.

When a logical terminal name message is sent, the physical terminal currently assigned to that logical terminal name receives the message. The system operator has commands that can be used to change the logical and physical terminal assignments at any time.

Logical terminal messages can be sent by MP and BMP programs, or by other terminals. When a terminal sends a logical terminal name message to another terminal, it performs a *terminal-to-terminal message switch*. The terminal operator (or software running in the terminal equipment) does this by beginning a message with a logical terminal name instead of a transaction code.

Defining Communications Resources to IMS-DC. Figure 10.3 shows a sample set of IMS system definition macros that could be used to define a very simple data communications network to IMS. There is a single line group consisting of two lines. Each has a single 3271 control unit attached to it. Each

```
LINEGRP       DDNAME=LINEDD,UNITYPE=3270
  LINE        ADDR=0C9
   CTLUNIT    ADDR=C1,MODEL=2
    TERMINAL  ADDR=40
     NAME     LTERM1
     NAME     LTERM2
    TERMINAL  ADDR=C1
     NAME     LTERM3
    TERMINAL  ADDR=C2
     NAME     LTERM4
  LINE        ADDR=0CA
   CTLUNIT    ADDR=C2,MODEL=2
    TERMINAL  ADDR=40
     NAME     LTERM5
    TERMINAL  ADDR=C1
     NAME     LTERM6
     NAME     LTERM7
     NAME     LTERM8
    TERMINAL  ADDR=C2
     NAME     LTERM9
```

Figure 10.3. IMS data communications macros

control unit supports three 3277 display terminals. The NAME macros define the logical terminal names that are initially assigned to each physical terminal.

DATA COMMUNICATIONS MESSAGES

The messages that flow through the IMS DB/DC system are divided into categories based on their destinations within the system. There are three message types. We have already briefly discussed two of them: transaction code messages and logical terminal name messages. The third type consists of IMS terminal commands. Let us look at each message type in detail.

Transaction Code Messages

A *transaction code message*, or *transaction* for short, has an MP or BMP program as its destination. A transaction can originate at a remote terminal, or in another application program. The following shows what a transaction code message might look like:

```
TRANS1(PASSWORD)THIS IS THE TEXT OF THE MESSAGE
```

The transaction begins with a one- to eight-character transaction code. This must be one of the valid transaction codes defined to IMS in a TRANSACT macro. The transaction code is followed by an optional one- to eight-character password in parentheses. A program called the *Security Maintenance Program*, or SMP, can be used to assign passwords to protect certain transaction codes. If this is done, a particular password must accompany the transaction code for the transaction to be accepted by IMS. The password (or transaction code if there is no password) is followed by the text of the message.

It is important to realize that the format of the actual information entered at the terminal by the operator might bear little resemblance to the transaction format as described above. Software running in the terminal equipment itself and software running in the central computer may be operating that translates the information entered by terminal operators into the required IMS transaction format. Message Format Service (MFS), which we introduce in Chapter 11, is an example of this type of software.

Message Segments. Messages can be broken into one or more *message segments*. Each group of message segments making up one message is transmitted at one time. In an MP or BMP program, application programs retrieve messages one segment at a time with calls to IMS, much as data base segments are retrieved; later in this chapter we will see in detail how this works. When IMS passes a message segment to the program, it strips off the transaction code and password and adds some control information to each segment.

Message Segments in the Application Program. Figure 10.4 shows a message segment as an MP or BMP program receives it. Each message segment consists of four bytes of control information, followed by the message segment text.

The first two bytes of control information in the message is a *message length* field. The length field contains a binary number that indicates the total length of the message segment, including the message text and the four bytes of control information. The second two bytes of control information, called the *ZZ field*, are normally manipulated by IMS. For an input message, the program ignores this two-byte field; for an output message, the program normally stores binary zeros in the ZZ field. An exception to this is when the program works directly with display terminals. With display terminals, the ZZ field is used to indicate where on the screen the message is written. The ZZ field is device dependent,

132 byte maximum length

Figure 10.4. Program view of message

and the *Application Programming Reference Manual* discusses how it is used. We discuss output messages next.

Logical Terminal Name Messages

A logical terminal name message has a logical terminal as its destination. As with transactions, logical terminal name messages can originate either in programs or at other logical terminals. The following shows what a logical terminal segment looks like to IMS:

```
LTERM1 THIS IS THE TEXT OF THE MESSAGE
```

Instead of a transaction code, the message segment begins with one of the valid logical terminal names. This must be one of the names defined during IMS system definition in a NAME macro. No password is allowed in a logical terminal name message. As with transactions, logical terminal name messages are often formatted by software running in the terminal equipment or in the central computing system. A logical terminal name message appears in the I/O area as shown in Figure 10.4. The logical terminal name does not appear in the I/O area; it is supplied in another way, which we discuss in Chapter 11.

IMS Terminal Commands

The third kind of message is represented by one of the IMS terminal commands. These begin with a slash followed by one of the valid terminal command verbs. These terminal commands are described in detail in the *Operator's Reference Manual* and are used to control the operation of the IMS DB/DC system. The following is an example of an IMS terminal command:

```
/DIS STATUS
```

The above DIS command is used to request a status display. IMS terminal commands are used most often by the IMS master terminal operator. The IMS master terminal is the main control center of the IMS DB/DC system, and is normally able to enter all of the IMS terminal commands. Usually, other remote terminals are able to enter only certain IMS terminal commands.

THE IMS DB/DC OPERATING ENVIRONMENT

In the DB/DC environment, multiple operating system regions are used for running MP and BMP programs. All of these regions are under the control of IMS. There are three types of region: the IMS control region, MP regions, and BMP regions. Figure 10.5 shows a typical IMS DB/DC region configuration.

Main or Virtual Storage

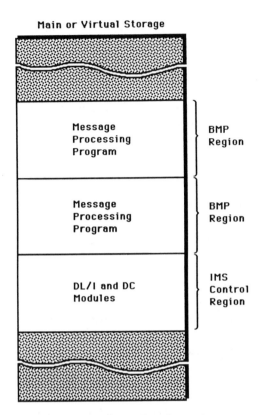

Figure 10.5. The IMS-DC runtime environment

We will look at each region type individually to see how the DB/DC system operates.

The IMS Control Region

The IMS control region handles all communication between IMS and remote terminals. The IMS control region also controls the use of the various MP regions in the system.

Message Processing Regions

The scheduling of MP programs into the MP regions is handled by the IMS control region. Each of the transaction codes defined to IMS is assigned to a transaction class identified with a number from 1 to 255. Each MP region is set up to process transactions from one to four of the transaction classes. Each time an MP region becomes available, IMS checks the message queues to see if a transaction of the appropriate class is available. If none is available, the region remains idle. If there are multiple transactions to choose from, IMS uses a priority scheme to select the highest priority transaction.

Messages are not always selected on a first-in/first-out basis. Rather, more important messages may be scheduled ahead of less important ones. We discuss this priority scheme later in this chapter.

Batch Message Processing Regions

In order to run BMP programs, one or more BMP regions must be made available. It is up to the system operator to schedule BMP programs into the BMP regions at the appropriate times.

BMP programs are used when it is necessary to receive information from remote terminals and each message might require substantial processing. It is desirable for each MP program to occupy a message processing region for as short a time as possible. In cases that require lengthy processing times but not immediate responses, a BMP program might better suit the application requirements. Batch message processing programs are often used when it is desirable to submit input from a terminal but a response back to the terminal is not required.

MESSAGE PROCESSING

Next, we will see how MP and BMP programs communicate with logical terminals. We will begin by examining messages and message segments in more detail.

Each message segment contains up to 130 bytes of text. In general, a message segment consists of a particular line of the total message. For example, if a terminal operator is required to send a message that consists of five individual lines, that message consists of five segments. In order for a program to send a message consisting of seven lines of data to a terminal or remote printer, the message will contain seven segments.

Receiving the First Message Segment

When a message processing program is loaded into a message processing region and control is passed to the MP program, there is always a transaction in the message queue waiting for it with one of that program's assigned transaction codes. An MP program normally begins by issuing a call to IMS to read in the first segment of the waiting message.

An MP program retrieves message segments by issuing calls to IMS in much the same way as data base segments are retrieved. The interface is designed so that the message queue behaves in a similar manner to a sequential file. The program reads the first segment of the message by issuing a Get-Unique call that references no SSAs (except in *conversational* programs which we discuss later in this chapter). The difference between a Get-Unique call for a message segment and a Get-Unique call for a data base segment is in the PCB the Get-Unique call is referenced. Data base calls reference *data base PCBs*; message segment calls reference *data communications PCBs*. One type of data communications PCB is called the *I/O PCB*. Later in this chapter we examine the format of data communications PCBs and see how they are passed to the program. Following is a Get-Unique call for the first segment of a message:

```
CALL 'CBLTDLI' USING  GET-UNIQUE
                      I-O-PCB
                      MESSAGE-AREA.
```

The GET-UNIQUE data name in the above call refers to a four-byte area containing the GU function code, the I-O-PCB data name refers to the PCB mask coding for a data communications PCB, and the MESSAGE-AREA data name refers to the I/O area into which the message segment should be placed.

Reading the Remaining Message Segments

Succeeding segments of the same message are read with a sequence of Get-Next calls. The following shows a call to read the second and any following message segments:

```
CALL 'CBLTDLI' USING  GET-NEXT
                      I-O-PCB
                      MESSAGE-AREA.
```

If the program issues a second Get-Unique call following the first one, all remaining segments of the message are deleted from the queue. If another message is waiting in the message queue, the first segment of *that* message is passed to the program. If no other message is waiting, IMS returns a GE status code.

Sending Information Back to the Terminal

An MP program uses Insert calls that reference the I/O PCB to send messages back to the terminal. The following is an example of an Insert call used to send a message segment back to the terminal:

```
CALL 'CBLTDLI' USING  INSERT
                      I-O-PCB
                      MESSAGE-AREA.
```

In most situations, MP programs send messages back to the same terminal that sent the input message. However, an MP program can send messages to other terminals, and they can also place messages back into the message queue to be read by other programs.

FLOW OF INFORMATION THROUGH THE SYSTEM

We next discuss how data flows through the system in the IMS DB/DC environment. We will see the sequence of events that takes place after a terminal operator enters a message at a terminal.

Message Input

The terminal operator sends a message by entering it at the keyboard and pressing the ENTER key. A program running in the IMS control region works together with data communications software that is part of the operating system to handle the actual transmission of the message from the remote terminal to the central computing system.

Each message that is received is accompanied by a transaction code and possibly a password. The transaction code and password are entered by the terminal operator or are supplied by software running either in the terminal equipment or in the central computing system.

After the message is received, the control region checks the transaction code against a list to see if the transaction code is valid; if required, it also verifies the password. If the transaction code and the password are valid, the message is stored in the appropriate message queue. Each transaction code and logical terminal name has its own message queue.

Message Selection

Another program in the IMS control region, running concurrently with the above program, selects messages from the message queues. When this program selects a message, it consults an internal list to see which MP program is associated with that message's transaction code. It then schedules that MP program for loading into an available MP region.

Message Processing

Once the message processing program is loaded into an MP region, a task is created, and control is passed to the MP program. The MP program then competes for system resources with all other tasks running in the system. The MP program begins by issuing a Get-Unique call for the first message segment. The program then processes the data in that message segment, which may require making any number of IMS data base calls. If the message consists of more than one segment, the program issues Get-Next calls for the remaining message segments. At any time, the program is able to make more data base calls.

Message Output

If the application determines that a reply is necessary, the MP program issues Insert calls to send messages back to the originating terminal. Optionally, the program can send messages to other terminals, and can also put messages back into the message queues to be read by other MP or BMP programs.

SENDING INFORMATION TO TERMINALS AND OTHER PROGRAMS

As we have seen, sending and receiving messages requires that the program issue Get and Insert calls that reference a data communications PCB. In this section we look at the various PCB types that can be used.

Sending Messages to the Originating Terminal

One of the simplest forms of message processing program receives a message from a terminal, processes one or more data base segments, and sends a message back to the same terminal. Two PCBs are required, one for the terminal and one for the data base.

Data Base PCBs. Data base PCBs are the PCBs that we discussed in Part I and Part II of this book. They describe the hierarchical structure of the sensitive segments and indicate the types of IMS calls that are valid. Data base PCBs are always defined in a PSB. The program's PSB contains all the data base PCBs that the program can reference.

Data Communications PCBs. Data communications PCBs allow the program to communicate with remote terminals. MP and BMP programs have access to at least one data communications PCB—the PCB that describes the logical terminal from which the input message is received. This PCB is called the *I/O PCB*. IMS automatically generates an I/O PCB for use by the program; the I/O PCB is not defined in the program's PSB. The I/O PCB is always the first PCB identified in the parameter list that is passed to an MP or BMP program.

In our example, the MP program that we are working with requires an I/O

```
PCB       TYPE=DB,DBDNAME=HOSPITAL,PROCOPT=A
SENSEG    ...
   .
   .

PSBGEN    LANG=COBOL,PSBNAME=MYPSB
END
```

Figure 10.6. PSB with no alternate PCB

PCB to send and receive messages to and from the originating terminal and a data base PCB to access an IMS data base. Figure 10.6 shows what the PSB might look like for this message processing program. Notice that there is only one PCB—the one for the data base; IMS supplies the I/O PCB automatically.

Figure 10.7 shows the entry coding for this MP program. Notice that the data base PCB parameter is the second one in the parameter list. The first parameter identifies the I/O PCB. (Chapter 11 discusses the format of the I/O PCB.)

Using the I/O PCB. The I/O PCB can be used to retrieve transaction messages segments sequentially from the message queue. It can also be used to transmit logical terminal name messages back to the originating terminal. One of the fields in the I/O PCB is the status code field, used, as with data base PCBs, to determine the result of each call. The I/O PCB is used with Get-Unique and Get-Next calls to retrieve messages from the message queue; it is used with Insert calls to transmit segments back to the originating terminal.

If an MP program simply sends responses back to the originating terminal, only data base PCBs are described in the program's PSB. IMS automatically generates the required I/O PCB. The only difference between a batch program and a data communications program, with respect to PCB references, is that the first data base PCB is the *second* PCB in the parameter list rather than the first.

```
LINKAGE SECTION.
01  DB-PCB.
       .
       .

01  I-O-PCB.
       .
       .

PROCEDURE DIVISION.
    ENTRY  'DLITCBL'  USING  I-O-PCB
                             DB-PCB.
```

Figure 10.7. Entry linkage

```
PCB       TYPE=TP,LTERM=T11234
PCB       TYPE=DB,DBDNAME=HOSPITAL,PROCOPT=A
SENSEG    ...
  .
  .

PSBGEN    LANG=COBOL,PSBNAME=MYPSB
END
```

Figure 10.8. PSB with alternate PCB

Sending Messages to Other Terminals

In addition to sending responses back to the originating terminal, a message processing program can route messages to other destinations in the system. To do this, the message processing program must have access to an *alternate PCB*.

Alternate PCBs. Alternate PCBs are defined in the program's PSB. Figure 10.8 shows the PSB for a program that sends messages to a destination other than to the terminal that sent the original message. This program is automatically provided with an I/O PCB, so it accesses three PCBs: the I/O PCB and the two PCBs identified in the PSB. In addition to receiving a message from the originating terminal, this program can send messages back to that same terminal and can send messages to the destination identified in the alternate PCB. Notice that a parameter in the alternate PCB identifies this destination.

Figure 10.9 shows the entry coding for the program that references the PSB in Figure 10.8. The first parameter in the parameter list identifies the I/O PCB, the alternate PCB is next, and the data base PCB is third.

```
LINKAGE SECTION.   .
01  DB-PCB.
        .
        .

01  ALT-PCB.
        .
        .

01  I-O-PCB.
        .
        .

PROCEDURE DIVISION.
    ENTRY  'DLITCBL'  USING  I-O-PCB
                             ALT-PCB.
                             DB-PCB.
```

Figure 10.9. Entry coding

Modifiable Alternate PCBs. In some cases, the destination of the messages sent by an MP program might not be fixed. For example, an MP program might have logic that determines where a particular message should be sent. *Modifiable* alternate PCBs are used for this purpose. The following is a PCB statement for a modifiable alternate PCB:

```
PCB  TYPE=TP,LTERM=T11234,MODIFY=YES
```

With the above PCB, the message processing program can issue a call with the CHNG function code to store the appropriate logical terminal name in the modifiable alternate PCB. In this way, a message processing program can send a message to any desired destination.

In many installations, the use of Change calls is discouraged. Installation standards normally document restrictions on the use of IMS calls that the installation does not wish programmers to use without authorization.

PROGRAM-TO-PROGRAM MESSAGE SWITCHING

We mentioned earlier that an MP program can send messages to other message processing programs as well as to logical terminals. To do this, an alternate PCB must be available to the program, and that alternate PCB must either be modifiable or must reference a *transaction code* rather than a logical terminal. When a MP program issues an Insert call to an alternate PCB specifying a transaction code rather than a logical terminal name, that message is placed in the appropriate message queue, rather than being sent to a terminal.

Messages that are placed in the message queue by MP programs are treated no differently from messages that come from remote terminals. Eventually, the particular message processing program associated with the message's transaction code is scheduled by IMS, and that program treats the message as if it had come from a terminal.

Some installations discourage the use of MP programs that send messages to other MP programs. This technique should be used only when necessary and only when permitted by the DBA.

IMS MESSAGE SCHEDULING TECHNIQUES

As we mentioned earlier, messages from terminals are stored into queues before they are passed to message processing programs. IMS uses a priority scheme in deciding which message to select next from the message queues. In this section we discuss the priority scheme that IMS uses.

Allocating the Message Processing Regions

One of the things that the DBA must decide when planning the data communications environment is how many MP regions to use. The DBA then decides which transaction codes each region should handle. Transactions are normally separated into classes based on their response requirements. For example, a particular environment may have a particular transaction type that occurs very frequently and must be given a fast response time. One or more MP regions might be set aside for that transaction type only. The MP regions are set up based on the requirements of the individual MP programs that run in the system.

Message Selection

IMS attempts to select a transaction for each of the message processing regions currently in operation. Each transaction type has two priorities associated with it: a *normal priority* and a *limit priority*. In addition, each transaction has a *limit count*. These three numbers are specified in the TRANSACT macro for each transaction type.

Within each message queue, messages are queued serially by transaction code. When an MP region becomes available, IMS examines the message queues to determine which messages can be handled by the available region. It then selects the transaction having the highest priority. To determine whether to use the normal priority or the limit priority, IMS looks at how many transactions with each transaction code are stored in each message queue. If the number of transactions in a particular queue is greater than or equal to that transaction code's limit count, the limit priority is used. If the number of messages queued is less than the limit count, the normal priority is used. A few examples will help make this clearer.

A Message Selection Example

Assume that a particular message processing region has become available, and that region is able to handle transaction T11234 and transaction T11432. Figure 10.10 shows what the message queues look like for those transaction codes. It shows the normal priority, the limit priority, and the limit count for those two transaction codes, and it shows the number of transactions for each of those transaction codes stored in the message queues.

Notice that the number of transactions of each of those transaction types has not yet exceeded the limit count. In determining which message to select, transaction T11234 has a normal priority of seven and T11432 has a normal priority of four, so the first transaction with transaction code T11234 is selected.

Figure 10.11 shows the condition of the message queues after a period of

Transaction Code	T11234	T11432
Normal Priority	7	4
Limit Priority	9	8
Limit Count	20	50
Entries in Queue	15	40

Figure 10.10. Message queues for T11234 and T11432

Transaction Code	T11234	T11432
Normal Priority	7	4
Limit Priority	9	8
Limit Count	20	50
Entries in Queue	13	50

Figure 10.11. Message queues after a time interval

time has passed. The number of transactions with transaction code T11432 now equals the limit count. IMS now compares the normal priority of transaction type T11234 with the limit priority of transaction type T11432. In this case, a transaction with transaction code T11432 is selected.

CONVERSATIONAL PROGRAMMING

The MP programs that we have looked at so far all process non-conversational transaction types. MP programs can also process conversational transaction types. Whether a transaction is conversational or non-conversational is determined by parameters that are coded in the TRANSACT macro.

The following is a summary of the sequence of events that occurs in processing a non-conversational transaction. The operator at a remote terminal enters a transaction at a remote terminal. This message is placed in the message queue, and eventually an MP program is scheduled to handle it. That program then processes the transaction and might send a response back to the terminal.

When the operator at the remote terminal sees the response, the choice might be made to enter another transaction. When this new transaction is processed by another MP program, or perhaps the same MP program, that MP program has no knowledge of any previous interaction with the operator.

In many cases, an MP program must engage in a dialog consisting of successive transactions and responses. One way IMS could have been designed to handle a continuous dialog is to have had the MP program reside permanently in the message processing region during the time the conversation is in progress. This is wasteful, however, because the time a terminal operator takes to formulate a reply might be thousands of times more than that which the MP program takes to generate the next message. The way that IMS actually implements conversational processing is through the use of a *scratch pad area* (SPA).

The Scratch Pad Area

The scratch pad area is stored in virtual storage or in direct access storage and is used to store the intermediate results of a series of executions of a message processing program. In the first execution of an MP program that handles a conversational transaction, the program might read in a transaction, and, based on the information in that transaction, store certain information in the SPA and send a response back to the terminal. When the MP program is brought in a second time, as a result of a conversational response by the terminal operator, the program reads in the scratch pad area to determine what happened during the previous execution of that program. The terminal operator can communicate with the MP program in a conversational manner even though the message processing program does not reside permanently in an MP region.

Writing Conversational Programs

The only major difference between an MP program that processes a non-conversational transaction, and one that processes a conversational transaction is in the use of the scratch pad area. The size and format of the SPA is defined by the DBA and must given to the application programmer. The first Get-Unique call that references the I/O PCB retrieves the SPA. This departs from the convention for nonconversational programs, where the Get-Unique call to the I/O PCB retrieves the first message segment.

In conversational programs all message segments, including the first one, are retrieved with Get-Next calls to the I/O PCB. Also, the first Insert call to the I/O PCB transfers the I/O area contents to the SPA.

Some installations use different techniques for implementing conversational transaction types that avoid the use of the scratch pad area. For example, a special data base segment can be set up for use by conversational MP programs to store intermediate results. Installation standards normally document how conversational transaction types are to be handled. We discuss conversational programming in detail in Chapter 11.

EXERCISES

1. List the three types of region that can be used in an IMS DB/DC system.

2. List the three types of PCBs that can be used in an MP program, and describe the purpose of each.

3. Match each of the terms below with the statement that best describes it. Each term matches one of the statements.

TERMS	STATEMENTS
D A. Physical terminal	a. Used to store information between two executions of a conversational message processing program.
C B. Logical terminal	
F C. Message queues	b. Control information in a message segment used to indicate where in a display screen the information should be written.
G D. Message processing program	
i E. Batch message processing program	c. Name by which message processing programs refer to terminals.
E F. Master terminal	
H G. Message segment	d. Name used to describe a hardware terminal.
J H. Password	e. Terminal used to control the IMS DB/DC system.
B I. ZZ field	
A J. Scratch pad area	f. Used to store messages from terminals before they are processed by message processing programs.
	g. Application program used to handle a particular type of transaction from a remote terminal.
	h. Portion of a message.
	i. Application program that runs in the batch mode but has access to a message queue.
	j. Used to protect the system from unauthorized access.

11
Message Processing Programs

In Chapter 10, we saw how IMS data communications facilities are implemented and, in general, how programs access them. In this chapter, we examine techniques used in implementing message processing programs. We look at a complete MP program that reads a one-segment transaction and sends a response back to the originating terminal. We then examine programming techniques for using alternate PCBs. We look at the format of the scratch pad area (SPA) used in writing conversational programs. We then list a number of hints for making MP programs efficient. This chapter concludes with a coding problem that describes a message processing version of the PATIENT segment retrieval program from Chapter 4.

A MESSAGE PROCESSING PROGRAM

We begin this chapter by examining a listing of a simple COBOL message processing program. The program reads a transaction that consists of a single message segment, the format of which is shown in Figure 11.1. The message text consists of a twenty-position hospital name followed by a two-position ward number.

The program reads the transaction and then retrieves the HOSPITAL and WARD segments from the data base corresponding to the hospital name and ward number in the transaction. The program then sends a response back to the originating terminal. Figure 11.2 shows the format of the first message segment of the response. This message segment displays the hospital name and ward number as verification to the operator.

Following this header message segment, the program sends a message segment for each PATIENT segment stored under that particular WARD segment. The format of PATIENT message segments is shown in Figure 11.3. The pro-

Figure 11.1. Message segment format

Figure 11.2. HOSPITAL and WARD message segment

Figure 11.3. PATIENT response format

gram sends to the terminal a complete listing of all patients in that ward. The listing consists of the patient name and bed identifier for each PATIENT segment. Following, in Figure 11.4, is the complete message processing program to produce this patient list. We will next examine each part of this message processing program.

Entry Coding

The program's entry coding sets up the necessary linkage to the I/O PCB and the data base PCB. (See Figure 11.5, p. 153) As discussed in Chapter 10, the I/O PCB is supplied by IMS and is not defined in the program's PSB. The I/O PCB is the first PCB passed to the program. We do not need an alternate PCB since we are only sending messages back to the originating terminal. The second PCB is for the data base.

The LINKAGE SECTION

Figure 11.6 (p. 154) repeats the LINKAGE SECTION coding. Notice that there are two PCB masks in the LINKAGE SECTION, one for the I/O PCB and one for the data base PCB. We will next look at the format of the I/O PCB.

```
000100 ID DIVISION.
000200 PROGRAM-ID.  CHAP11.
000300 AUTHOR.      JOE LEBEN.
000400 DATE COMPILED.
000500
000600 REMARKS.  THIS IS A SIMPLE IMS-DC PROGRAM.  IT DOES VERY LITTLE
000700           ERROR CHECKING.  IT READS AN INPUT TRANSACTION,
000800           WHICH HAS THE FOLLOWING FORMAT:
000900
001000           POSITIONS  1 -  2  TRANSACTION LENGTH
001100                      3 -  4  ZZ FIELD
001200                      5 - 24  HOSPITAL NAME
001300                     25 - 26  WARD NUMBER
001400
001500           FOR EACH TRANSACTION, THE PROGRAM SENDS A CONFIRMING
001600           MESSAGE BACK TO THE TERMINAL REPEATING THE HOSPITAL
001700           NAME AND WARD NUMBER AND THEN LISTS ALL THE PATIENT
001800           SEGMENTS UNDER THAT WARD AND HOSPITAL SEGMENT.
001900
002000 ENVIRONMENT DIVISION.
002500 DATA DIVISION.
002600 WORKING-STORAGE SECTION.
002700
002800 01  TERM-IN.
002900
003000     03  IN-LENGTH           PIC S9999  COMP.
003100     03  IN-ZZ               PIC XX.
003200     03  HOSPNAME-TERM       PIC X(20).
003300     03  WARDNO-TERM         PIC XX.
003400
003500 01  TERM-OUT-PATIENT-HOSPITAL.
003600
003700     03  OUT-LENGTH          PIC S9999  VALUE +30   COMP.
003800     03  OUT-ZZ              PIC XX     VALUE SPACE.
003900     03  HOSPITAL-INFO       PIC X(20).
004000     03  FILLER              PIC X(4)   VALUE SPACE.
004100     03  WARD-INFO           PIC XX.
004200
004300 01  TERM-OUT-PATIENT.
004400
004500     03  OUT-LENGTH          PIC S9999  VALUE +129  COMP.
004600     03  OUT-ZZ              PIC XX.
004700     03  PATIENT-INFO        PIC X(125).
004800
004900 01  GET-NEXT-P              PIC X(4)   VALUE 'GNP '.
005000 01  GET-UNIQUE              PIC X(4)   VALUE 'GU  '.
005100 01  INSERT-FUNCTION         PIC X(4)   VALUE 'ISRT'.
005120
005200 01  P-Z-D                   PIC X      VALUE SPACE.
005210 01  BAD-DATA  REDEFINES  P-Z-D.
005211     03  FILLER              PIC S9.
005300 01  PACKED-ONE              PIC S9     VALUE +1.
```

Figure 11.4. Retrieval MP program (page 1 of 4)

```
005400
005500 01  HOSPITAL-SSA.
005600        03  FILLER              PIC X(21)   VALUE 'HOSPITAL*D(HOSPNAME ='.
005700        03  HOSPNAME-SSA        PIC X(20).
005800        03  FILLER              PIC X       VALUE ')'.
005900
006000 01  WARD-SSA.
006100        03  FILLER              PIC X(21)   VALUE 'WARD      (WARDNO   ='.
006200        03  WARDNO-SSA          PIC X(2).
006300        03  FILLER              PIC X       VALUE ')'.
006400
006500 01  PATIENT-SSA             PIC X(9)    VALUE 'PATIENT  '.
006900
007000 01  I-O-AREA   COPY   PATIENT.
007100
007200 01  HOSPITAL-INPUT.
007220
007300        03  HOSPITAL.
007400            05  HOSPNAME          PIC X(20).
007500            05  HOSP-ADDRESS      PIC X(30).
007600            05  HOSP-PHONE        PIC X(10).
007610            05  ADMIN             PIC X(20).
007620
007700        03  WARD.
007800            05  WARDNO            PIC XX.
007900            05  TOT-ROOMS         PIC XXX.
008000            05  TOT-BEDS          PIC XXX.
008100            05  BEDAVAIL          PIC XXX.
008200            05  WARDTYPE          PIC X(20).
008300
008400 LINKAGE SECTION.
008420
008500 01  DB-PCB   COPY   MASKC.
008600
008700 01  I-O-PCB.
008720
008800        03  LTERM-NAME          PIC X(8).
008900        03  FILLER              PIC XX.
009000        03  I-O-STAT-CODE       PIC XX.
009100        03  INPUT-PREFIX.
009200            05  PREF-DATE         PIC S9(7)   COMP-3.
009300            05  PREF-TIME         PIC S9(7)   COMP-3.
009320            05  PREF-SEQ          PIC S9(7)   COMP-3.
009340
```

Figure 11.4. Retrieval MP program (page 2 of 4)

In Figure 11.6, the first eight bytes of the I/O PCB contain the logical terminal name for input and output messages. When an I/O PCB is used, the input destination and the output destination are always the same.

The next field is a two-byte field reserved for IMS. The program should not modify this field.

Next is the two-byte status code. The status code field is used in much the same way as it is used in data base PCBs.

```
009500 PROCEDURE DIVISION.
009700 ENTRY-LINKAGE.
009900     ENTRY 'DLITCBL' USING I-O-PCB DB-PCB.
009920
009940 MAIN PROGRAM.
009960
010000     PERFORM GET-MESSAGE THRU GET-MESSAGE-EXIT
010020             UNTIL I-O-STAT-CODE EQUAL 'QC' OR 'QD'.
010100     GOBACK.
010200
010300 GET-MESSAGE.
010400
010500     CALL 'CBLTDLI' USING GET-UNIQUE
010600                          I-O-PCB
010700                          TERM-IN.
010800
010900     IF I-O-STAT-CODE EQUAL 'QC'
010920
010940        GO TO GET-MESSAGE-EXIT.
010960
011000     IF I-O-STAT-CODE NOT EQUAL SPACE
011100
011200        MOVE I-O-PCB TO PATIENT-INFO
011300        PERFORM SEND-PAT-RTN
011400        MOVE SPACE TO PATIENT-INFO
011500        GO TO GET-MESSAGE-EXIT.
011600
011700     MOVE HOSPNAME-TERM  TO HOSPNAME-SSA.
011800     MOVE WARDNO-TERM    TO WARDNO-SSA.
011900
012000     CALL 'CBLTDLI' USING GET-UNIQUE
012100                          DB-PCB
012200                          HOSPITAL-INPUT
012300                          HOSPITAL-SSA
012400                          WARD-SSA.
012500
012600     IF STATUS-CODE NOT EQUAL SPACE
012610
012700        MOVE 'NO HOSPITAL OR WARD' TO PATIENT-INFO
012800        PERFORM SEND-PAT-RTN
012810        MOVE SPACE TO PATIENT-INFO
012900        GO TO GET-MESSAGE-EXIT.
013000
013100     MOVE HOSPNAME TO HOSPITAL-INFO.
013200     MOVE WARDNO   TO WARD-INFO.
013300
013400     CALL 'CBLTDLI' USING INSERT-FUNCTION
013500                          I-O-PCB
013600                          TERM-OUT-PATIENT-HOSPITAL.
013700
013800     IF I-O-STAT-CODE NOT EQUAL SPACE
013802
013900        ADD PACKED-ONE TO BAD-DATA.
013920
014000     PERFORM GET-PATIENT THRU GET-PATIENT-EXIT
014010                         UNTIL STATUS-CODE EQUAL 'GE'.
014100
014200 GET-MESSAGE-EXIT.
014300     EXIT.
```

Figure 11.4. Retrieval MP program (page 3 of 4)

```
014400
014500 GET-PATIENT.
014600
014700     CALL  'CBLTDLI'  USING  GET-NEXT-P
014800                             DB-PCB
014900                             I-O-AREA
015000                             PATIENT-SSA.
015100
015200     IF STATUS-CODE EQUAL 'GE'
015220
015240         GO TO GET-PATIENT-EXIT.
015260
015300     IF STATUS-CODE NOT EQUAL SPACE
015400
015500         MOVE DB-PCB TO TERM-OUT-PATIENT
015600         PERFORM SEND-PAT-RTN
015700         MOVE SPACE TO TERM-OUT-PATIENT
015800         GO TO GET-MESSAGE.
015900
016000     PERFORM SEND-PAT-RTN.
016100
016200 GET-PATIENT-EXIT.
016300     EXIT.
016400
016500 SEND-PAT-RTN.
016600
016700     CALL  'CBLTDLI'  USING INSERT-FUNCTION
016800                            I-O-PCB
016900                            TERM-OUT-PATIENT.
017000
017100     IF I-O-STAT-CODE NOT EQUAL SPACE
017200
017300         ADD PACKED-ONE TO BAD-DATA.
```

Figure 11.4. Retrieval MP program (page 4 of 4)

```
009500 PROCEDURE DIVISION.
009700 ENTRY-LINKAGE.
009900     ENTRY 'DLITCBL' USING I-O-PCB DB-PCB.
```

Figure 11.5. Entry coding

Following the status code (in Figure 11.6) are three fields that form the message's *input prefix*, which contains the current date, the current time, and an input message sequence number. The date is stored as a packed-decimal number in the form 00YYDDD. The time is also a four-byte packed-decimal number in the format HHMMSS.S. (The decimal point is implied and is not actually a part of the time field.) The sequence number is a four-byte binary number.

Following the input prefix is an eight-position field that is used only when the Message Format Service (MFS) facility is being used. (MFS is introduced later in this chapter.) This field contains the name of the an MFS control block called the *Message Output Descriptor* (MOD).

```
008400 LINKAGE SECTION.
008420
008500 01  DB-PCB  COPY  MASKC.
C*000010 01  DB-PCB.
C 000020    03  DBD-NAME              PIC X(8).
C 000030    03  LEVEL-NUMBER          PIC XX.
C 000040    03  STATUS-CODE           PIC XX.
C 000050    03  PROC-OPTIONS          PIC XXXX.
C 000060    03  JCB-ADDRESS           PIC XXXX.
C 000070    03  SEGMENT-NAME          PIC X(8).
C 000080    03  LEY-LENGTH            PIC S9(5) COMP.
C 000090    03  NUMBER-SEGS           PIC S9(5) COMP.
C 000100    03  KEY-FEEDBACK.
C 000110        05  HOSPNAME-KEY      PIC X(20).
C 000120        05  WARDNO-KEY        PIC XX.
C 000130        05  BEDIDENT-KEY      PIC X(4).
008600
008700 01  I-O-PCB.
008720
008800    03  LTERM-NAME         PIC X(8).
008900    03  FILLER             PIC XX.
009000    03  I-O-STAT-CODE      PIC XX.
009100    03  INPUT-PREFIX.
009200        05  PREF-DATE      PIC S9(7)  COMP-3.
009300        05  PREF-TIME      PIC S9(7)  COMP-3.
009320        05  PREF-SEQ       PIC S9(7)  COMP-3.
```

Figure 11.6. Linkage section

Input and Output Message Format

The DATA DIVISION coding shows the format of the input and output messages. The program coding allows for the two-position length field, and the two-position ZZ field, in both the input and output messages. A fixed-length value is stored in each of the output message types, since each message has a fixed length. This length field could be modified by the program if it were designed to send messages of varying length. In this simple example, the ZZ field contains binary zeros.

The PROCEDURE DIVISION coding contains a Get-Unique call for retrieving the first message segment from the message queue. It also contains Insert calls for sending message segments back to the originating terminal. Notice that the Get-Unique and Insert calls reference the I/O PCB. The Get calls for retrieving data base segments reference the data base PCB.

After the complete patient list has been sent back to the terminal, the program repeats the Get-Unique call to the I/O PCB. This is a useful convention that is normally followed in MP programs. It saves the overhead of loading this program back into an MP region should there be another message of the same transaction code waiting in the message queue.

```
LINKAGE SECTION.
01  ALT-PCB.
        .
        .

01  I-0-PCB.
        .
        .

01  DB-PCB
        .
        .

PROCEDURE DIVISION.
    ENTRY  'DLITCBL'  USING  I-0-PCB
                             ALT-PCB
                             DB-PCB.
        .
        .

    CALL  'CBLTDLI'  USING  INSERT-FUNCTION
                            ALT-PCB
                            OUT-MESSAGE.
```

Figure 11.7. Using an alternate PCB

Using Alternate PCBs

The program we have just examined shows the basics of writing an MP program that simply sends a response back to the originating terminal. We next discuss techniques for using alternate PCBs. We begin by looking at coding to send a message using an alternate PCB that defines the destination of the message. Figure 11.7 shows the partial coding for such a program.

Alternate PCB Coding

The entry coding and the LINKAGE SECTION define three PCBs. The first is the I/O PCB, the second is the alternate PCB, and the third is the data base PCB. If more than one alternate PCB are used, they follow the I/O PCB in the parameter list in the order in which they appear in the PSB.

The Alternate PCB Mask

We next look at the PCB mask that is used to describe alternate PCBs. It consists of only three fields: the name of the output destination, the two-byte reserved field, and the two-byte status code field.

The coding for an Insert to the alternate PCB is similar to the coding for an Insert call for the I/O PCB; the only difference is in the name of the PCB mask.

```
WORKING-STORAGE SECTION.
77  CHANGE     PIC X(4)  VALUE 'CHNG'.
77  NEW-TERM   PIC X(8)  VALUE 'T11432  '.
            .
            .

    CALL  'CBLTDLI'  USING  CHANGE
                            I-O-PCB
                            NEW-TERM.
```

Figure 11.8. Modifying the alternate PCB

Modifying the Alternate PCB

In an alternate PCB, the first eight positions contain either a logical terminal name or a transaction code. If this field contains a logical terminal name, the message is directed to the appropriate logical terminal. If it contains a transaction code, the message is stored in the appropriate transaction code message queue. The message is then later read by the appropriate MP or BMP program. (As we mentioned in Chapter 10, the use of this technique is discouraged in many installations.)

If the alternate PCB has been defined in the PSB as *modifiable*, the program can store a logical terminal name or transaction code into the alternate PCB before issuing Insert calls. This allows the program itself to dynamically specify the destination of the output message. The program does not, however, simply store the destination name directly into the PCB. The destination is set by issuing a Change call (a call that references the CHNG function code). Figure 11.8 shows the coding for a Change call.

A CHNG call references no SSAs, and the I/O area parameter references an eight-position field that contains the logical terminal name or transaction code. The Change call stores that eight-position field into the alternate PCB.

As mentioned in Chapter 10, some installations discourage the use of Change calls and allow them only with special authorization.

MESSAGE PROCESSING PROGRAM STATUS CODES

There are a number of status codes that MP programs can receive when issuing Get calls to the I/O PCB. The three status codes shown below are helpful in implementing programs that read message segments from the message queue:

- Blanks—Call was successful
- QD   —No more message segments
- QC   —No more messages

The status code of *blanks*, as with data base calls, indicates that the call was successful and that a message segment was retrieved by the call.

The QD status code indicates that all the message segments associated with the current message have been read.

The QC status code indicates that there are no more messages in the message queue of the program's transaction type. IMS returns the QC status code if the program repeats the Get-Unique call in attempting to retrieve another message and there are no messages available at this time.

There are many other status codes that IMS can return in a message processing program, but most of them indicate programming errors; the *Application Programming Reference Manual* contains descriptions of these codes.

Many installations have a special routine that must be called when an MP program encounters a status code that it is not designed to handle. Installation standards normally document how status code checking is to be handled by MP programs.

Additional MP Program Techniques

In this section we discuss more programming techniques that can be used in writing MP programs. We discuss the PURG function code used to cause message segments to be transmitted to their destination at a predetermined time. We then look at the format of the scratch pad area and discuss some programming techniques used in writing conversational MP programs. Finally, we list a variety of techniques that can be used to increase the efficiency of MP programs.

The Purge Call

When the program issues Insert calls, either to the I/O PCB or to an alternate PCB, the message segments that the program sends are held in message buffers. They are not actually transmitted until the program finishes working with its input transaction. There are two methods that the program can use in indicating to IMS that it is finished processing the transaction. One method is to terminate the MP program and return control to IMS; the other method is to issue another Get-Unique call to the I/O PCB. Either of the two above events causes IMS to transmit all the output message segments to their destinations.

Under certain circumstances it is useful to explicitly tell IMS to transmit all pending message segments. If the program determines that pending message segments should be transmitted, it issues a Purge call (a call that references the PURG function code). This directs IMS to transmit all pending message segments. The Purge call allows an MP program to transmit more than one mes-

```
WORKING-STORAGE SECTION.
77 PURGE     PIC X(4) VALUE 'PURG'.
              .
              .

       CALL  'CBLTDLI' USING PURGE-FUNCTION
                             I-O-PCB.
```

Figure 11.9. Using the PURG call

sage for each Get-Unique call to the I/O PCB. Figure 11.9 shows the coding for the Purge call.

Many installations discourage the use of the Purge call and allow it to be used only with special authorization. Installation standards should be consulted before using the Purge call.

The Scratch Pad Area

As we discussed in Chapter 10, the scratch pad area (SPA), held in main or virtual storage or in direct access storage, can be used to save information between individual executions of an MP program that processes a conversational transaction. In Chapter 10 we discussed some of the differences between non-conversational and conversational MP programs. We next describe the format of the SPA and show how conversational MP programs work. Figure 11.10 shows the format of the SPA.

Scratch Pad Area Format. The first two bytes give the length (in binary) of the SPA. This length is that of the user work area plus all the control information, including the length field.

Following the length field is a four-position field reserved for IMS. This four-position field should not be modified by the MP program.

Next is an eight-position transaction code field. This contains the transaction code associated with this particular conversation. When the first message segment is read, this transaction code is the same as the transaction code associated with the input transaction. The transaction code normally remains unchanged throughout the conversation. This means that each new transaction sent by the operator causes the same MP program to be scheduled again.

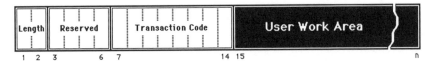

Figure 11.10. Scratch pad area

It is possible, however, that during the conversation the program may determine that some other MP program should take over the next time the operator enters a transaction. The program can store a new transaction code in this field to indicate which MP program should be executed next.

Following the three control fields in the SPA is the *user work area*. The format of this area is determined by the designer of the MP program. When the scratch pad area is read in by the first execution of the MP program, the user work area contains binary zeros.

Using the Scratch Pad Area. The scratch pad area is similar in format to an input message. In a conversational MP program, the scratch pad area is read by issuing a Get-Unique call to the I/O PCB. Message segments are then read with Get-Next calls to the I/O PCB. This is different from a non-conversational program, in which the Get-Unique call retrieves the first message segment. The scratch pad area is written by issuing an Insert call to the I/O PCB. All subsequent Insert calls to the I/O PCB send message segments.

Terminating the Conversation. There are two ways that a conversation can be terminated. First, the terminal operator can end the conversation by entering the appropriate IMS terminal command. When that happens, IMS stops scheduling the MP program for loading. Second, the MP program itself can terminate the conversation by storing binary zeros in the transaction code field in the scratch pad area. When the scratch pad area is then returned to IMS with an insert call, IMS stops scheduling the MP program for loading.

EFFICIENCY TECHNIQUES

Execution efficiency is an important factor for MP programs. In most cases, a large number of MP programs compete with one another for system resources. If the total system is to meet the response time objectives that installation management has set, MP programs must be designed to occupy message processing regions for as short a period of time as possible. The following are a number of hints that can be used to help increase the efficiency of message processing programs and of the system as a whole:

- **Get-Unique Call to the I/O PCB.** The first IMS call issued in an MP program should be the Get-Unique call to the I/O PCB. The reason for this is that IMS preloads the first message segment into a buffer in anticipation of this call. If the MP program makes some other call before issuing the Get-Unique call to the I/O PCB, the message segment is overlaid and IMS has to retrieve it from the message queue and load it into the buffer a second time when the Get-Unique call to the I/O PCB is finally issued.

- **Repeating the Get-Unique Call.** A useful technique, which we have already discussed, is to repeat the Get-Unique call after the program has finished processing a transaction. In case there is another message of the program's transaction type waiting, the message can be processed immediately. This saves IMS the overhead of bringing the MP program back into an MP region.

- **BMP Programs.** For transaction types that require a large amount of processing time, the use of a BMP program to process that transaction type should be considered. A BMP program can often be used when immediate responses are not required.

- **MP/BMP Combinations.** In some cases only a portion of the processing for a particular input message needs to be done immediately. In this case the MP program can do some of the processing immediately and send a response back to the terminal. The message processing program can then take whatever information from the message is needed for later processing and send that information back to the message queue in a transaction. The transaction can then be read later by a BMP program, and the rest of the processing can be done in the batch mode.

- **Reentrant or Serially Reusable.** MP programs should be either reentrant or serially reusable. Reentrant programs can be made permanently resident in main or virtual storage. For some MP programs that are used very frequently, this can increase the program's efficiency.

- **Rapid Responses.** It is important for an MP program to send its response back to the originating terminal as quickly as possible. In many cases, IMS prevents the terminal operator from entering further input until the response is received.

- **Call Clustering.** Whenever possible, an MP program should make all required calls to the I/O PCB to retrieve all segments of a message without making intervening data base calls. Efficiency of the system as a whole is increased if MP programs cluster their calls to the I/O PCB.

- **Data Base Call Limitations.** Many installations enforce a limit of perhaps twenty data base calls per input message. Installation limitations such as these should be observed whenever possible, because they contribute to achieving the installation's response time objectives.

- **Message Length Field.** If a program sends message segments of varying lengths, it is important for the program to appropriately adjust the message length field in the I/O area for each message segment that is sent. Sending extraneous data at the end of each message segment decreases overall system efficiency.

- **Load Module Size.** Many installations enforce a limitation of perhaps

48K for MP program load module size. Exceeding installation size limitations can drastically reduce the efficiency of the MP program.

- **System Service Functions.** In designing MP programs, the following assembler language macros (and their equivalent high-level language functions) should be avoided because of the excessive system overhead they incur: WTO, WTOR, ABEND, TIME, LOAD, LINK, ATTACH, XCTL, SPIE, STAE, GETMAIN. If the date and time are required, they can be obtained from the I/O PCB. If messages must be issued to the system operator, they should normally be sent via an alternate PCB using Insert calls.

MESSAGE FORMAT SERVICE (MFS)

A powerful facility provided by IMS is called *Message Format Service*, or *MFS* for short. This facility is most useful in helping to format messages that will be transmitted to and from display screens. When MFS is used, the program only works with certain fields of data in the screen. IMS inserts and removes filler characters and control characters that will actually be used to format the screens at the terminal.

Input Message Formatting

When display terminals are used, messages to be sent to the message processing program from the terminal often consist of full screens of information. These screens often contain a lot of descriptive information that helps make the screen readable. MFS provides two control blocks, set up by macros, to separate out information of direct interest to the MP or BMP program.

One control block, called the *Message Input Descriptor* (MID) is used to describe an input message as the program would like to see it. The MID describes just those fields on the screen in which the program is interested. Another control block, called the *Device Input Format*, or *DIF* describes the screen format as the terminal operator formats it.

Output Message Formatting

Two other MFS control blocks are used to help format screens that will be transmitted from the program to a display terminal. The *Message Output Descriptor*, or *MOD*, describes the message as the program formats it. Another control block, called the *Device Output Format* or *DOF*, describes the screen format as it will appear on the screen. MFS uses the MOD and DOF to translate the data fields that the program places in the output message into a complete screen format as it will appear on the display screen.

MFS Advantages

MFS allows a program to work with information on the data field level, avoiding concern over where on the screen the information is stored or should appear. It allows complex screen formats to be used without tying the application program to the screen area where the pertinent information is stored.

The subject of screen formatting, and the writing of the four control blocks that MFS uses to help format display terminal screens, is almost the subject of a book in itself; we will not go into MFS in any more detail here. If an installation uses MFS, the data base administration group can be consulted to learn more about how it is used in that installation.

CODING PROBLEM

In this coding problem, the PATIENT segment retrieval program from Chapter 4 should be converted to an MP program. That program reads a series of input records, each containing a hospital name, a ward number, and a patient name, and prepares a listing of some of the information in the PATIENT segments for the patients identified in the input records.

The MP program should process messages consisting of a single message segment. The format of this message segment is shown in Figure 11.11. Notice that the same information is supplied to the MP program as is supplied to the batch program. The program should send a message to the originating terminal. Its format is shown is Figure 11.12. Store binary zeros in the ZZ field bytes following the length field of the output message.

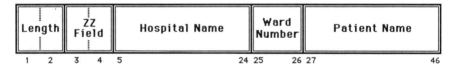

Figure 11.11. Input message segment

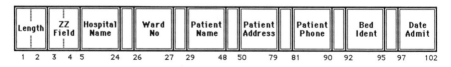

Figure 11.12. Output message format

Part IV
Advanced Techniques

12
IMS Access Methods

The access method chosen for a data base is not normally a major concern of the application programmer. Usually it is determined by the data base administrator, and is transparent to application programs. However, there are efficiency considerations that the application programmer should be aware of with respect to the choice of an access method, and the access method chosen may restrict the use of some IMS facilities.

In this chapter, we provide an overview of the main access methods that IMS uses and discuss those characteristics of the access methods that are of the most interest to application programmers.

STORAGE ORGANIZATIONS AND ACCESS METHODS

At the heart of IMS are the access methods that retrieve and manipulate the segments stored in a data base. IMS supports two major methods for organizing data bases. These two storage organization methods are the *Hierarchical Sequential Organization* (HS organization) and the *Hierarchical Direct Organization* (HD organization). Each of these organizations is supported by a set of IMS access methods. The Hierarchical Sequential Organization is supported by HSAM, for *Hierarchical Sequential Access Method* and HISAM, for *Hierarchical Indexed Sequential Access Method*. The Hierarchical Direct Organization is supported by HDAM, for *Hierarchical Direct Access Method*, and HIDAM, for *Hierarchical Indexed Direct Access Method*.

In addition to the two forms of storage organization and the four major access methods, IMS supports a fifth access method called GSAM, for *Generalized Sequential Access Method*. GSAM is a special-purpose access method that is discussed in Appendix C.

The Hierarchical Sequential Organization

With the Hierarchical Sequential Organization, using either HSAM or HISAM, segments within a data base record are related to each other by physical adjacency on the storage medium. In other words, segments are arranged physically in hierarchical sequence. The major difference between HSAM and HISAM is in the way that root segments are retrieved. In HSAM data bases, no provision is made for directly accessing a particular root segment. All segments, including root segments, are stored in hierarchical sequence, and random retrieval of a root segment is performed by scanning through all the segments up to that root. In an HISAM data base, either an ISAM or VSAM index contains pointers to all the root segments. The index is used to gain direct access to root segments.

The Hierarchical Direct Organization

In the Hierarchical Direct Organization, IMS uses direct address pointers to chain together in hierarchical sequence all the segment occurrences in a data base record. As in the Hierarchical Sequential Organization, the main difference between HDAM and HIDAM is in the way that an individual root segment is accessed.

With HDAM, a software routine called a *randomizing module* is used to translate a root key value into the actual physical location of that root segment. With HIDAM, IMS uses a separate index data base to locate root segments.

The IMS Physical Access Methods

To implement the various access methods, IMS uses most of the standard operating system access methods, including QSAM, BSAM, VSAM, and ISAM. IMS also employs a special IMS physical access method called OSAM, for *Overflow Sequential Access Method.*

In general, OSAM combines many of the good features of the sequential access methods and of BDAM. An OSAM data set looks like a sequential data set to the operating system and can be read with BSAM or QSAM. Like the sequential access methods, OSAM allows either fixed-length records or fixed-length blocked records, and an OSAM data set does not have to be preformatted. However, like a BDAM data set, OSAM allows direct access to records.

THE TWO HIERARCHICAL SEQUENTIAL ACCESS METHODS

As we mentioned earlier, the Hierarchical Sequential Organization supports two major access methods, HSAM and HISAM. In both access methods, the seg-

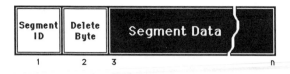

Figure 12.1. Hierarchical sequential segment format

ments within each data base record are stored in hierarchical sequence on the storage medium. HISAM supports an index, which IMS uses to locate root segments, but HSAM does not. We will look first at the physical format of segments as they are stored in either HSAM or HISAM data bases.

The Hierarchical Sequential Segment Format

HSAM and HISAM segments have the same format. Each segment consists of a segment prefix followed by data. (See Figure 12.1.) In both HSAM and HISAM, the segment prefix is two bytes in length. The first byte of the prefix contains a binary number called a segment code which identifies the segment type. The segment codes of each segment type are assigned automatically during DBDGEN. They correspond to the hierarchical sequence of the segment types, as defined by the sequence of the SEGM statements in the DBD. For example, the root segment always has a segment code of 1. The second segment type defined has a segment code of 2, and so on.

The second byte of the prefix is the delete byte. This byte is maintained by IMS and is used in handling segment deletions.

Neither of the two prefix bytes is available to the application program when retrieving or manipulating segments. The first byte of the data portion of the segment is the first byte that is stored in the application program's I/O area.

HSAM—Hierarchical Sequential Access Method

HSAM uses one of the standard operating system Sequential Access Methods, either BSAM or QSAM. HSAM is used mainly for applications that require very little random access to segments and that process segments mainly in hierarchical sequence. HSAM is generally considered to be a special-purpose access method because it imposes restrictions too severe for most data base applications.

HSAM Data Base Example. Figure 12.2 shows how HOSPITAL data base segment occurrences are stored in an HSAM data base. We will assume here that the data base consists only of HOSPITAL, WARD, and FACILITY seg-

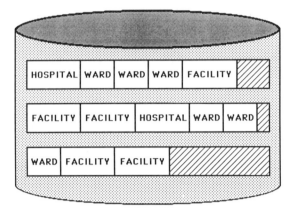

Figure 12.2. HSAM data base

ments. The data base consists of a standard sequential file containing fixed-length, unblocked records. Segments are stored in hierarchical sequence, and each block contains as many segments as will fit. Segments cannot span more than one block, so if a new segment will not fit at the end of the current block, the segment is put at the beginning of the next block.

Notice that root segments are treated no differently from dependent segments. The root segment for the second data base record is stored immediately after the last dependent segment from the first data base record. If there is room for it in the current block, it is placed there; if not, it is written in a new block.

Only certain IMS calls are valid for HSAM data bases. These are Get-Next, Get-Unique, and Insert in the load mode. HSAM segments cannot be deleted or replaced and new segment occurrences cannot be inserted into an existing HSAM data base. To update an HSAM data base, an application must process the old HSAM data base as input and create a new version of the HSAM data base using Insert Calls in the load mode.

HSAM DBD and PSB Statements. Figures 12.3 and 12.4 illustrate HSAM processing. Figure 12.3 shows a possible DBD and PSB for an HSAM data base; Figure 12.4 shows parts of a sample update program using that PSB.

Notice that in the DBD two DD names are specified in the DATASET statement. One DD name, named DD1, is for the input data base; the other, named DD2, is for the output data base. Notice also that the PSB contains two PCBs. The first PCB is for the input data base and the second is for output.

The update program issues a series of Get-Next calls using the first PCB and a series of Insert calls using the second PCB. In this way the application program reads the old version of the data base and writes out a new version,

```
DBD       NAME=HOSPITAL,ACCESS=HSAM
DATASET   DD1=INPUT,DD2=OUTPUT,DEVICE=TAPE
SEGM      ...
  .
  .

FIELD     ...
DBDGEN
FINISH
END


PCB       TYPE=DB,PROCOPT=G,NAME=HOSPITAL
SENSEG    ...
  .
  .

SENSEG    ...

PCB       TYPE=DB,PROCOPT=LS,NAME=HOSPITAL
SENSEG    ...
  .
  .

SENSEG    ...

PSBGEN    LANG=COBOL,PSBNAME=HSAMPSB
END
```

Figure 12.3. DBD and PSB coding for HSAM


```
LINKAGE SECTION.
01   INPUT-PCB.
       .
       .

01   OUTPUT-PCB.
       .
       .

PROCEDURE DIVISION.
     ENTRY  'DLITCBL'  USING  INPUT-PCB
                              OUTPUT-PCB.
       .
       .

     CALL  'CBLTDLI'  USING  GET-NEXT
                            INPUT-PCB
                            INPUT-AREA.
       .
       .

     CALL  'CBLTDLI'  USING  INSERT
                            OUTPUT-PCB
                            OUTPUT-AREA
                            UNQUAL-SSA.
```

Figure 12.4. HSAM Program

processing whatever updates are required. An HSAM data base update program operates in a similar manner to a program that updates a sequential file.

Since Delete calls are not allowed for HSAM data bases, IMS does not manipulate the delete byte in the prefix of an HSAM segment. It is there for compatibility with the other access methods.

Get-Unique Processing with HSAM. The following discussion of how HSAM handles Get-Unique calls illustrates how inefficient HSAM can be for random retrieval. The first Get-Unique call that the application program makes causes IMS to start at the beginning of the HSAM data base. IMS then scans forward until the requested segment is located. The result of subsequent Get-Unique calls depends on the following factors:

- Whether there is a key field defined for the root segment. (HSAM is the only access method that does not require a key field for the root segment.)
- Whether the processing option is defined as PROCOPT=G or PRO-COPT=GS.
- Whether there is a sequence field defined for the root segment, and how the root key value compares with the key value specified in the previous Get-Unique call.

If there is no key field defined for the root segment, IMS starts at the beginning of the data base for each Get-Unique call. If the root segment has a key field defined, then IMS attempts to make use of current position in handling Get-Unique calls. If the second Get-Unique call specifies a root key that is greater than the root key specified in the previous Get-Unique call, IMS moves forward in the data base from current position.

When the program directs IMS to move backward in the data base by specifying a root key value that is less than the root key value of the previous segment retrieved, the search is handled differently depending on whether a processing option of G or GS is specified in the PCB. If a processing option of G is specified, IMS scans backward in the data base from current position in searching for the requested segment. If a processing option of GS is specified, IMS starts at the beginning of the data base.

HSAM data bases are most often used when it is necessary to maintain data in the form of an IMS data base, but the data is not used very often, such as in the case of historical data. HSAM data bases are also sometimes used when it is necessary to maintain IMS data on a sequential device, such as a tape drive.

SHSAM—Simple HSAM. There is a variation of HSAM that is used for compatibility with standard operating system data sets. A SHSAM data base is a data base consisting of only root segments that do not contain segment prefixes.

This makes the segment occurrences look exactly like records in a standard operating system data set. With SHSAM, a root-only data base can be loaded using IMS calls, and the data base can later be processed by a non-IMS program using standard operating system access methods.

HISAM—Hierarchical Indexed Sequential Access Method

HISAM is a more commonly used IMS access method that, although still oriented to sequential processing of segments, allows the use of all IMS calls. The main difference between HSAM and HISAM is in the way that root segments are accessed. With HISAM, a VSAM or ISAM index is used to locate root segments. Dependent segments within each data base record are stored sequentially, as in an HSAM data base.

HISAM Data Set Structure. An HISAM data base always consists of at least two data sets. The DBD for an HISAM data specifies that either VSAM or the ISAM/OSAM combination be used to implement the data base. (See Figure 12.5.) If VSAM is chosen, the data base consists of a KSDS and an ESDS. If the ISAM/OSAM combination is chosen, an ISAM data set and an OSAM data set are used to store the segments.

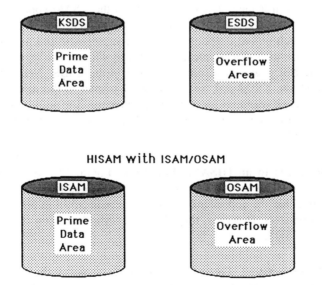

Figure 12.5. HISAM data set configuration

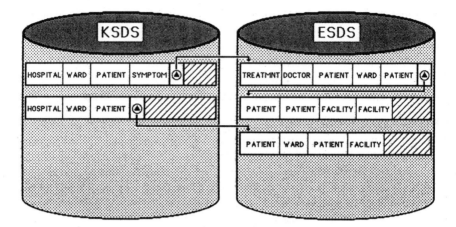

Figure 12.6. HISAM with VSAM

The KSDS or ISAM portion of an HISAM data base contains all of the root segments and as many dependent segments as will fit. The KSDS or ISAM index contains a pointer to each root segment within the data portion of the KSDS or ISAM data set. The ESDS or OSAM data set contains all of the dependent segments that do not fit in the KSDS or ISAM data set.

Figure 12.6 shows how a portion of an HISAM data base looks after the data base has been loaded. The example shows the VSAM configuration; the ISAM/OSAM version is similar. There is one record in the KSDS for each data base record. Each record contains at least a root segment and as many of its dependent segments, in hierarchical sequence, as will fit. The segments that do not fit in the KSDS logical record are stored in the ESDS. Notice that each record in both the KSDS and the ESDS has a pointer to the next record that contains dependent segments for that data base record. The need for this pointer will be clearer after we see what happens when a few segments are added to a data base record.

Adding Segments to an HISAM Data Base. Figure 12.7 shows what can happen in the ESDS after a PATIENT segment is added to the first data base record. Notice that the dependent segments are maintained in hierarchical sequence with pointers. However, they do not necessarily remain in physical sequence in the ESDS.

HISAM Disadvantages. Figure 12.7 illustrates some of the drawbacks of HISAM. Suppose we want to access the FACILITY segments for a particular hospital, but we are not interested in any of the WARD, PATIENT, SYMP-

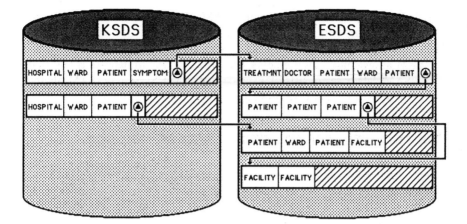

Figure 12.7. Adding PATIENT segment

TOM, TREATMENT, or DOCTOR segments. Since all segments in a data base record are maintained in hierarchical sequence, it is necessary to read through all preceding segment occurrences to get to the first occurrence of the FACILITY segment. As it is likely that each data base record is large in an actual implementation of the HOSPITAL data base, HISAM would probably be inefficient for random retrieval of FACILITY segments. HISAM also tends to be inefficient when the data base is subject to a lot of additions and deletions.

In general, HISAM is a good access method to use when random access is required to root segments and when data base records are fairly small, or when access to dependent segments is always sequential.

HISAM DBD Statements. Figure 12.8 shows a DBD for an HISAM data base. Notice that two DD statements are specified. The first, named DD1, describes either the KSDS or the ISAM data set. The second DD statement, named OVFLW, describes either the ESDS or the OSAM data set.

```
DBD      NAME=HOSPITAL,ACCESS=(HISAM,ISAM)
DATASET  DD1=PRIME,OVFLW=OVERFLOW,DEVICE=3350
SEGM     ...
  .
  .
FIELD    ...
DBDGEN
FINISH
END
```

Figure 12.8. DBD statements for HISAM

SHISAM—Simple HISAM. As with HSAM, HISAM has a variation that provides compatibility with standard operating system access methods. A SHISAM data base consists only of root segments that do not contain prefixes. Since SHISAM allows only root segments, the ESDS or OSAM data set is not used. A SHISAM data base consists of a standard VSAM KSDS or an ISAM file that can be processed by non-IMS programs using VSAM or ISAM.

THE TWO HIERARCHICAL DIRECT ACCESS METHODS

The hierarchical direct organization supports two access methods: HDAM for Hierarchical Direct Access Method and HIDAM for Hierarchical Indexed Direct Access Method. With either of the hierarchical direct access methods, segments are stored in a VSAM ESDS or in an OSAM data set.

HD Segment Format

As we have just seen, segments in an hierarchical sequential data base are related to each other by their physical sequence in the data base. The physical sequence of segments in a hierarchical direct data base does not normally correspond to hierarchical sequence. Hierarchical sequence is maintained in a hierarchical direct data base through the use of direct address pointers that are stored within each segment occurrence.

Figure 12.9 shows the format of a hierarchical direct data base segment occurrence. The first two bytes of the segment prefix contain the segment code and the delete byte. Following those two bytes is an area reserved for the direct address pointers used to chain segments together. This area varies in format depending on the types of pointers that have been requested in the DBD for each segment type. Following the pointer area in the prefix is the data area of the segment occurrence.

HD Access Method Characteristics

HD data base performance frequently depends on the size of the data base records and the types of pointers that are specified. In general, however, direct

Figure 12.9. Hierarchical direct segment format

access to segments in a hierarchical direct data base record can often be much faster than direct access in an equivalent hierarchical sequential data base. Both HDAM and HIDAM work similarly within a data base record. The difference between the two access methods is in the way that root segments are accessed.

HDAM Root Segment Access. In HDAM, a randomizing module, identified in the DBD, is used to access root segments. A randomizing module is a special program, usually written by a system programmer, that converts a root-key value into the actual location within the data base where the corresponding root segment is stored.

A problem with randomizing modules is that they invariably produce *synonyms*. A synonym occurs when the randomizing routine produces the same storage address for more than one root-key value. HDAM is designed to handle synonyms; however, too many synonyms can cause inefficiencies. A good randomizing module uses an algorithm that is designed to produce as few synonyms as possible.

After a data base has been loaded using a randomizing module to generate storage addresses, the physical sequence of the root segments is generally different from root-key sequence. For this reason, HDAM is poorly suited to sequential processing of root segments. If a series of Get-Next calls is issued for root segments, IMS retrieves root segments in a sequence roughly equivalent to the sequence in which they are stored on the storage medium and not in root key sequence. This produces undesirable results in applications that require access to root segments in root-key sequence. With an HDAM data base, root segments cannot be retrieved in key sequence unless all of the key values are known.

HDAM DBD Statements. DBD statements for HDAM and HIDAM data bases allow pointer types to be specified in the SEGM statements for each segment type. Because pointers are chosen in the same manner for both HDAM and HIDAM data bases, we will first examine the differences between DBD statements for HDAM and HIDAM data bases. After that we will see how pointer types are specified. Figure 12.10 shows the statements in an HDAM DBD.

The ACCESS parameter specifies that the data base is an HDAM data base. The RMNAME operand is required for HDAM. The first subparameter specifies the load module name of the randomizing module that HDAM is to use in accessing root segments. The numbers following the randomizing module name specify information about the physical nature of the ESDS or OSAM data set that is used to store segments. Values for these parameters are normally chosen by the DBA, and are beyond the scope of this book.

```
DBD        NAME=HOSPITAL,ACCESS=HDAM,RMNAME=(RANDMOD,1,125,400)
DATASET    DD1=HDAMDD,DEVICE=3350
SEGM       ...
 .
 .
FIELD      ...
DBDGEN
FINISH
END
```

Figure 12.10. DBD statements for HDAM

HIDAM Root Segment Access. An HIDAM data base consists of a combination of two data bases. A separate index data base is used to point to root segments. Figure 12.11 shows an HIDAM data base that uses VSAM or the ISAM/OSAM combination.

With VSAM, a combination of a KSDS and an ESDS is used to maintain an index data base that points to root segments. The root segment occurrences themselves are stored in a separate data base that is implemented as an ESDS data set. The index portion of an HIDAM data base is actually a separate data base and can be processed apart from the data for some applications.

The ISAM/OSAM combination works in a similar manner. A combination of an ISAM data set and an OSAM data set makes up the index, which points to root segment occurrences that are stored in a separate OSAM data set.

A rarely employed data set combination uses a VSAM data set to maintain the index portion of the data base and an OSAM data set for segment occurrences.

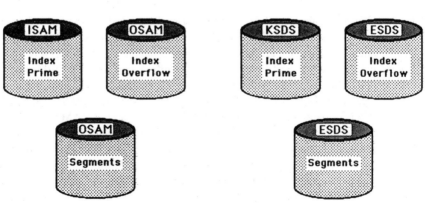

Figure 12.11. HIDAM data set configurations

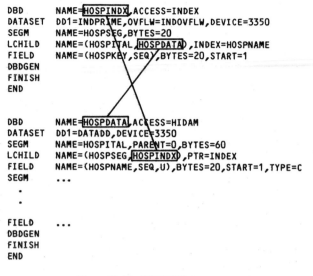

```
DBD       NAME=HOSPINDX,ACCESS=INDEX
DATASET   DD1=INDPRIME,OVFLW=INDOVFLW,DEVICE=3350
SEGM      NAME=HOSPSEG,BYTES=20
LCHILD    NAME=(HOSPITAL,HOSPDATA),INDEX=HOSPNAME
FIELD     NAME=(HOSPKEY,SEQ),BYTES=20,START=1
DBDGEN
FINISH
END


DBD       NAME=HOSPDATA,ACCESS=HIDAM
DATASET   DD1=DATADD,DEVICE=3350
SEGM      NAME=HOSPITAL,PARENT=0,BYTES=60
LCHILD    NAME=(HOSPSEG,HOSPINDX),PTR=INDEX
FIELD     NAME=(HOSPNAME,SEQ,U),BYTES=20,START=1,TYPE=C
SEGM      ...
           .
           .

FIELD     ...
DBDGEN
FINISH
END
```

Figure 12.12. DBDGEN statements

HIDAM handles synonyms and also allows root segments to be retrieved in key sequence. It is well suited to applications that require both sequential and random retrievals. The tradeoff is that random access to root segments is through an index, which requires storage space.

HIDAM DBD Statements. Figure 12.12 shows the main DBD statements for an HIDAM data base. Notice that an HIDAM data base requires two separate and distinct DBDs. The first DBD is for the HIDAM index, and the second is for the data portion.

The boxes in the diagram show how the various DBD statement operands hook the two DBDs together. The LCHILD DBD statement is used to connect the index portion of the data base to the data portion. Notice also that the AC-CESS operands are used to distinguish between the index portion of the data base and the data portion.

Hierarchical Direct Pointers

When a hierarchical direct data base is defined, pointers are chosen individually for each segment type. The more pointers that are chosen, the faster access will be to segments within a data base record. On the other hand, the more pointers that are specified, the more space will be taken up within each segment occurrence for pointers. Each pointer occupies four bytes in a segment's prefix.

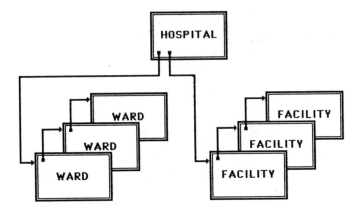

Figure 12.13. Physical-child-first and physical-twin-forward

We will next look at the kinds of pointers that can be specified for segments in the hierarchical direct organization. To simplify things, we will look at a physical data base that consists only of HOSPITAL, WARD, and FACILITY segments. We will begin by looking at the *physical-child-first* and *physical-twin-forward*. These are the default pointers that are chosen when information about pointers is omitted. Physical-child-first and physical-twin-forward pointers are shown in Figure 12.13.

Physical-Child-First and Physical-Twin-Forward Pointers. The pointers from the HOSPITAL segment occurrence to the WARD and FACILITY segment occurrences are physical-child-first pointers. They point from a parent segment to the first occurrence of each of that parent's physical child segment types.

The other pointers are physical-twin-forward pointers. Figure 12.13 shows that there are three WARD segment occurrences stored under the HOSPITAL segment occurrence. The physical-twin-forward pointers point from each occurrence of a particular segment type to the next occurrence of that same segment type, thus forming a twin chain.

Figure 12.13 also shows physical-twin-forward pointers for the FACILITY segment. Physical-child-first pointers and physical-twin-forward pointers work together. If a particular segment type has a physical-child-first pointer pointing to it from its parent, it must also have physical-twin-forward pointers. If there is only a single occurrence of a child segment type, space is still reserved for a physical-twin-forward pointer. It indicates the end of the twin chain.

Hierarchical Pointers. Figure 12.14 shows another type of pointer that can be used instead of the physical-child-first and physical-twin-forward combination.

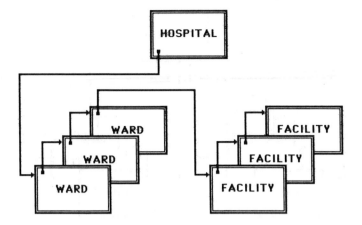

Figure 12.14. Hierarchical pointers

They are called *hierarchical* pointers. On first glance, hierarchical pointers look very similar to the physical-child-first/physical-twin-forward combination. The difference is that there is only a single pointer in the parent segment rather than one for each child segment type. In the example, the first FACILITY segment is pointed to by the last occurrence of the WARD segment. With hierarchical pointers, all the segments are chained together in hierarchical sequence. With physical-child-first pointers, IMS can get directly to the first occurrence of the WARD segment or to the first occurrence of the FACILITY segment without accessing any intervening segments. With hierarchical pointers, IMS must read through all the WARD segments before it can get to the first FACILITY segment.

Hierarchical pointers chain segments together in the sequence in which they would be physically stored in an HSAM or HISAM data base. However, in the hierarchical direct organization they are chained together with pointers and are not necessarily stored in *physical* sequence.

Physical-child-first pointers are normally used when direct access is required to occurrences of a particular segment type. Hierarchical pointers can be used in portions of a data base record where access is normally sequential. Later in this chapter, we will see how different types of pointers can be requested in different portions of a data base record. Now we will look at some variations of the three main pointer types.

Pointer Variations. Each of the three types of pointers, physical-child-first, physical-twin-forward, and hierarchical, has a second variation. When physical-child pointers are used, either *physical-child-first* pointers or *physical-child-*

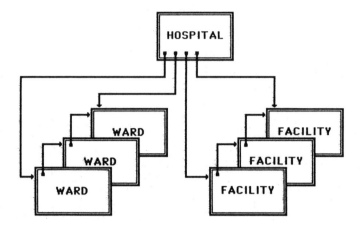

Figure 12.15. Physical-child-first and -last pointers

first-and-last pointers can be specified. Physical-child-first-and-last pointers are shown in Figure 12.15.

When physical-child-first-and-last pointers are specified, each HOSPITAL segment occurrence has four pointers in its prefix rather than only two when physical-child-first pointers are used. There is a pointer to the first occurrence of each child segment type and also a pointer to the last occurrence of each child segment type. When physical-child pointers are used, either physical-child-first pointers or physical-child-first-and-last pointers can be specified. Physical-child-last pointers cannot be used alone. Physical-child-last pointers allow quicker access to the last occurrence of a particular segment type. This helps increase efficiency when new segments must be inserted at the ends of long twin chains.

Physical-twin pointers also have two variations. In addition to the physical-twin-forward pointers that we have already seen, *physical-twin-forward-and-backward* pointers can also be specified. Figure 12.16 shows these for WARD segments. In addition to a set of pointers pointing forward along the twin chain, a second set of pointers points backward along the twin chain. The combination of physical-twin-forward-and-backward pointers can improve performance when segment occurrences are deleted from long twin chains.

The second variation of hierarchical pointers is called *hierarchical-forward-and-backward*. Hierarchical-forward-and-backward pointers work in a similar manner to physical-twin-forward-and-backward pointers. Figure 12.17 shows this pointer variation. In addition to a set of pointers pointing forward along the hierarchical path, there is also a set of pointers pointing backward. Again, the main use for hierarchical-forward-and-backward pointers is to improve segment deletion performance in long twin chains.

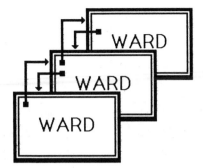

Figure 12.16. Physical-child-forward and -backward pointers

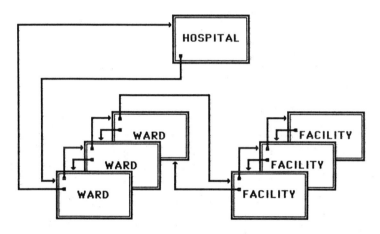

Figure 12.17. Hierarchical-forward and -backward pointers

Pointer Combinations. Figure 12.18 shows a portion of an entire HOSPITAL data base record. For simplicity, we are not showing all occurrences of each segment type. The segment occurrences that are shown illustrate how different pointer types can be chosen for different segment types. In the example, physical-child-first pointers are used in the HOSPITAL segment to point to both the WARD and the FACILITY segments. However, both physical-child-first and physical-child-last pointers have been chosen to point from the WARD segment to the PATIENT segment.

Also, physical-twin-forward-and-backward pointers are shown for the PA-TIENT segment, although physical-child-first pointers only are specified for the WARD and FACILITY segments. And finally, hierarchical pointers have been chosen for the SYMPTOM, TREATMNT, and DOCTOR segments. This is a

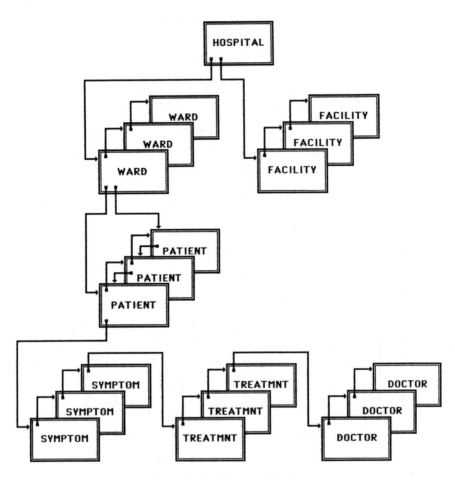

Figure 12.18. Pointer combinations

good choice if we always process these segment occurrences sequentially, and we will not process a DOCTOR segment without first processing the SYMPTOM and TREATMNT segments.

In this particular example we do not have an example of hierarchical-forward-and-backward pointers, which is a little-used pointer combination.

Choosing Pointer Types. As mentioned earlier, pointer types are specified in the SEGM statements of the DBD for the data base. Figure 12.19 shows the SEGM statements for the pointer combination in Figure 12.18. The PARENT

```
SEGM   NAME=HOSPITAL,PARENT=0

SEGM   NAME=WARD,PARENT=(HOSPITAL,SNGL),PTR=TWIN

SEGM   NAME=PATIENT,PARENT=(WARD,SNGL),PTR=TB

SEGM   NAME=SYMPTOM,PARENT=(PATIENT,SNGL),PTR=HIER

SEGM   NAME=TREATMNT,PARENT=PATIENT,PTR=HIER

SEGM   NAME=DOCTOR,PARENT=PATIENT,PTR=HIER

SEGM   NAME=FACILITY,PARENT=(HOSPITAL,SNGL),PTR=TWIN
```

Figure 12.19. SEGM statements for pointer combination example

and POINTER operands are used to specify pointer types for each segment type.

Pointer Selection Rules

Physical-child-first and physical-twin-forward pointers are chosen if no mention of pointers is made in the SEGM statements for an HD data base. Three simple rules govern the the pointer combinations that can be explicitly chosen for each segment type:

- **Pointer Rule 1.** For a given segment type, the physical-child/physical-twin combination and hierarchical pointers are mutually exclusive.
- **Pointer Rule 2.** The POINTER parameter is used to specify physical-twin pointers or hierarchical pointers. These pointers reside in occurrences of the segment type identified by the SEGM statement that contains the POINTER parameter.
- **Pointer Rule 3.** The second subparameter of the PARENT operand is used to select physical-child pointers. These pointers reside in occurrences of the segment type identified in the PARENT parameter. Since physical-child/physical-twin pointers and hierarchical pointers are mutually exclusive, physical-child pointers cannot be specified in the PARENT operand if that segment's parent has hierarchical pointers specified in its POINTER operand.

DATA SET GROUPS

Most access methods allow different segment types to be separated into *data set groups*. Each group of segments can be stored in its own data set or group of data sets. This is sometimes done when different segment types have different maintenance requirements. For example, only a few segment types may require frequent updating, while the rest of the data base might remain essentially static. It is best to create one or more data set groups for segments that are subject to heavy maintenance requirements, because often it is possible to reorganize only a single data set group rather than the entire data base.

EXERCISES

1. Match each access method below with the statement or statements that best describe it.

ACCESS METHODS	STATEMENTS
A. HSAM	a. Access to root segments is via an index.
B. HISAM	b. Access to all segments is sequential.
C. HDAM	c. Dependent segments are accessed via direct address pointers.
D. HIDAM	d. Segments have a two-byte prefix area.
	e. Simple root-only data bases are supported where segments have no prefix area.
	f. Get-Next calls do not retrieve root segments in key sequence.
	g. Dependent segments are accessed sequentially.
	h. Normally the best access methods to use for a mixture of sequential and direct retrievals.
	i. Segment prefix normally bigger than two bytes.
	j. Normally the best access method if all or most retrievals are random.
	k. Normally used only for sequential retrieval or for historical files.
	l. Best for limited random retrievals and low volume of updating.
	m. Root segments are accessed via a randomizing module.
	n. Requires pointers in segment occurrences.

2. List each pointer combination below with the statement that best describes it. Each pointer combination matches one statement.

POINTERS	STATEMENTS
A. Physical-child-first	a. Segments are chained in a forward direction in hierarchical sequence.
B. Physical-twin-forward	
C. Hierarchical	b. Pointers are maintained in both forward and backward directions along a twin chain.
D. Physical-child-first-and-last	
E. Physical-twin forward-and-backward	c. A parent segment contains a pointer to the first occurrence of each of its dependent segment types on the next lower level.
F. Hierarchical-forward-and-backward	d. Segments are chained in both forward and backward directions in hierarchical sequence.
	e. A parent segment contains pointers to the first and last occurrence of its dependent segment types at the next lower level.
	f. Pointers are maintained in a forward direction along a twin chain.

13
Secondary Indexing

Sequential retrievals are normally made using key sequence. The secondary indexing feature allows the program to sequentially retrieve segments, or search for segments, in a sequence other than key sequence. In most cases, the use of a secondary index is transparent to the application program, but there are some cases in which application programmers must be aware of them. In this chapter we define the terms used to describe secondary indexes, show how they can be used, and see how they can be accessed in application programs.

SECONDARY INDEX IMPLEMENTATION

A secondary index is implemented in the form of a self-contained data base that stores a series of pointers which point to segments in the data base being indexed. The secondary index allows the program to process segments in a sequence other than key sequence. Since a secondary index is a separate data base, each secondary index is described by its own individual DBD. Secondary index data bases are connected to the main data base through the use of DBDGEN parameters. The definitions of some new terms, along with examples, will illustrate how secondary indexes are used.

SECONDARY INDEX TERMINOLOGY

A secondary index is in many ways similar to the index used to implement an HIDAM data base. Figure 13.1 shows the relationship between the index and the data portion of an HIDAM data base. We saw in Chapter 12 that in an HIDAM data base the keys of all the root segments are collected and stored in an index data base. The index data base contains index pointer segments corresponding to the root segments stored in the data portion of the HIDAM

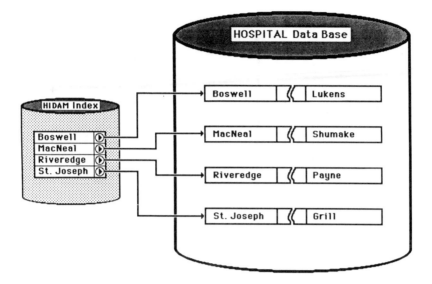

Figure 13.1. HIDAM index

data base. Each index pointer segment contains a key value and a pointer to a root segment.

The ADMINDX Secondary Index

To show a simple example of a secondary index, we will index the root segments in the HOSPITAL data base on the administrator's name field, which we will assume is different for each hospital. Figure 13.2 shows what this secondary indexing relationship looks like. The secondary index contains an index pointer segment for each root segment in the data base. The key fields in these pointer segments contain administrator names rather than hospital names. Each segment in the secondary index data base points to its corresponding HOSPITAL segment in the HOSPITAL data base. This secondary index can be used in three ways by an application program. First, an application program could use a sequence of Get-Next calls to retrieve HOSPITAL segments in administrator name sequence rather than in hospital name sequence.

```
GN      HOSPITAL
```

Notice that the Get-Next call does not reference the secondary index. The above use of the secondary index is transparent to the application program. In order to tell IMS that the secondary index should be used in making each se-

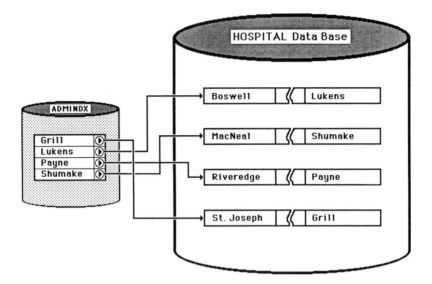

Figure 13.2. ADMINDX secondary index

quential retrieval, the call must reference a PCB that specifies the secondary index. The following is the PCB statement that directs IMS to access the HOS-PITAL data base using the secondary index:

```
PCB     TYPE=DB,NAME=HOSPITAL,
        PROCOPT=A,PROCSEQ=ADMINDX
```

The PROCSEQ parameter names the DBD that defines the secondary index. When a secondary index is used in this way, we are accessing the data base using a *secondary processing sequence*.

Referencing the Indexed Field

A second way to use the secondary index is to issue a call that references a PCB that does not identify the secondary index and references a special field called the *indexed field* in an SSA. The following SSA shows an example of this.

```
GU      HOSPITAL(XADMIN   =LUKENS                    )
```

The XADMIN field is a special field specified in the DBD for the data base being indexed. Because the indexed field is referenced in the SSA, this use of the secondary index is not transparent to the application program. The application programmer must know the name of the indexed field in order to access the secondary index in this manner.

Processing the Secondary Index as Data

In addition to using a secondary processing sequence or referencing the indexed field name, a third alternative for using a secondary index is to directly access the pointer segments stored in the secondary index data base. When this is done, the application program works directly with the secondary index and does not necessarily reference the data base that it indexes. A possible use for processing the ADMINDX secondary index as data is to prepare a listing of administrator names in alphabetical sequence.

Secondary Index Terms

Figure 13.3 shows a diagram of the ADMINDX secondary index that illustrates four important secondary indexing terms. The *index source segment* is the segment from which the information to be stored in the secondary index is taken. In this example, the HOSPITAL segment is the index source segment because

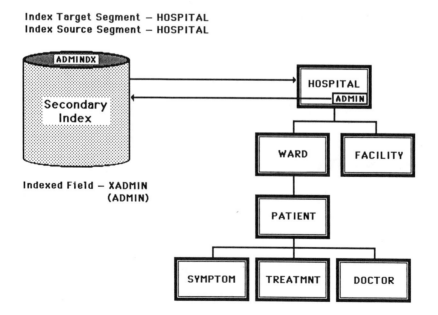

Figure 13.3. Secondary index relationships

the ADMIN field, which is stored in the secondary index, comes from the HOSPITAL segment.

The *index target segment* is the segment being indexed by the secondary index. In this example, the index target segment is the same as the index source segment, because a HOSPITAL segment occurrence is pointed to by each entry in the secondary index. Later in this chapter, we will see that it is not required for the index source segment and the index target segment to be the same segment.

The *indexed field* is a new field defined in the DBD for the data base being indexed. It describes the information from the data base being indexed that is to be stored in the secondary index. In this example, the indexed field, named XADMIN, consists of a single field from the index source segment, the ADMIN field. An indexed field can also be made up of two or more fields taken from the index source segment.

The *index pointer segment* is the segment type that is actually stored in the secondary index data base. Each occurrence of the index pointer segment contains information from an index source segment and a pointer to its corresponding index target segment.

PATINDX Secondary Index

A second secondary index that might be useful with the HOSPITAL data base indexes PATIENT segments based on patient names. The relationships implemented by this secondary index, called PATINDX, are shown in Figure 13.4.

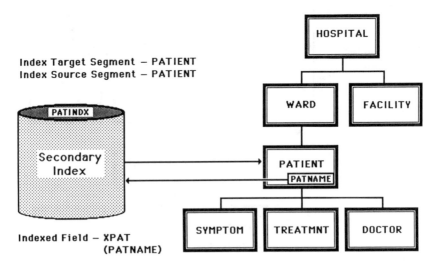

Figure 13.4. PATINDX secondary index

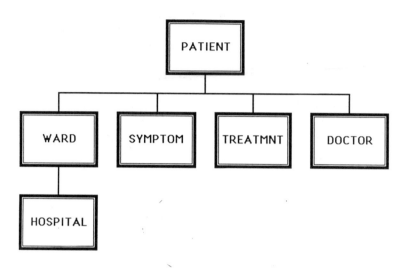

Figure 13.5. PATINDX hierarchical structure

Notice that with this secondary index, the index target segment is below the level of the root segment.

When the index target segment is below the root segment, the secondary index gives the user a new view of the data base. If PATINDX is used to provide a secondary processing sequence, a new hierarchical structure is created with the PATIENT segment at the root level. The new hierarchical structure created by PATINDX is shown in Figure 13.5. All segments below PATIENT in the original hierarchy keep their same relationships to the PATIENT segment. All segments that were above the PATIENT segment are inverted and appear as dependents of PATIENT in the new structure. Notice, however, that not all of the segment types are included in the new structure. Specifically, segments that are dependents of the segment types above the index target segment in the original hierarchy are excluded from the new structure. In our example, the FACILITY segment is not part of the restructured hierarchy.

Figure 13.6 shows a few index pointer segments from the PATINDX secondary index and the corresponding segment occurrences in the HOSPITAL data base that they point to.

DATEINDX Secondary Index

A given segment type can be indexed by any number of secondary indexes. For example, Figure 13.7 shows another secondary index, DATEINDX, for the

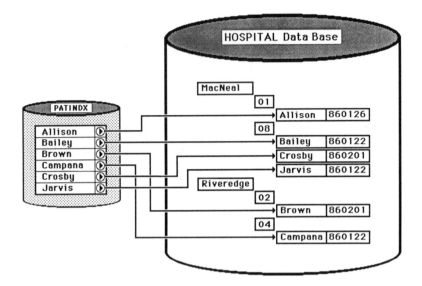

Figure 13.6. PATINDX index pointer segments

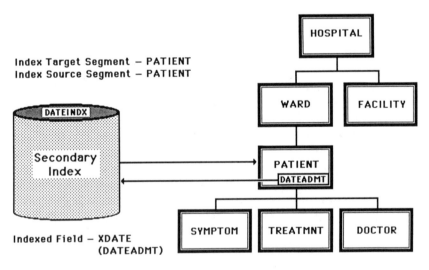

Figure 13.7. DATEINDX secondary index

PATIENT segment that might be useful. In this example the indexed field, XDATE, consists of the DATEADMT field from the PATIENT segment. Because the index source segment and the index target segment are again the PATIENT segment, each index pointer segment consists of a patient's date of admittance and a pointer to the corresponding PATIENT segment.

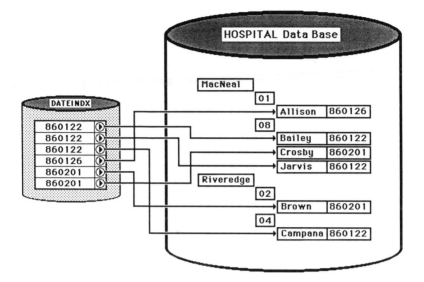

Figure 13.8. DATEINDX index pointer segments

The DATEINDX secondary index allows an application program to retrieve PATIENT segments in the order in which they were admitted. Figure 13.8 shows a few DATEINDX index pointer segments and the corresponding segments in the HOSPITAL data base that they point to. The hierarchical structure created by DATEINDX is the same as for the PATINDX secondary index.

DIAGINDX Secondary Index

Figure 13.9 shows a fourth secondary index in which the index source segment and the index target segment are different segment types. In this example the information used to construct the secondary index *comes from* the SYMPTOM segment type, but the secondary index *points to* PATIENT segments. The index source segment is the SYMPTOM segment and the index target segment is the PATIENT segment.

The indexed field, XDIAG, is made up of the DIAGNOSE field from the SYMPTOM segment. There is an index pointer segment for each occurrence of the SYMPTOM segment in the data base. These will be sequenced by diagnosis type. Since there can be multiple SYMPTOM segment occurrences for each PATIENT segment occurrence, each index source segment can be pointed to by multiple index pointer segments.

This secondary index can be used to obtain a list of all patients having a particular diagnosis. The application program would issue a sequence of Get-Next calls using a fully-qualified SSA referencing the indexed field and speci-

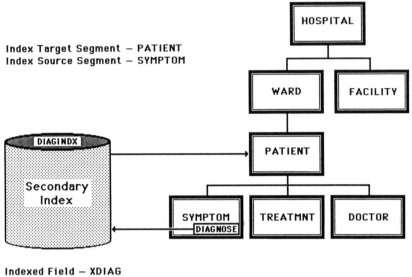

Index Target Segment — PATIENT
Index Source Segment — SYMPTOM

Indexed Field — XDIAG
          (DIAGNOSE)

Figure 13.9. DIAGINDX secondary index

fying the desired diagnosis. Figure 13.10 shows a few index pointer segments from DIAGINDX and the corresponding segment occurrences in the HOSPITAL data base that they point to.

Note that the indexed field is considered to be a field of the indexed target segment, PATIENT, even though the information used to construct it comes from the index source segment, SYMPTOM. Get-Next calls are used because there will often be multiple index pointer segments with the same diagnosis, each pointing to a different PATIENT segment.

Since the PATIENT segment is again the index target segment, the PATIENT segment becomes the root segment in a new hierarchical structure when DIAGINDX is used to provide a secondary processing sequence.

PROGRAMMING WITH SECONDARY INDEXES

As we have already indicated, the PCBs and SSAs referenced by IMS calls control the way in which secondary indexes are used. Suppose the PSB specifies that the program will use the secondary processing sequence defined by the ADMINDX secondary index. That would be done by including a PCB statement like the following in the PSB:

    PCB   TYPE=DB,PROCOPT=1,NAME=HOSPITAL,PROCSEQ=ADMINDX

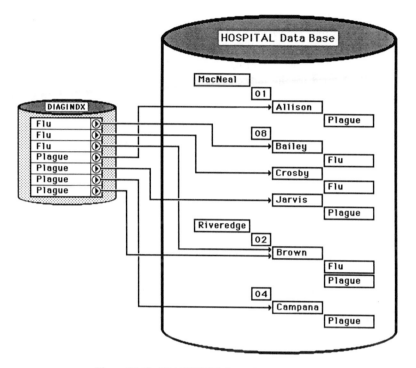

Figure 13.10. DIAGINDX index pointer segments

When an application program issues a call that references a PCB specifying a secondary processing sequence, SSAs can be coded without reference to the secondary index. The PROCSEQ parameter in the PCB statement causes IMS to search the secondary index in satisfying all calls for the index target segment. As a quick review, suppose we issue a sequence of the following Get-Next calls:

```
GN       HOSPITAL
^^^^     ^^^^^^^^^^
```

As we learned earlier, the above call causes IMS to retrieve HOSPITAL segments in sequence according to ADMIN field values rather than in HOSP-NAME sequence.

When the PCB statement specifies the PROCSEQ parameter, we are also allowed to code the indexed field name in an SSA. This causes the program to explicitly request that IMS search the secondary index in satisfying the call.

Suppose we are referencing a PCB that specifies PROCSEQ=PATINDX. We could then code the Get-Unique call:

```
GU       PATIENT  (XPAT    =BROWN                    )
^^^^     ^^^^^^^^^^^^^^^^^^^^^^^^^^^^^^^^^^^^^^^^^^^^^^^
```

The above call causes IMS to search the secondary index for an index pointer segment that has the value *Brown*. If it finds one, it uses the pointer in the index pointer segment to locate the PATIENT segment for *Brown*. Notice that the XPAT field name is a new field name for the PATIENT segment. It is a field name that is defined for the index target segment in the DBD.

Referencing the indexed field in an SSA explicitly directs IMS to use the secondary index in satisfying that call. The application programmer must determine whether it is more efficient for IMS to search for a segment via the secondary index or to search for it the normal way. IMS makes no attempt to determine which is most efficient.

Using the Indexed Field Name

The indexed field name that is defined by a secondary index can be used in SSAs only if statements in the PSB reference the secondary index. We have already seen that one way to do that is to include the PROCSEQ parameter in the PCB statement. We can cause the program to use the normal processing sequence by omitting the PROCSEQ parameter and still give the program the option to reference the indexed field in SSAs. This is done by including the INDICES parameter in the SENSEG statement for the index target segment. For example, suppose we wanted a program to be able to use the ADMINDX secondary index, but did not want the program to use the secondary processing sequence for all IMS calls. We would code the INDICES parameter in the SENSEG statement for the HOSPITAL segment as follows:

```
SENSEG   NAME=HOSPITAL,PARENT=0,INDICES=ADMINDX
```

Now suppose the application program issues a series of Get-Next calls for HOSPITAL segments:

```
GN       HOSPITAL
```

This would cause the program to retrieve HOSPITAL segments in HOSP-NAME sequence. This is because the PCB statement specified the normal processing sequence by omitting the PROCSEQ parameter. The program can still use the secondary index, but would have to request it specifically by referencing the indexed field in an SSA, as in the following example:

```
GU       HOSPITAL(XADMIN   =LUKENS                 )
```

Because the SSA references the indexed field, XADMIN, IMS searches for the segment via the ADMINDX secondary index. The INDICES parameter in the SENSEG statement allows the programmer to use the indexed field in an SSA, even though the secondary processing sequence is not used for other calls.

If we wanted to access a HOSPITAL segment occurrence based on an administrator's name, but we did not want IMS to use the secondary index, we could code a normal Get-Unique call qualified on the ADMIN field:

```
GU     HOSPITAL(ADMIN    =LUKENS                   )
```

For the above call, IMS searches for the segment by scanning through the data base, examining each HOSPITAL segment until it finds a match on the ADMIN field. Since the SSA does not reference the indexed field and the secondary processing sequence was not specified in the PCB, the secondary index is not used in satisfying the call.

Using the Independent-AND Boolean Operator

The Independent-AND boolean operator (#) can be used to retrieve data in situations where more than one index pointer segment can point to a given index target segment. The DIAGINDX secondary index provides an example of this kind of relationship. (See Figures 13.9 and 13.10.) Suppose we wanted to obtain a list of all patients who have been diagnosed as having both *Plague* and *Flu*. The following is an example of a call that uses a conventional AND operator (*) to attempt the above retrieval:

```
GU     PATIENT (XDIAG    =PLAGUE       *XDIAG    =   FLU    )
```

The above call would not produce the desired result. In effect, the above use of the AND operator directs IMS to look for a *single* index pointer segment whose indexed field, XDIAG, is equal to *Plague* and *Flu* at the same time. Clearly, this is an impossibility. The conventional AND operator should not be used in the above manner. For cases such as the above, the Independent-AND operator does produce the desired result. The following is an example:

```
GU     PATIENT (XDIAG    =PLAGUE       #XDIAG    =   FLU    )
```

The above call causes IMS to look for a single index target segment that has at least two different index pointer segments pointing to it, one of which has the value *Plague* and the other of which has the value *Flu*. The Independent-AND operator causes IMS to look for a single target segment pointed to by multiple index pointer segments. In the above example, IMS returns the PATIENT segment for *Brown*. That segment occurrence satisfies both conditions of the qualification statement.

Multiple Secondary Indexes

The Independent-AND operator can also be used when the program has access to multiple secondary indexes. Suppose we have access to both the DATEINDX secondary index and the DIAGINDX secondary index. Access to both secondary indexes is provided by including the names of both secondary indexes in the INDICES parameter in the PATIENT segment SENSEG statement. We can then direct IMS to search for a particular PATIENT segment based on a patient's date of admittance and also based on diagnosis type. The following call provides an example of this type of search:

```
GU    PATIENT (XDIAG   =PLAGUE                #XDATE   <860101)
```

The above call directs IMS to look for a PATIENT segment occurrence that is pointed to by at least two index pointer segments. One is for a patient who has been diagnosed as having *Plague* and one for a patient who was admitted to the hospital prior to January 1, 1986 (*860101*). The above call could have alternatively been coded with a conventional AND operator, as in the following example:

```
GU    PATIENT (XDIAG   =PLAGUE                *XDATE   <860101)
```

The Independent-AND operator is *required* only when the same indexed field name is specified in both qualification statements. The conventional AND, in that case, causes IMS to look for a single index pointer segment satisfying both qualification statements. The Independent-AND operator causes IMS to make two independent scans of the index, looking for a target segment that is pointed to by more than one index pointer segment, each satisfying one of the qualification statements. When multiple secondary indexes are referenced by specifying more than one indexed field name in an SSA, the conventional AND operator and the Independent-AND operators produce the same results.

Secondary Indexing Restrictions

When the secondary processing sequence is used, there are some restrictions in the types of call that can be issued. Any type of call can be issued for segments below the index target segment. Delete and Insert calls cannot be made for the index target segment or any of its parents in the original hierarchy.

Secondary Indexing Relationships

The information in the secondary index and in the data base being indexed can form either a one-to-one relationship or a one-to-many relationship. This depends on how the index target segment and the data elements that make up the indexed field have been chosen.

For example, the ADMINDX example forms a one-to-one relationship if we assume a different administrator for each hospital. Each pointer segment contains a unique key field and there is an index pointer segment for each root segment in the data base being indexed. The DIAGINDX example forms a one-to-many relationship. In this relationship the index pointer segment does not contain unique key fields. Each particular DIAGNOSE value references many PATIENT segments in the data base being indexed. Thus there may be many index pointer segments having the same indexed field value.

Non-Unique Key Fields in Pointer Segments

If the index pointer segments contain unique keys as in the ADMINDX example, IMS stores all the occurrences of the index pointer segments in the KSDS portion of the secondary index data base.

When the occurrences of the index pointer segments do not all have unique keys, IMS uses a KSDS and an ESDS to implement the secondary index. When multiple occurrences of an index pointer segment contain the same key value, only the first one is stored in the KSDS. All other occurrences are stored in the ESDS.

Index Pointer Segment Format

Figure 13.11 shows the physical format of the index pointer segment. The first field is a four-byte pointer to the ESDS. This is present only if the key field is not unique. Following the pointer is the index pointer segment's prefix. It normally consists of a delete byte followed by a four-byte pointer to the index target segment. This four-byte pointer is not used if the data base being indexed is an HISAM data base.

The data portion of the pointer segment can begin with an optional one-byte constant. This is used when more than one secondary index shares the physical secondary index data base.

The field following the optional constant is called the *search field*. It con-

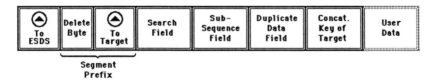

Figure 13.11. Index pointer segment format

tains the data identified as the indexed field in the index source segment. It can contain from one to five fields from the source segment and is normally the field referenced in an SSA qualified on the indexed field.

Next is an optional subsequence field. This field can consist of one to five additional fields from the source segment. All or a part of the subsequence field can be included in the key of the index pointer segment to help make the key field unique.

After that is the duplicate data field. This is an optional field in which another one to five fields from the index source segment can be stored. These fields are available only when the secondary index is processed as data.

Following the duplicate data field is an optional field in which the concatenated key of the index target segment can be stored. This is used when an HISAM data base is indexed and is used instead of the direct address pointer field at the beginning of the index pointer segment.

The last field is called the user data field and it is not maintained by IMS. This field must be added after the secondary index has been created by running a user-supplied program that reads the index as data and writes out a new index which includes the user data.

Index Pointer Segment Examples

Figure 13.12 shows the index pointer segment format in the ADMINDX secondary index. This example assumes HDAM or HIDAM is used to store the data base and that the index pointer segment key field is unique.

The index pointer segment begins with the delete byte. Following that is the four-byte pointer to the index target segment in the HOSPITAL data base.

Following the prefix is the ADMIN field from the index source segment. That is all which is stored in the data portion of the index pointer segment. The entire data portion of the segment makes up the key field.

Figure 13.13 shows the format of the index pointer segment when HISAM is used to store the HOSPITAL data base. The index pointer segment prefix consists of only the delete byte. The key field is followed by the concatenated key of the index target segment, in this case simply the hospital name value.

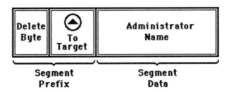

Figure 13.12. ADMINDX index pointer segment

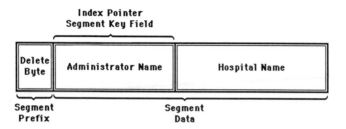

Figure 13.13. HISAM index pointer segment

When an HISAM data base is being indexed, the concatenated key field is used to locate the index target segment in the data base being indexed.

EXERCISES

1. Answer true or false to the following statements concerning secondary indexing.

   a. The index source segment points to the segments being indexed.
   b. The index pointer segments contain pointers to the data base being indexed.
   c. You are allowed to reference the indexed field in an SSA only when the PCB specifies the secondary processing sequence.
   d. The index target segment must be below the root segment in the hierarchy.
   e. The index source segment and index target segment must be the same segment in the hierarchy.
   f. The indexed field must consist of fields defined in the index source segment.
   g. The secondary index can be transparent to individual applications.
   h. The Independent-AND boolean operator is useful only when you are using secondary indexing.
   i. You must reference the indexed field in an SSA in order for IMS to use the secondary index.

2. Below is a list of terms used to describe the secondary indexing feature and a list of statements. Match each term with the statement that best describes it.

TERMS	STATEMENTS
A. Index pointer segment	a. Defined for the index target segment, but data comes from the index source segment
B. Index source segment	
C. Index target segment	b. Points to segments in the data base being indexed.
D. Indexed field	c. Data from this segment is used to construct the secondary index.
E. Secondary processing sequence	
	d. The secondary index indexes these segments.
	e. Defined in the PCB statement in the PSB.

3. Your PSB contains a PCB specifying a secondary processing sequence using the DATEINDX secondary index. (See Figure 13.7 and Figure 13.8.) Write the internal representation of the function code and SSAs that you would use to retrieve PATIENT segments in sequence by date of admittance.

4. Your PSB contains a PCB specifying a secondary processing sequence using the ADMINDX secondary index. (See Figure 13.2 and Figure 13.3.) Write the internal representation of the function code and SSAs that you would use to retrieve the HOSPITAL segment whose administrator is named *Lukens*.

14
Logical Relationships— Concepts

This chapter is the first of two on IMS *logical relationships.* The purpose of this chapter is to discuss the major uses for logical relationships, define many of the terms used to describe this powerful feature of IMS, and introduce the major concepts involved with logically related data bases.

LOGICAL DATA BASES

In Chapter 3, we said that DBDGEN control statements are used to define *physical* and *logical* data bases. An example of a physical data base is the HOSPITAL data base we have been working with throughout this book. In this chapter we will introduce the concept of a logical data base.

Suppose we need a PSB that provides access to the logical data structure shown in Figure 14.1. The BILLING segment type contains information used in preparing hospital bills. We could provide access to the BILLING segment by adding it to the hierarchical structure of the HOSPITAL data base, performing a new DBDGEN, and reloading the data base including the new BILLING segment occurrences. The new data base would then contain the billing information, as shown in Figure 14.2. But suppose that billing information already exists in some other physical data base, for example a HISTORY data base, shown in Figure 14.3.

If the billing information already exists, it would be redundant to store it again in the HOSPITAL data base. We should instead find a way to combine the data from the two physical data bases.

One way that we can gain access to both data bases is to code a PSB that contains two PCBs, one for each physical data base. Our application programs could then provide the program logic to tie together the two data bases. We would not get the logical data structure shown in Figure 14.1. We would instead

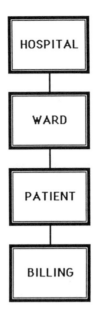

Figure 14.1. Accessing billing information

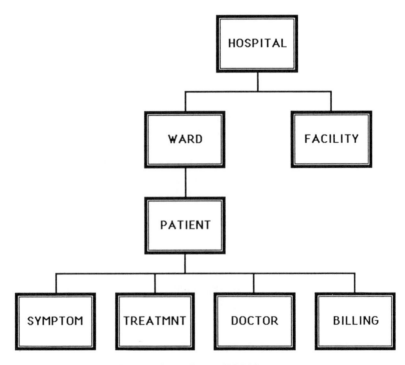

Figure 14.2. Adding a BILLING segment

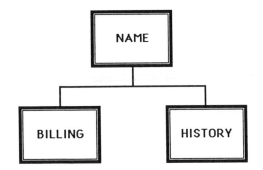

Figure 14.3. HISTORY data base

get two separate logical data structures: one with segments from the HOSPI-
TAL data base and one with segments from the HISTORY data base.

Logical relationships provide a method for hooking two or more data bases
together in such a way that application programs can work with them as if they
implemented a single logical data structure. To do this, the physical DBD coding for the HOSPITAL and HISTORY data bases would be modified to create
a physical structure something like the one shown in Figure 14.4. Here a logical
path is created from the HOSPITAL data base to the HISTORY data base.
Instead of duplicating the BILLING segment in the HOSPITAL data base, we
create a new pointer segment type. Each occurrence of the pointer segment

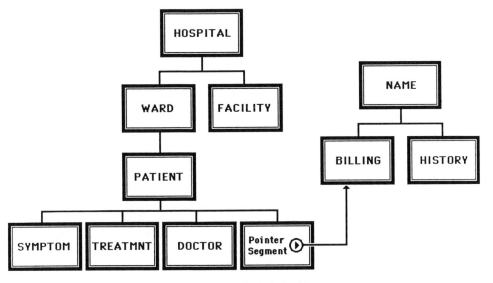

Figure 14.4. Logical relationship

points to an appropriate occurrence of the BILLING segment in the HISTORY data base.

A logical DBD is required that maps against the two physical DBDs. This logical DBD defines the logical structure shown in Figure 14.1. PSBs requiring access to that logical structure would reference the logical DBD rather than either of the two physical DBDs.

In logical relationship terminology, the pointer segment in the HOSPITAL physical data base is called a *logical child* segment. The segment it points to— the BILLING segment—is called a *logical parent*.

The advantage to using a logical relationship is that the BILLING information can be stored in a single place. However, the application program has access to it as if it were a part of the HOSPITAL data base. When the BILLING data base is updated, the logical child segments will point to the updated information.

The example we just looked at is an example of the simplest kind of logical relationship and is called a *unidirectional logical relationship*. There are more complex types of logical relationships that allow data bases to be connected in two directions, and we will discuss them later in this chapter.

LOGICAL DATA BASE TERMINOLOGY

In Chapter 3, we introduced the following four important terms that define the way data stored in IMS data bases can be viewed:

- Logical data structure
- Application data structure
- Physical data base
- Logical data base

We will next review these terms because they are particularly important when discussing logically-related data bases.

Logical Data Structure

A *logical data structure* is the view that an application program has of a particular IMS data base. In terms of IMS control blocks, a logical data structure is the structure of data as defined by a single data base PCB within a PSB. A logical data structure is often referred to as an *application view* of the data in an IMS data base.

Application Data Structure

An *application data structure* consists of one or more logical data structures. From the viewpoint of IMS control blocks, an application data structure is the collection of data base PCBs defined in a single PSB. It is the collection of logical views of data that a particular application program has access to. The various logical data structures in a single application data structure can present different views of the *same* data base to the application program. They can also present logical views of *different* data bases to an application program.

Physical Data Base

The physical data base represents the view of the data as the data base administrator sees it. A physical data base describes how data is actually stored in an IMS data base. A physical DBD is used to describe this view of the data. A physical data base is often known as the *physical view* of the data.

When logical relationships are not used, the above three terms (logical data structure, application data structure, and physical data base) are the only ones we need to talk about data in IMS data bases. The DBD describes the data as it is stored, and the PCBs in PSBs describe the views of that data as application programs see it. Figure 14.5 shows these relationships.

Logical Data Base

As we saw in the BILLING segment example above, it is not always enough to be able to access subsets of the segments defined in physical data bases. We sometimes need to use logical relationships to define *logical data bases* that define new hierarchical structures. There are two main uses for logical data bases.

Restructuring a Hierarchy. Logical relationships can be used to rearrange the hierarchical structure of a single physical data base in order to better meet the needs of a particular application. In a case like this, the DBA defines a *logical data base* that uses logical relationships which map against the segments defined in a single physical DBD. A logical data structure can then be defined by a PCB that maps against the segments defined in the logical data base. Figure 14.6 shows a possible set of relationships between physical DBDs, logical DBDs, PCBs, and a PSB.

Connecting Physical Data Bases. Logical relationships can also be used to hook together segments from two or more physical data bases. A single logical

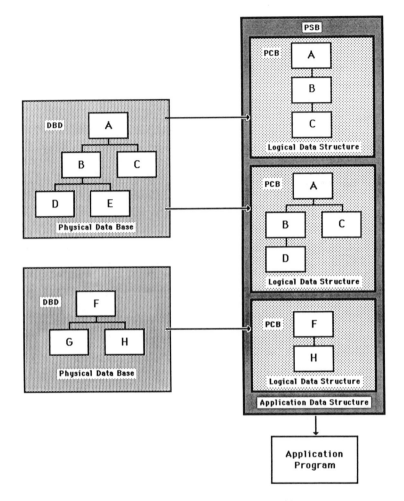

Figure 14.5. Physical data base relationships

data base can then be defined that identifies segments stored in multiple physical data bases. A PCB within a PSB can map against the segments defined in this logical data base just as if the logical data base were a single physical data base. A possible set of relationships illustrating this is shown in Figure 14.7.

PATIENT and DOCTOR Data

To illustrate some of the different types of logical relationships that can be defined, Figure 14.8 shows two possible views of the PATIENT and DOCTOR

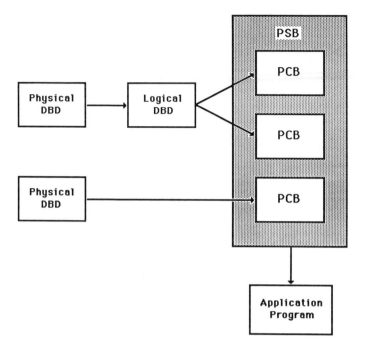

Figure 14.6. Logical data base relationships

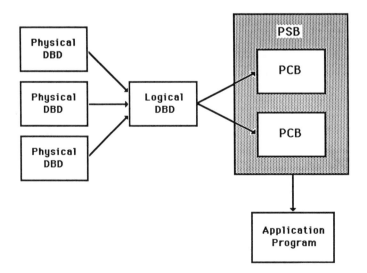

Figure 14.7. Logical data base relationships

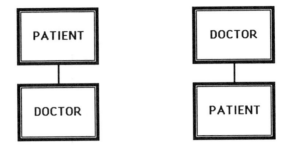

Figure 14.8. Two views of patient and doctor data

data from our HOSPITAL data base. Given the first view, we can find out which doctors each patient has. Given the second view we can find out which patients each doctor treats.

Figure 14.9 shows a few of the segment occurrences that would be stored if the two views were implemented as separate physical data bases. Notice that there is some data redundancy. The *Abrams* DOCTOR segment is stored twice in the first data base and the *Curtis* PATIENT segment is stored twice in the second data base. Taken together, the two physical data bases represent even more data redundancy. For example, DOCTOR segments are stored twice, once as root segments of one physical data base and again as dependent segments in the other.

Redundant data wastes storage space and causes difficulties in updating. For

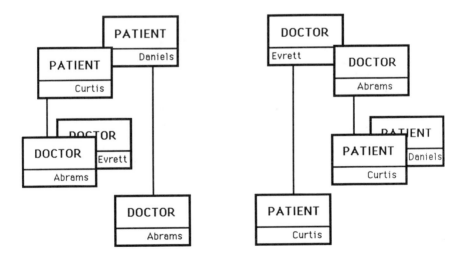

Figure 14.9. Data base segment occurrences

example, what happens if we update a piece of data in one data base and forget to update it in the other? Logical relationships can help to avoid this type of problem, because they allow a segment to be stored in only one place and still provide the capability for constructing an application view that best serves the needs of each application program.

A Unidirectional Logical Relationship

The first type of logical relationship that we will look at is called a *unidirectional* logical relationship. We introduced an example of this type of logical relationship earlier in this chapter. To begin, let us create two separate data bases, each having only one segment type, as shown in Figure 14.10. Our PATIENT segments are stored as root segments of a physical data base called PAT; our DOCTOR segments are stored as root segments of a physical data base called DOC.

Now we can define a unidirectional logical relationship that allows us to keep track of the doctors each patient has. To do that, we create a new segment type under PATIENT, which we call PTRDOC, as shown in Figure 14.11. The PTRDOC segment occurrences contain pointers to the appropriate occurrences of the DOCTOR segment type. Figure 14.12 shows what a few segment occurrences in our PAT and DOC physical data bases might now look like. The PTRDOC segment type, whose occurrences contain pointers into the DOC data base, is the *logical child*. The DOCTOR segment, which is pointed to by the logical child segment, is the *logical parent*.

This type of logical relationship is called *unidirectional* because we can only get from a particular PATIENT occurrence to its related DOCTOR segment occurrences; we cannot get from a DOCTOR segment back to its related PATIENT segment occurrences.

Figure 14.13 shows five different views of the data that we can define using the logically related PAT and DOC physical data bases. We can code a PSB that gives a program only the root segment of either of the physical data bases. We can also provide the program with a view that lets the program access the PTRDOC logical child segment. Using the logical relationship implemented by

Figure 14.10. Two physical data bases

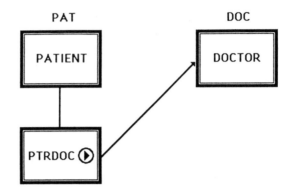

Figure 14.11. Pointer segment type

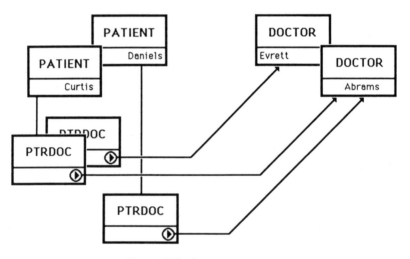

Figure 14.12. Segment occurrences

the PTRDOC logical child segment, we can provide a logical view that makes the data base look to the program as if the DOCTOR segment were dependent on the PATIENT segment. In this view, the application program does not retrieve occurrences of the PTRDOC logical child segment. The logical child segment is, in fact, somewhat transparent to the application program. Finally, we can provide the program with a view of the data that implements a *concatenated segment* consisting of the logical child and the logical parent connected together as if they were a single segment type.

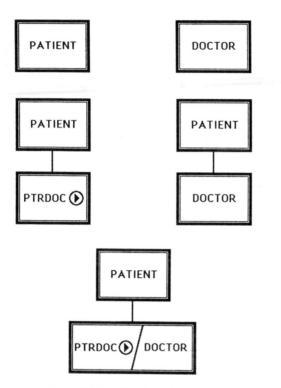

Figure 14.13. Five alternative views

Logical, Physical, and Application Views

Figure 14.14 shows the *physical view* of the data in our two data bases. Notice that it consists of two separate physical data bases: a PAT data base and a DOC data base.

The following is typical DBD coding for the PAT data base:

```
DBD      NAME=PAT,ACCESS=HDAM,RMNAME=(DFSHDC40,5,18)
DATASET  DD1=PAT,DEVICE=3350
SEGM     NAME=PATIENT,BYTES=125,PARENT=0
   FIELD    NAME=(BEDIDENT,SEQ,U),BYTES=4,START=61,TYPE=C
   FIELD    NAME=PATNAME,BYTES=20,START=1,TYPE=C
   FIELD    NAME=DATEADMT,BYTES=6,START=65,TYPE=C
SEGM     NAME=PTRDOC,BYTES=28,
         PARENT=((PATIENT,SNGL),(DOCTOR,PHYSICAL,DOC))
   FIELD    NAME=(DOCTKEY,SEQ),BYTES=20,START=1
DBDGEN
FINISH
END
```

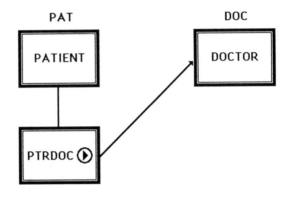

Figure 14.14. Physical data bases

Notice in the above example that the PARENT operand in the SEGM statement for the PTRDOC logical child segment connects the segment to both the PATIENT segment in the PAT data base (its physical parent) and to the DOCTOR segment in the DOC data base (its logical parent).

The following is a typical set of DBD coding for the DOC data base:

```
DBD      NAME=DOC,ACCESS=HDAM,RMNAME=(DFSHDC40,5,18)
DATASET DD1=DOC,DEVICE=3350
SEGM     NAME=DOCTOR,BYTES=80,PARENT=0
  LCHILD  NAME=(PTRDOC,PAT)
  FIELD   NAME=(DOCTNAME,SEQ),BYTES=20,START=1,TYPE=C
  FIELD   NAME=SPECIALT,BYTES=20,START=61,TYPE=C
DBDGEN
FINISH
END
```

Notice in the above coding that the LCHILD statement following the SEGM statement for the DOCTOR segment connects the DOCTOR segment to its logical child segment in the PAT data base.

Figure 14.15 shows one of the above five possible *logical views* of the data in the PAT and DOC physical bases. The following is a typical set of DBD coding for this logical data base:

```
DBD      NAME=LAUTO,ACCESS=LOGICAL
DATASET LOGICAL
SEGM     NAME=PATIENT
         SOURCE=((PATIENT,DATA,PAT))
SEGM     NAME=DOCTOR,
         SOURCE=((PTRDOC,KEY,PAT),(DOCTOR,DATA,DOC))
DBDGEN
FINISH
END
```

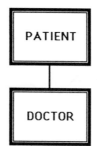

Figure 14.15. Logical Data Base

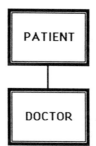

Figure 14.16. Application view

Figure 14.16 shows a particular *application view* of the data in the logical data base. Notice that it has the same structure as the logical data base itself (Figure 14.15). In a more complex example, only a subset of the segments defined in a logical data base might be described in a particular application view. As in data bases without logical relationships, the application view is described to IMS through the PSB.

A Second Unidirectional Relationship

Figure 14.17 shows our two data bases with logical child segments connecting them in both directions. This can be done with two unidirectional logical relationships. Figure 14.18 shows two of the many different views of the data that our two unidirectional logical relationships implement. One view shows DOCTOR segments dependent on PATIENT segments; the other shows PATIENT segments dependent on DOCTOR segments.

At first glance, it appears that these two unidirectional logical relationships allow us to satisfy two requirements: finding the doctors each patient has and

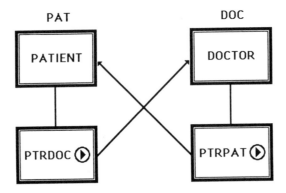

Figure 14.17. Two unidirectional relationships

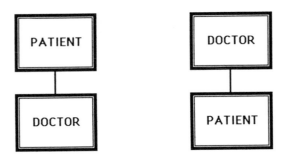

Figure 14.18. Two logical views

finding the patients each doctor treats. But maintenance problems occur when we use two unidirectional logical relationships.

Figure 14.19 shows what might happen when a new PTRDOC logical child segment occurrence is added under *Daniels* to point to the *Everett* DOCTOR segment. It now appears that *Daniels* has both *Abrams* and *Everett* as doctors. However, to accurately describe the situation that actually exists when Everett becomes one of Daniels' doctors, we must also insert a PTRPAT logical child segment occurrence into the DOC data base under the *Everett* DOCTOR segment to point to *Daniels*. With a set of two unidirectional logical relationships, inserting a new occurrence on one side does not automatically cause a new segment occurrence to be inserted on the other side.

Bidirectional Logical Relationships

In order to cause IMS to handle this double updating for us automatically, we would use a single *bidirectional* logical relationship instead of two unidirec-

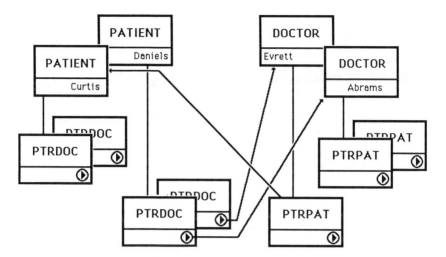

Figure 14.19. Adding a logical child occurrence

tional logical relationships. There are two varieties of bidirectional logical relationship, one with *physical pairing* and one with *virtual pairing*.

Physical Pairing

Figure 14.20 shows that when the logical child segments are properly inserted in both physical data bases, there is an equal number of them on each side. For each logical child segment on the PATIENT side there is a corresponding one on the DOCTOR side, so the logical child segments are considered paired. With a *physically paired bidirectional* logical relationship, IMS maintains the pairing between logical child segments. If a program inserts a logical child on the PATIENT side, IMS automatically inserts another one on the DOCTOR side, and vice versa. The same amount of updating takes place as if two unidirectional logical relationships were used, but it is less work for the application program. A single Insert call causes IMS to insert both logical child segment occurrences.

Intersection Data

Intersection data consists of information that is unique to the relationship between a single occurrence of a logical child segment and its logical parent segment occurrence (the segment it points to). An example of possible intersection data in our PATIENT and DOCTOR example is the fee a doctor charges a particular patient.

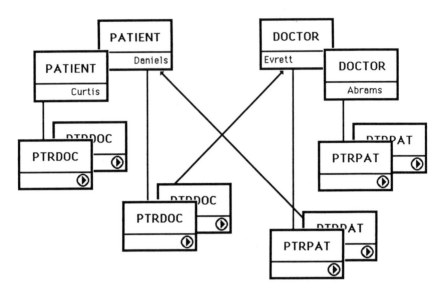

Figure 14.20. Paired logical child occurrences

Fixed Intersection Data. It would not make sense to store fee data in the PATIENT segment because all of a patient's doctors would have to charge that patient the same fee. It would not make sense to store fee data in the DOCTOR segments either. That would mean that all patients would have to pay a given doctor the same fee. A better place to store fee information is in the PTRDOC and PTRPAT segments, as shown in Figure 14.21. This allows us to store a separate FEE value for each doctor and for each of a doctor's patients. Data that is stored in the logical child segment itself is called *fixed intersection data*.

Variable Intersection Data. With a physically paired bidirectional logical relationship, using fixed intersection data causes the intersection data to be duplicated on both sides of the logical relationships. This is a form of data redundancy that IMS maintains for us. If we change the intersection data in the logical child on one side, IMS automatically changes it in its pair on the other side.

To avoid this redundancy, we can store intersection data in a separate segment type that is dependent on one of our logical child segments. This is shown in Figure 14.22. Intersection data that is stored in a separate segment type is called *variable intersection data*. With variable intersection data, intersection data is stored under only one of the logical child segments. However, IMS makes that segment type available from both sides of the logical relationship. It actually looks as if the variable intersection data is stored under both logical child segments as shown in Figure 14.23.

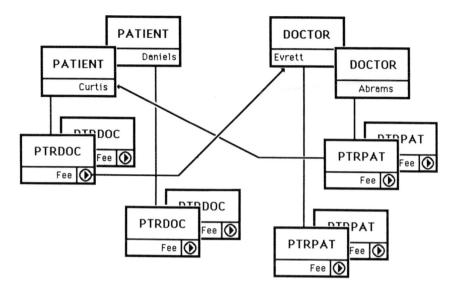

Figure 14.21. Fixed intersection data

Virtual Pairing

Next, we introduce a bidirectional logical relationship with *virtual pairing*. In a *virtually paired bidirectional* logical relationship, a single logical child segment is used to provide a two-way path between the two data bases, as shown in Figure 14.24. An extra set of pointers is maintained in the logical child segment in order to simulate the existence of the second logical child, as shown in Figure 14.25. PTRDOC, the logical child that is actually stored in the data base, is called a *real logical child*. PTRPAT, the simulated logical child, is called a *virtual logical child*.

We can think of virtual pairing as if we were trying to simulate a physically paired relationship by using a single logical child. This relationship is shown in Figure 14.26. The PTRDOC segment actually exists, and is stored in the data base. The PTRPAT segment, although it is defined in the DOC physical DBD, does not physically exist and is not stored in the data base. The relationship functions, however, as if it does exist. The diagram in Figure 14.26 shows how a virtually paired relationship *appears* to the programmer.

A standard form of diagram for a virtually paired relationship is as shown previously in Figure 14.24. This makes the virtually paired relationship more easily distinguishable from a physically paired one. It also more accurately describes how the relationship is implemented. As we mentioned earlier, a second set of pointers is maintained to hook the segments together in the opposite di-

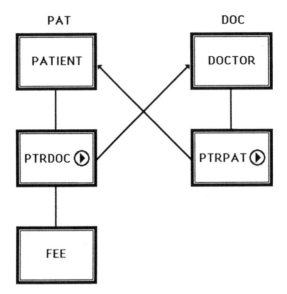

Figure 14.22. Variable intersection data

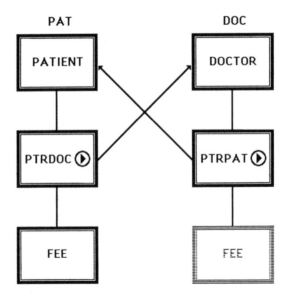

Figure 14.23. Apparent physical structure

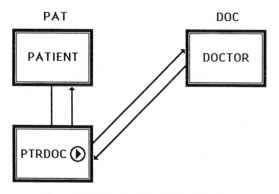

Figure 14.24. A virtually paired relationship

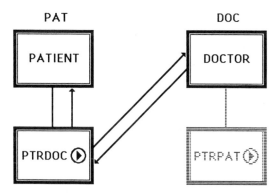

Figure 14.25. The virtual logical child

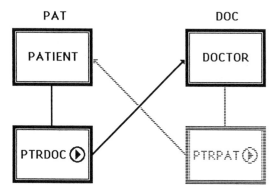

Figure 14.26. Virtual pairing

PAT

DOC

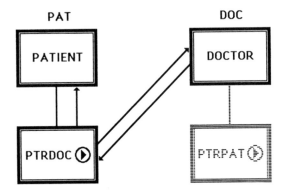

Figure 14.27. Virtual pairing

rection. But this form of diagram does not show the virtual logical child, and we often add it with dashed lines as in Figure 14.27. Since we must sometimes know the name of the virtual logical child, this is the most useful way to diagram a virtually paired bidirectional logical relationship.

The Destination Parent

Previously, we defined the logical child segment type and the logical parent segment type. To review, a *logical child* is a segment type that contains a pointer to another segment type, thus implementing a logical relationship. The PTRDOC and PTRPAT segments are examples of logical child segments. The logical child creates a *logical path* between one segment type and another.

The *logical parent* is the segment pointed to by a logical child. In our previous physically paired bidirectional logical relationship examples, both the PATIENT and DOCTOR segments are logical parents. Note that a segment is not considered a logical parent unless some logical child is actually pointing at it. In a virtually paired relationship, we have a segment type that behaves like a logical parent, but does not actually have a real logical child pointing to it. This type of segment is called a *destination parent*. A destination parent is actually any segment that can be gotten to via a logical path. A destination parent segment is either a logical parent, or it is the physical parent of the real logical child in a virtually paired logical relationship.

To illustrate this, examine the virtually paired logical relationship shown in Figure 14.28. The PATIENT and DOCTOR segments are both destination parents. The PATIENT segment is only a destination parent, and not a logical parent. But the DOCTOR segment is both a logical parent and a destination parent. Even though both PATIENT and DOCTOR are destination parent segments, it is customary to call DOCTOR a logical parent and only PATIENT a

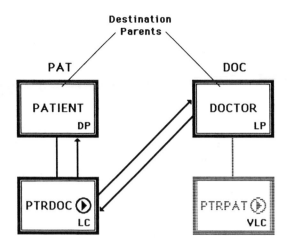

Figure 14.28. The destination parent

destination parent. But depending on the usage, we sometimes use the term *destination parent* to refer to either segment in a virtually paired relationship.

POINTERS IN LOGICAL RELATIONSHIPS

A brief introduction to the pointers used in implementing logical relationships will help to show the difference between physical and virtual pairing, and how the virtual logical child is simulated.

Pointers in Physical Pairing

Figure 14.29 shows most of the pointers used to hook the segments together in a physically paired logical relationship. Notice that there is a separate set of logical child segments on each side of the logical relationship. Assume that we issued Get-Next calls for the DOCTOR segment under a particular PATIENT segment when coming into the data base from the PAT side. The physical twin chain of the PTRDOC logical child segments under the PATIENT segment would be used to determine in what sequence DOCTOR segments are retrieved.

Let us say we then issued Get-Next calls for the PATIENT segments under a particular DOCTOR segment when coming into the data base from the DOC side. This time the physical twin chain of the PTRPAT logical child segments would be used to determine the sequence in which PATIENT segments are retrieved.

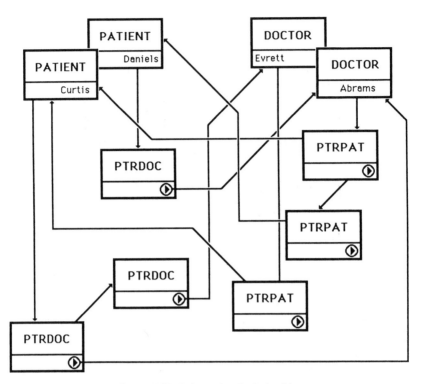

Figure 14.29. Pointers for physical pairing

Pointers in Virtual Pairing

In physical pairing, there are two sets of logical child segments. One set maintains a physical twin chain to sequence one logical parent, and the other maintains a physical twin chain to sequence the other logical parent.

In virtual pairing, IMS must maintain two different twin chains and two different sets of pointers using a single set of logical child segments. Figure 14.30 shows how the logical parent pointers and the physical twin chain of the real logical child (PTRDOC) are used to point to, and sequence, occurrences of the logical parent (DOCTOR). These pointers are the same as those on one side of a physically paired relationship.

Figure 14.31 shows how a different set of pointers in the same set of logical child segments maintains the other side of the virtually paired relationship. The following pointers are used in implementing the DOC side of the virtually paired logical relationship:

- Logical child pointers that point back from each logical parent (DOCTOR) to its logical child (PTRDOC).

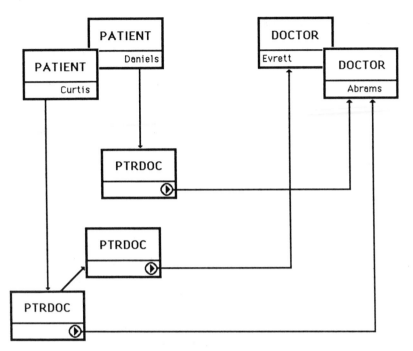

Figure 14.30. Accessing the logical parents

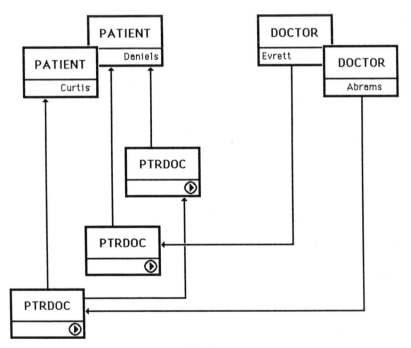

Figure 14.31. Accessing the destination parents

- Logical twin pointers that maintain the twin chain of the virtual logical child (PTRPAT).
- Physical parent pointers that point up to the physical parent (PATIENT) of each logical child.

These pointers are used to simulate the existence of the virtual logical child. As far as the application program is concerned, the result is no different from physical pairing.

LOGICAL DATA BASES

Once physical data bases have been defined and logical relationships specified, the data base administrator must decide how those segments will be combined in defining logical data bases. There is a set of rules that the DBA must follow to combine segments and choose hierarchical paths in logical data bases.

In general, the DBA can follow any physical or logical path in a logical relationship. A physical path is generally one that is maintained by a physical pointer. A logical path is generally one that is maintained by one of the pointers that implements a logical relationship.

The Concatenated Segment

In combining segments in a logical data base, a segment that is not a logical child or a logical parent appears in a logical data base by itself, just as it does in a physical data base. When a logical relationship is crossed, a concatenated segment is formed, combining a logical child and a logical parent.

Example of a Concatenated Segment

Figure 14.32 shows our two physical data bases with a unidirectional logical relationship defined. This logical relationship gives us a logical path from PA-TIENT to DOCTOR. Figure 14.33 shows a possible logical data base that can be formed from the segments in our two physical data bases. The segment we have named CONCAT in the logical data base is a combination of the logical child (PTRDOC) and the logical parent (DOCTOR).

In defining a logical data base, there are three choices for how the concatenated segment should appear to an application program that retrieves it. The logical DBD can specify that the program's I/O area contain the logical child segment alone (PTRDOC), the logical parent segment alone (DOCTOR), or a combination of both PTRDOC and DOCTOR (CONCAT). This is shown in Figure 14.34.

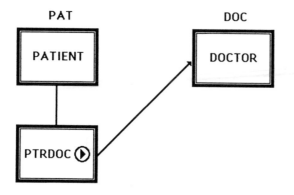

Figure 14.32. Two physical data bases

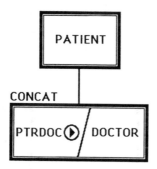

Figure 14.33. Logical data base

Diagramming a Concatenated Segment

In all three cases, CONCAT is referred to as the concatenated segment, no matter which option is chosen for retrieval. Any name can be chosen for the concatenated segment type, even the same name as either the logical child or the logical parent. So, although the standard form of diagram for the concatenated segment is as shown in Figure 14.33, two alternative ways of drawing a logical data base are shown in Figure 14.35. In the diagram on the left, the concatenated segment has the same name as the logical child; in the diagram on the right, it has the same name as the logical parent.

In order to avoid confusion, and to clearly identify the concatenated segment, the diagrams shown in Figure 14.36 are useful. In the first example, the concatenated segment for retrieval consists of both the logical child and the logical parent. In the second example, the I/O area contains only the logical parent, but for clarity we show the logical child with broken lines. In the third

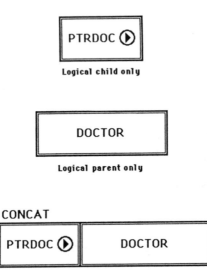

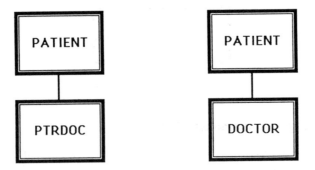

Figure 14.34. Concatenated segment I/O area options

Figure 14.35. Two logical data bases

example, the I/O area contains only the logical child, but we show the logical parent with broken lines.

Concatenated Segments with Virtual Pairing

In virtual pairing, the concatenated segment consists of the real logical child (PTRDOC) and the logical parent (DOCTOR) if the data base is entered from the side that has the real logical child. This is shown in Figure 14.37. In this

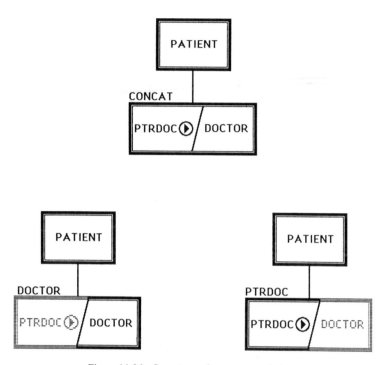

Figure 14.36. Concatenated segment symbology

example, the concatenated segment is formed in the same way as it is for a unidirectional or physically paired relationship.

If the data base is entered from the opposite side, as in Figure 14.38, the concatenated segment consists of the virtual logical child (PTRPAT) and the destination parent (PATIENT). Note that IMS creates an actual occurrence of the virtual logical child in the I/O area, even though it does not physically exist in the data base. If the option of making the logical child transparent to the program has not been chosen, an occurrence of the virtual logical child will be placed in the I/O area, and it will be available to the application program, just as if it had actually been retrieved from the data base.

The point to remember is that to an application program a bidirectional logical relationship with virtual pairing looks and behaves in an identical manner to one with physical pairing.

Physical Pairing Efficiencies

The main difference between physical pairing and virtual pairing is efficiency. Physical pairing results in generally equal retrieval performance on either side

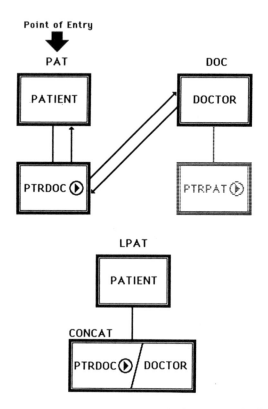

Figure 14.37. Concatenated segment with the real logical child

of the logical relationship. This is because each side has its own set of logical child segments. However, physical pairing requires that two sets of logical child segments be maintained, occupying twice as much direct access storage space for the logical child segment occurrences as for virtual pairing. Physical pairing also affects update performance. For example, when something is updated in one logical child segment, the corresponding logical child on the other side of the logical relationship must be updated as well.

Virtual Pairing Efficiencies

With virtual pairing, only one set of logical child segments is maintained, thus saving direct access space. Virtual pairing can also save processing time in some types of update operations. However, retrieval efficiency depends on which side of the relationship the data base is entered. If the data base is entered from the side that has the real logical child, the performance is the same as it

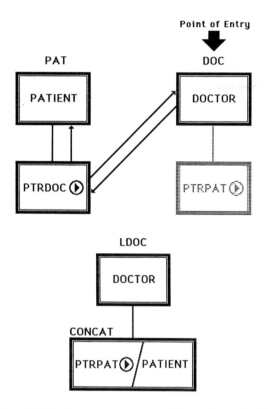

Figure 14.38. Concatenated segment with virtual logical child

would be for physical pairing. This is because the logical child points directly to a logical parent. However, if the data base is entered from the side that has the virtual logical child, more I/O activity may be required to get to the destination parent. This is because the twins tend to be scattered throughout the data base.

EXERCISES

1. Below are ten terms and ten statements. For each term, choose the statement that best describes it.

TERMS	STATEMENTS
A. Logical relationship	a. Creates a logical path from one segment to another, which alters the hierarchical relationships in one or more physical data bases.
B. Logical child	

TERMS	STATEMENTS
C. Application data structure	b. Can be reached via a logical path, but is not necessarily a logical parent.
D. Variable intersection data	
E. Fixed intersection data	c. Data unique to a logical relationship that is stored in a logical child segment.
F. Concatenated segment	
G. Destination parent	d. Data as described in a PSB.
H. Physical data base	e. Implements a logical path by pointing to a logical parent.
I. Logical parent	f. Data as described by a physical DBD.
J. Logical data base	
	g. Data unique to a logical relationship that is stored in segments dependent on a logical child.
	h. Can be reached via a logical path created by a logical child.
	i. Data as described by a logical DBD.
	j. Segment in a logical data base consisting of a logical child and a logical parent from one or more physical data bases.

15
Logical Relationships— Programming

This chapter presents the specific information needed to write application programs that issue IMS calls against logically related data bases. We will see how to interpret the information found in DBDs for physical and logical data bases to make decisions about application programs. These decisions involve the format of the I/O area when retrieving a concatenated segment type, and data stored in the PCB key feedback area. We will also see some choices the DBA has for specifying pointers in the logical child, and some considerations for segment sequencing and status codes for logically related data bases.

DATA BASE EXAMPLES

In this chapter, we will use for examples the PATIENT and DOCTOR data from the HOSPITAL data base broken into two separate physical data bases. The main example we will use is the unidirectional logical relationship repeated in Figure 15.1. Figure 15.2 shows the structure of a possible logical data base we can create using our two logically related physical DBDs.

PATIENT and DOCTOR Data

Figure 15.3 shows the physical DBDs for the PAT and DOC physical data bases. Look first at the SEGM statement for the PTRDOC logical child segment in the PAT DBD. Notice that the PARENT parameter has two subparameter strings. The presence of the second subparameter identifies this segment type as a logical child. It names this logical child segment's logical parent (the DOCTOR segment defined in the DOC data base). The first subparameter string of PARENT names the logical child segment's physical parent and, since this is an HD data base, its physical pointer type.

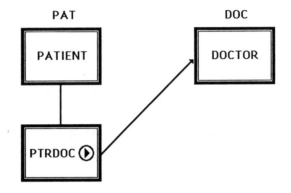

Figure 15.1. Unidirectional logical relationship

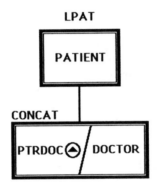

Figure 15.2. Logical data base

Now examine the physical DBD for the DOC data base. The LCHILD statement tells IMS that the segment identified in the preceding SEGM statement has a logical child pointing to it. The LCHILD statement says that the name of the logical child segment is PTRDOC and the physical DBD that defines it is named PAT.

Logical Data Bases

We will next look at various logical data bases that we can define using the PAT and DOC physical DBDs. Figure 15.4 shows the five different logical structures that we can define from our two physical data bases.

```
DBD      NAME=PAT,ACCESS=HDAM,
         RMNAME=(DFSHDC40,5,18)
DATASET DD1=PAT,DEVICE=3350
SEGM     NAME=PATIENT,BYTES=125,PARENT=0
  FIELD    NAME=(BEDIDENT,SEQ,U),BYTES=4,START=61,TYPE=C
  FIELD    NAME=PATNAME,BYTES=20,START=1,TYPE=C
  FIELD    NAME=DATEADMT,BYTES=6,START=65,TYPE=C
SEGM     NAME=PTRDOC,BYTES=28,
           PARENT=((PATIENT,SNGL),(DOCTOR,PHYSICAL,DOC))
  FIELD    NAME=(DOCTKEY,SEQ),BYTES=20,START=1
DBDGEN
FINISH
END


DBD      NAME=DOC,ACCESS=HDAM,
         RMNAME=(DFSHDC40,5,18)
DATASET DD1=DOC,DEVICE=3350
SEGM     NAME=DOCTOR,BYTES=80,PARENT=0
LCHILD  NAME=(PTRDOC,PAT)
  FIELD    NAME=(DOCTNAME,SEQ),BYTES=20,START=1,TYPE=C
  FIELD    NAME=SPECIALT,BYTES=20,START=61,TYPE=C
DBDGEN
FINISH
END
```

Figure 15.3. Physical data base DBD coding

Determining I/O Area Contents

In order to determine what the I/O area layouts should be in an application program, we must look at the logical DBD coding, the PSB coding, and also the physical DBD coding. The logical DBD coding defines the segment types that are potentially available to the application program.

The Concatenated Segment

Figure 15.5 shows the logical DBD coding. It defines a concatenated segment type in which both the logical child and the logical parent segments appear in the I/O area on retrieval. In the example, the concatenated segment type is named CONCAT. In a logical DBD, the SEGM statements give names to the segments just as they do in the physical DBD. The SEGM statements also tell in which physical DBDs those segments are defined. The segment name in a SEGM statement in a logical DBD can be the same as the segment name in a physical DBD, or the names can be different.

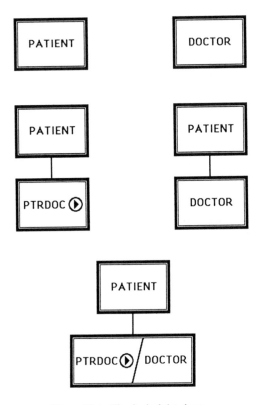

Figure 15.4. Five logical data bases

```
DBD      NAME=LPAT,ACCESS=LOGICAL
DATASET  LOGICAL
SEGM     NAME=PATIENT,
         SOURCE=((PATIENT,DATA,PAT))
SEGM     NAME=CONCAT,
         SOURCE=((PTRDOC,DATA,PAT),(DOCTOR,DATA,DOC))
DBDGEN
FINISH
END
```

Figure 15.5. Logical DBD Coding

In the first SEGM statement, the name of the segment is PATIENT. It comes from a physical DBD named PAT, and the segment name in that DBD is also PATIENT. The DATA keyword in the SOURCE parameter indicates that this segment is to be placed in the I/O area for retrieval calls. If KEY is coded in place of DATA, the segment is not placed in the I/O area. This subparameter is most important in a description of the concatenated segment type.

Defining the Concatenated Segment

The second SEGM statement identifies the concatenated segment type. In the example in Figure 15.5 its name is CONCAT. The SOURCE parameter contains two subparameter strings. The first one identifies the source of the logical child, and the second one identifies the source of the logical parent. Since we have included the DATA subparameter in both strings, IMS places both the logical child and the logical parent into the I/O area when we make a retrieval call for the CONCAT segment type.

Coding for a Transparent Logical Child

Figure 15.6 shows the logical DBD coding that makes the logical child segment transparent to the application program with respect to the I/O area contents. Notice that this time the concatenated segment type has the same name as the logical parent: DOCTOR. The second SEGM statement is still defined as a concatenated segment type, and it has a SOURCE subparameter string for both the logical child and the logical parent. But this time, the subparameter string for the logical child specifies KEY instead of DATA. This tells IMS to place only the logical parent in the I/O area and not the logical child. However, the key of the logical child *is* placed into the key feedback area in this situation.

Coding for Logical Child Only

Figure 15.7 shows the logical DBD coding we would use to retrieve only the logical child segment and not the logical parent. Notice that this time the KEY subparameter is used in the SOURCE subparameter string for the logical parent. Since DATA is specified solely for the logical child, the I/O area will contain

```
DBD     NAME=LPAT,ACCESS=LOGICAL
DATASET LOGICAL
SEGM    NAME=PATIENT,
        SOURCE=((PATIENT,DATA,PAT))
SEGM    NAME=DOCTOR,
        SOURCE=((PTRDOC,KEY,PAT),(DOCTOR,DATA,DOC))
DBDGEN
FINISH
END
```

Figure 15.6. Logical DBD for transparent logical child

```
DBD       NAME=LPAT,ACCESS=LOGICAL
DATASET LOGICAL
SEGM      NAME=PATIENT,
          SOURCE=((PATIENT,DATA,PAT))
SEGM      NAME=PTRDOC,
          SOURCE=((PTRDOC,DATA,PAT),(DOCTOR,KEY,DOC))
DBDGEN
FINISH
END
```

Figure 15.7. Logical DBD for logical child only

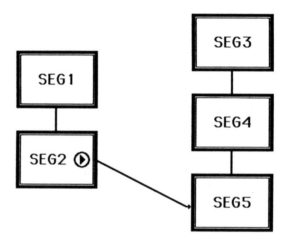

Figure 15.8. Sample physical data bases

only the logical child and not the logical parent when this concatenated segment is retrieved.

Format of the I/O Area

Figure 15.8 shows two physical data bases that we will use to illustrate the contents of the I/O area and the PCB key feedback area when the concatenated segment type is retrieved.

Figure 15.9 shows the structure of a logical data base that can be derived from the two physical data bases in Figure 15.8. The following is the SOURCE parameter for the concatenated segment type in the logical DBD:

```
SOURCE=((SEG2,DATA,DBD1),(SEG5,DATA,DBD2))
```

At the bottom Figure 15.9 is a diagram showing what the I/O area would look like if we retrieved the concatenated segment. Notice that the logical child

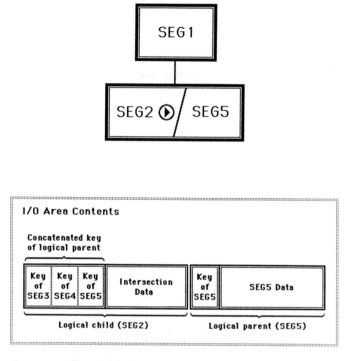

Figure 15.9. Concatenated segment in I/O Area

segment appears first in the I/O area and begins with the complete concatenated key of the logical parent. Next comes the logical child segment's intersection data. Last comes the logical parent segment. Notice that the concatenated key of the logical parent is nothing more than a combination of the key fields of its physical parents. This is no different from the concatenated key of any other segment type.

The PCB Key Feedback Area

Figure 15.10 shows another logical data base that can be derived from our two physical data bases. The following is the SOURCE parameter used to define the concatenated segment for this logical data base:

```
SOURCE=((SEG2,KEY,DBD1),(SEG5,DATA,DBD2))
```

Figure 15.10 shows both the I/O area contents and the format of the PCB key feedback area for concatenated segment retrievals using this logical data base. In this example we are assuming that the key field of the logical child

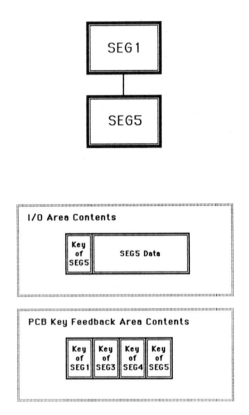

Figure 15.10. I/O area and PCB key feedback area contents

segment in the physical DBD is defined as the entire concatenated key of the logical parent.

Notice that the key feedback area does not contain simply the key of SEG1 followed by the key of SEG5, as it would be if SEG1 and SEG5 were defined in a single physical data base. Instead, the key feedback area contains the key of SEG1 followed by the fully concatenated key of the logical parent. In this case, this is the key of SEG3, followed by the key of SEG4, followed by the key of SEG5.

Other PCB Key Feedback Area Examples

The key feedback area contains different values depending on the key defined for the logical child. In Figure 15.11 the logical child segment is defined with no key field. In this example the fully concatenated key of the logical child segment consists simply of the key of SEG1.

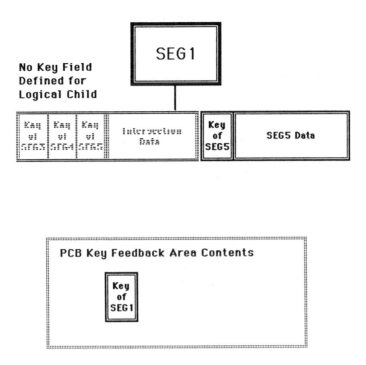

In Figure 15.12 the key of the logical child segment is defined as only the third field from the logical child. This consists of the key of SEG5. In this example, the fully concatenated key of the concatenated segment is the key of SEG1, followed by the key of SEG5. In this case, the key feedback area will look exactly as if the logical data base consisted of a single physical data base. So the use of a logical relationship in this particular example would be transparent to an application program, both with respect to the I/O area contents and to the PCB key feedback area.

As we have seen, for retrieval calls, the DBA has the choice of passing to an application program either the logical child and logical parent, or both concatenated together in the I/O area. But, for most calls other than retrieval calls, the I/O area must contain both the logical child and the logical parent, no matter what option has been chosen for the concatenated segment for retrieval.

POINTERS FOR THE LOGICAL CHILD

The DBA has another choice that must be made for the logical child segment. The logical child segment must contain a pointer to the logical parent. In the

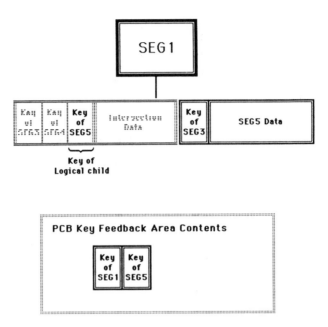

Figure 15.12. Transparent logical relationship

physical DBD that defines the logical child segment, the DBA must specify what type of pointer is to be used. Pointers can be either *symbolic* or *direct*.

Symbolic Pointers

If the data base containing the logical parent is an HISAM data base, the pointers in the logical child segments pointing to that logical parent must be *symbolic pointers*. A symbolic pointer consists of the concatenated key of the logical parent. When a logical child is retrieved, the I/O area always begins with the concatenated key of the logical parent. In HISAM, this is also the pointer IMS uses to locate the logical parent. Figure 15.13 shows the format of the logical child as it is stored in the data base and its format in the I/O area. The following is the SEGM statement used to define it:

```
SEGM  NAME=PTRDOC,BYTES=28,
   PARENT=((PATIENT),(DOCTOR,PHYSICAL,DOC))
```

The keyword PHYSICAL in the second subparameter of PARENT indicates that a symbolic pointer should be used. This pointer option must be specified for HISAM, but it is also a valid option for HD data bases.

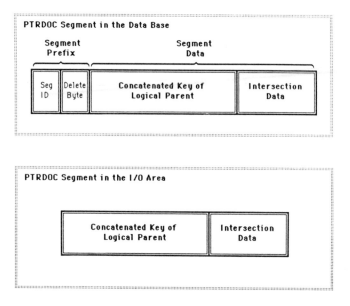

Figure 15.13. PTRDOC segment with symbolic pointer

Direct Pointers

In an HD data base, the DBA can alternatively specify that a *direct pointer* be used to point to the logical parent. The following shows the SEGM statement coding for a direct pointer to the logical parent:

```
SEGM  NAME=PTRDOC,BYTES=28,
   PARENT=((PATIENT),(DOCTOR,VIRTUAL,DOC)),
   POINTER=(LPARNT,TWIN)
```

The keyword VIRTUAL in the second subparameter of PARENT indicates that the symbolic pointer is to be omitted. The POINTER parameter must then be included to indicate that the logical parent pointer should be included in the segment's prefix, as shown in Figure 15.14. The logical child, as it is stored in the data base, does not contain the concatenated key of the logical parent. The direct pointer in the segment's prefix contains all the information necessary to locate the logical parent.

Even if a direct pointer is specified for the logical child, the logical child, as it appears to the program in the I/O area, will always begin with the fully concatenated key of the logical parent, whether that concatenated key is stored in the data base or not. If it is not stored in the data base, IMS constructs it before the logical child is placed in the I/O area.

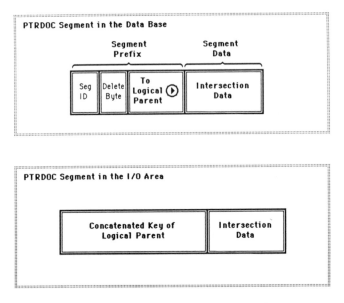

Figure 15.14. PTRDOC segment with direct pointers

Both Symbolic and Direct Pointers

Since the construction of the concatenated key requires additional processing, IMS gives the DBA the option of specifying that both a direct pointer and a symbolic pointer be stored. This takes more storage space, but processing overhead is lower since IMS does not have to construct a concatenated key each time a logical child segment is retrieved. This pointer configuration is shown in Figure 15.15. The SEGM statement coding for both pointer types is as follows:

```
SEGM  NAME=PTRDOC,BYTES=28,
  PARENT=((PATIENT),(DOCTOR,PHYSICAL,DOC))
  POINTER=(LPARNT,TWIN)
```

In the above example, the PHYSICAL keyword in the second subparameter of PARENT indicates that the symbolic pointer is to be included and the POINTER parameter includes the LPARNT keyword as well.

No matter what choice the DBA has made for the logical child pointer type, the contents of the I/O area are the same. The logical child in the I/O area *always starts with the fully concatenated key of the destination parent* and ends with the intersection data, if any. The important thing is the choice the DBA has made in the *logical DBD* for the concatenated segment type. We must know

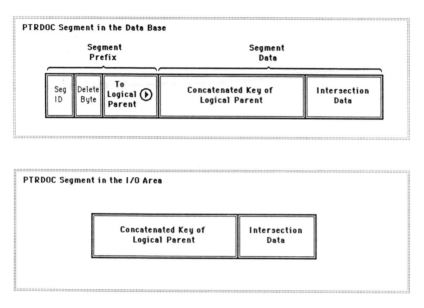

Figure 15.15. Both symbolic and direct pointers

for retrieval whether the I/O area will contain the logical child, the logical parent, or both.

CONCATENATED SEGMENT KEY FIELD

It is the key of the logical child segment, as defined in the physical DBD for the logical child, that determines the sequence in which we will retrieve concatenated segments when using a logical DBD. As we have already seen, the proper choice of a key field for the logical child makes it possible for the DBA to make the logical relationship transparent to the application program. Let us see some of the restrictions the DBA has in choosing key fields for the logical child.

Key of the Real Logical Child

Figure 15.16 shows a virtually paired logical relationship. Towards the bottom of the figure is a diagram showing the format of the real logical child for that logical relationship. The following is the coding that defines the real logical child segment type in the physical DBD:

```
SEGM   NAME=PTRDOC,BYTES=28,
  PARENT=((PATIENT),(DOCTOR,VIRTUAL,DOC)),
  POINTER=(LPARNT,LTWIN,TWIN)
  FIELD  NAME=(DOCTKEY,SEQ,U),BYTES=20,START=1
```

When choosing a key field for the real logical child, the DBA can select any contiguous set of bytes within the data area of the logical child to be its key. Then, in a logical data base using that logical child segment, the key field of the *concatenated segment* will be that same field. In other words, the key of a concatenated segment is always the key of the logical child. And that is true no matter which option for the concatenated segment has been chosen for the contents of the I/O area.

Concatenated Key Restriction

When choosing the key of the logical child, the DBA has complete freedom in specifying which bytes of the logical child will be the key. However, if any

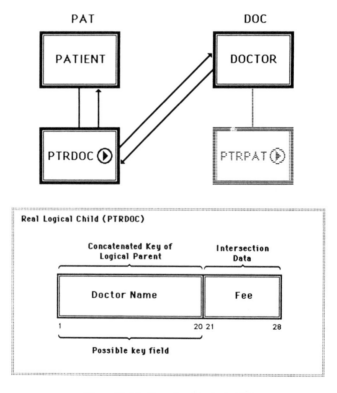

Figure 15.16. Key of real logical child

portion of the logical parent's concatenated key is chosen as part of the key field, the physical DBD must specify that a symbolic pointer be included in the logical child. If only data included in intersection data is chosen as the key of the logical child, the DBA can choose a direct pointer, a symbolic pointer, or both for the logical child. The DBA cannot include as part of the key field any portion of the logical child that does not physically exist *as stored in the data base*.

The Key of the Virtual Logical Child

The virtual logical child in a virtually paired logical relationship is very different from other segment types in a set of logically related data bases. In no case does any portion of the virtual logical child physically exist; its existence is simulated through a set of pointers in the real logical child. Since the virtual logical child does not really exist, no pointer types are specified for it when it is defined in the physical data base. Figure 15.17 shows the virtual logical child for our sample data base. The following shows the physical DBD coding for the DOC physical data base:

```
DBD      NAME=DOC,ACCESS=HDAM,RMNAME=(DFSHDC40,5,18)
DATASET  DD1=PAT,DEVICE=3350
SEGM     NAME=DOCTOR,BYTES=80,PARENT=0
  LCHILD NAME=(PTRDOC,PAT),PAIR=PTRPAT,POINTER=SNGL
  FIELD  NAME=(DOCTNAME,SEQ),BYTES=20,START=1,TYPE=C
  FIELD  NAME=SPECIALT,BYTES=20,START=61,TYPE=C
SEGM     NAME=PTRPAT,BYTES=12,PARENT=DOCTOR,
         SOURCE=(PTRDOC,DATA,PAT),POINTER=PAIRED
  FIELD  NAME=(PATKEY,SEQ,U),BYTES=4,START=1
DBDGEN
FINISH
END
```

When the DBA defines logical data bases using virtually paired relationships, the virtual logical child is treated as if it actually exists. The concatenated segment consists of the virtual logical child and the destination parent. The key field of the concatenated segment type is the key field of the virtual logical child. Since the virtual logical child does not actually exist, and no pointer types are specified for it, the DBA has more choices in defining the key field of the virtual logical child. In fact, a unique feature is implemented for the virtual logical child: *its key field does not have to be contiguous*.

Scattered Key Field

Figure 15.18 illustrates a scattered key field for a virtual logical child. The following is the part of the physical DBD coding that defines this virtual logical child:

```
SEGM     NAME=VIRSEG,BYTES=45,
         PARENT=ROOTSEG,
         SOURCE=(REALSEG,DATA,DBD2),
         POINTER=PAIRED
  FIELD    NAME=(KEYA,SEQ,U,BYTES=4,START=24
  FIELD    NAME=(KEYB,SEQ,U,BYTES=4,START=10
  FIELD    NAME=(KEYC,SEQ,U,BYTES=4,START=20
```

Notice that there are three FIELD statements following the SEGM statement for the virtual logical child, all specifying that they are key fields. Each FIELD statement defines one portion of the virtual logical child's key. Remember, this option exists only for a virtual logical child. A real logical child must have a contiguous key field defined with a single FIELD parameter.

Using a Scattered Key Field in SSAs

When coding calls that use SSAs qualified on the scattered key field, the normal case is to use only the name in the first FIELD statement following the SEGM

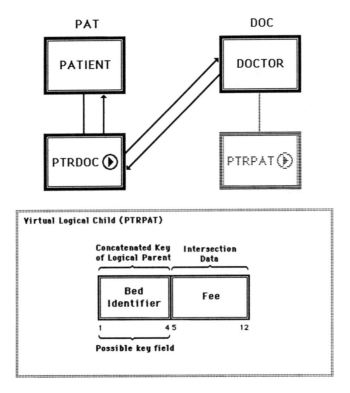

Figure 15.17. Virtual logical child

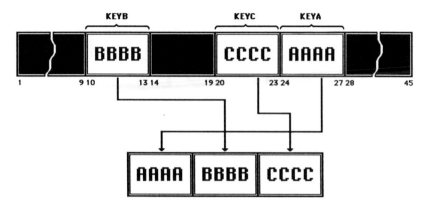

Figure 15.18. Scattered key field

for the virtual logical child. The key is then the combination of all the parts of the key. The following shows an example:

```
GU   VIRSEG  (KEYA     =AAAABBBBCCCC)
```

If we specify the field name defined in one of the other FIELD statements, the SSA should be qualified on only a portion of the full key field. For example, if we specify the name of the second key field, KEYB, we must supply only eight bytes of key information, as follows:

```
GU   VIRSEG  (KEYB     =BBBBCCCC)
```

And, if we use the third key field name, KEYC, we must supply qualification information only for the last piece of the key field described by that portion of the key:

```
GU   VIRSEG  (KEYC     =CCCC)
```

SEGMENT SEQUENCING

When accessing segments via a logical data base, the options chosen for the logical relationships determine the sequence in which segments will be retrieved when sequential retrieval calls are issued. The segments that give the most difficulty are the concatenated segments. Let us look at some examples.

Figure 15.19 shows a unidirectional logical relationship in which we are storing fixed intersection data in the PTRDOC segment. The intersection data

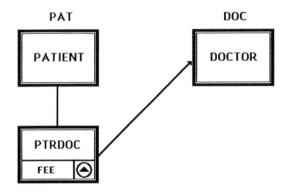

Figure 15.19. Unidirectional logical relationship

contains a fee value for the doctor to which each logical child points. In our first example, the DBA has defined the key field of the logical child to be the concatenated key of the logical parent portion of the logical child, as shown in Figure 15.20.

Figure 15.21 shows a possible logical data base that we might use to retrieve segments from our two physical data bases. In this case the DBA has chosen to make the logical child segment transparent to the application program. The name of the concatenated segment has been selected as DOCTOR, the same as its SOURCE segment in the DOC data base. The application program could issue a Get-Unique call for any particular PATIENT segment and then issue a series of Get-Next-Within-Parent calls for DOCTOR segments using a conventional unqualified SSA. The program would then retrieve DOCTOR segments in sequence by doctor name. The result of sequential retrieval in this particular logical data base would be very similar to if we had used a physical data base that looked like the one in Figure 15.22. In this case, the use of the logical relationship would be somewhat transparent to the application program.

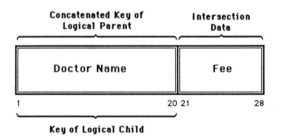

Figure 15.20. PTRDOC logical child segment

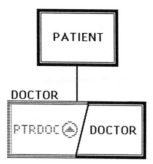

Figure 15.21. A possible logical data base

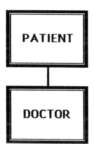

Figure 15.22. Equivalent physical data base

We will next look at another example in which the logical relationship is not transparent. In Figure 15.23, the DBA has chosen the fee value in the intersection data as the key field of the logical child. The logical data base this time says that both the logical child and the logical parent will be placed in the I/O area on retrieval. Also, notice that the name of the concatenated segment this time is CONCAT, different from either PTRDOC or DOCTOR. Now, to sequentially retrieve DOCTOR segments, we would issue a Get-Unique call for a particular PATIENT segment and then issue a series of the following Get-Next-Within-Parent using an unqualified SSA for the CONCAT segment type. For each call, we would retrieve not only a DOCTOR segment, but a PTRDOC segment as well. Also, we would get concatenated segment occurrences in sequence by the fee value in the logical child segments, not in doctor name sequence as in the previous example.

The above two examples show that the DBA can cause a program to vary its behavior by making different choices in the physical and logical DBD coding. In the last example the logical relationship is not transparent to the application program, and the programmer needs detailed information on the nature

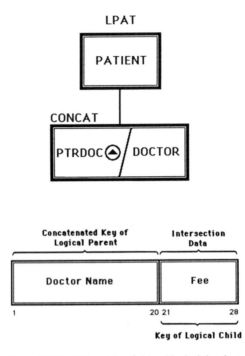

Figure 15.23. Different key field and logical data base

of the logical relationship in order to write a program that accesses the concatenated segment.

STATUS CODES

When segments that participate in logical relationships are retrieved, there are some differences in the status codes that IMS returns. When segments are updated, there are even more status code differences. We will discuss the simpler case of segment retrieval. The complex problems of updating segments that participate in logical relationships are beyond the scope of this book.

Retrieval Status Codes

There is only one significant difference in the status codes that are obtained when segments that participate in logical relationships are retrieved. This dif-

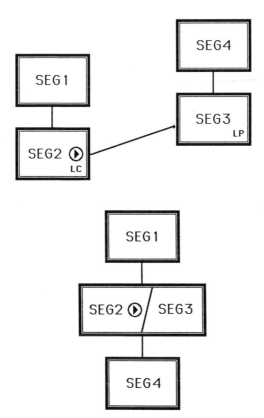

Figure 15.24. Levels in physical and logical data bases

ference involves the GA and GK status codes that are received as a result of unqualified Get-Next calls. The rule to keep in mind is that the GA status code indicates we have gone up level in the *physical* data base, not in a *logical* data base. Figure 15.24 shows a set of physical data bases, and a logical data base derived from it.

Assume that we are issuing unqualified Get-Next calls and are currently retrieving occurrences of the concatenated segment type. When we retrieve the last occurrence of the concatenated segment type under a particular parent and then next retrieve an occurrence of SEG4, we have gone down a level in the logical data base. However, in the physical data base, we have actually gone up a level from SEG3 to SEG4. In this case, we receive a GA status code and not a status code of blanks.

When issuing unqualified Get-Next calls with logical data bases, it is necessary to be familiar with the structures of the physical data bases to be able to predict the status codes that will be obtained.

Update Status Codes

When segment insertion, replacement, and deletion in logical data bases are performed, a lot more status code conditions can occur. Segment updating is more complex for logical data bases because a logical parent or destination parent segment can be accessed from at least two different paths. So there have to be rules about the directions from which we are allowed to process updates. For example, the DBA can specify, through the use of logical update rules, that a particular logical parent segment can be inserted only via its physical parent, and not via its logical parent. As another example, the DBA can specify that a particular logical parent segment must already have been deleted via its physical path before a Delete call can be accepted for it via a logical path.

Logical update rules are complex and allow the DBA to build elaborate updating precautions in logically related data bases. This allows better control with the result that multiple applications can access the data without interfering with one another.

EXERCISES

1. Answer true or false to the following statements concerning logical relationships.

   a. The logical child segment is always present in the I/O area when the concatenated segment type is retrieved.
   b. The size and field structure of a segment is defined in the physical DBD and not in the logical DBD.
   c. The DATA keyword of the SOURCE parameter in the logical DBD coding causes a segment type to be stored in the I/O area upon retrieval.
   d. A symbolic pointer must always be included in a logical child segment.
   e. The DBA has free choice in determining the key of a logical child segment type.
   f. Either a real logical child or a virtual logical child can have a scattered key field.

2. Which of the following determines the contents of the I/O area when the concatenated segment type is retrieved?

   a. The SEGM statements in the physical DBD
   b. The SEGM statements in the logical DBD
   c. The SENSEG statements in the PSB
   d. The SSA referenced by the retrieval call
   e. All of the above
   f. None of the above

3. Which of the following determines the sequence in which segment occurrences are retrieved when a sequence of Get-Next calls are issued for the concatenated segment type?

   a. The key values in logical parent segment occurrences
   b. The key values in logical child segment occurrences
   c. The sequence of the SENSEG statements in the PSB
   d. All of the above
   e. None of the above

16
Fast Path Data Bases

The Fast Path feature of IMS provides two types of high-performance data base that can be used to increase the performance of certain types of data base application. These data base types are called *data entry data bases* and *main storage data bases*. A feature called *Expedited Message Handling* is also provided to increase the performance of message processing programs. In this chapter, we introduce these facilities.

MAIN STORAGE DATA BASES

A main storage data base (MSDB) is a data base that consists of a root segment type only and is organized in a similar manner to a SHISAM root-only data base. An MSDB is used to store frequently accessed data and employs two facilities to greatly increase retrieval and update performance. First, the entire data base is loaded into main storage at the beginning of processing, and remains there as long as it is needed. Second, data base updates are not made immediately after each update call. Instead, all updates requested by a given application program are performed at one time, after a *synchronization point* has been reached. In a message processing program, a synchronization point occurs each time the program issues a Get-Unique call to the I/O PCB. In a batch program, a synchronization point is reached each time the program issues an IMS SYNC call.

There are two different types of MSDB that can be used. These are terminal-related MSDBs and non-terminal-related MSDBs. We will discuss each type.

Terminal-Related MSDB

In a terminal-related MSDB, each segment occurrence in the data base is owned by a specific logical terminal, as shown in Figure 16.1. The key of each MSDB record occurrence consists of the logical terminal name of its owner. However,

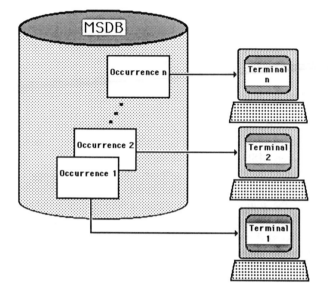

Figure 16.1. Terminal-related MSDB

the logical terminal name does not reside in the segment occurrence itself; the logical terminal name simply serves as the mechanism for locating individual segment occurrences in the MSDB.

Only the logical terminal assigned to a specific segment occurrence is allowed to update the data in that segment occurrence. All logical terminals, however, are allowed to retrieve any MSDB segment occurrence.

There are two types of terminal related MSDB: *fixed* and *dynamic*. In a fixed terminal-related MSDB, there is a separate segment occurrence in the data base for each logical terminal. Occurrences can not be inserted or deleted; they can be retrieved and updated only. In a dynamic terminal-related MSDB, an application program is allowed to insert and delete the segment occurrence that is related to the logical terminal invoking the program. This facility is sometimes used to implement a facility similar to the scratch pad area discussed in Part III. The scratch pad area facility itself is not available for Fast Path transaction types.

Non-Terminal-Related MSDB

With a non-terminal-related MSDB, segment occurrences are not associated with specific logical terminals. A Fast Path application program can read and update any segment occurrence in the data base. The key can be chosen in any desired manner by the DBA. The DBA can use the logical terminal name as a record key, in which case the logical terminal name does not reside in the segment itself. Alternatively, the DBA can choose as the key all or part of the segment's sequence field.

The Field Call

The Fast Path feature provides an additional call that can be used to update data in an MSDB segment occurrence. The Field call is used to update the data in a specific field in an MSDB segment occurrence.

As you learned in Part II, the normal method used to update a segment occurrence is to retrieve it using a Get-Hold call, thus preventing other users from accessing the segment. The segment is then updated and the lock on the record is removed. In order to increase performance, the Field call allows several users to access the same MSDB segment occurrence at the same time by allowing applications to update the segment occurrence at the field level. There are two types of Field call: *Change* Field calls and *Verify* Field calls.

Change Field Calls. A Change Field call allows an application program to perform the following three types of modification to a specific field in an MSDB segment occurrence:

- Add a specific value to the contents of an arithmetic field
- Subtract a specific value from the contents of an arithmetic field
- Replace the contents of a field with a new value

Verify Field Calls. Because segment occurrences in an MSDB are actually physically updated in the data base only after a synchronization point has been reached, an application program must have a way of determining that the same conditions exist at the synchronization point as existed at the time that the update was made. For example, if one application program processes an update to a segment occurrence, it is possible that a second application program may also process an update to the same field and reach its synchronization point before the synchronization point for the first program occurs. Since the segment has already been updated by the second program, the first program will cause double updating to take place after it reaches its synchronization point. The Verify Field call can be used to determine if updating has taken place since the first program's update call was issued.

The ROLB Call. The Fast Path feature provides an additional call, having function code ROLB, that can be used to remove from the update buffers any data that is awaiting synchronization point processing. It can be used by an application program when a Verify Field call fails and determines that a field has in fact been updated between the time that an update was made and the time that the synchronization point has been reached.

DATA ENTRY DATA BASES

A data entry data base (DEDB) is a more conventional type of data base than an MSDB. It is structured in a similar manner to an HDAM data base and is maintained in direct access storage rather than in main storage. However, the characteristics of a data entry data base make it well suited for high-performance applications that must provide very rapid response times.

A DEDB can be designed using any desired hierarchical structure. However, a DEDB is best suited for storing data bases that use simple hierarchical structures. In early versions of the Fast Path feature, only a two-level hierarchical structure consisting of a root segment and up to seven dependent segment types was allowed for DEDBs. In the latest versions of IMS/VS, this restriction has been lifted.

DEDB Areas

Although a DEDB behaves to the application program in a similar manner to an HDAM data, its physical structure is quite different. In a conventional HDAM data base, the entire logical data base structure is spread across the whole data base. If multiple data sets are used, the structure is broken up on a segment basis, and parts of each data base record (a root segment occurrence and all of its dependents) may be contained in multiple data sets. Figure 16.2 shows how the HOSPITAL data base might be divided into separate data sets.

In a DEDB, multiple data sets can also be used, with each data set designated as an *area*. Each area contains segment occurrences of all types, and all segment occurrences that make up a given data base record are always stored in the same physical area. Figure 16.3 shows how the same hierarchical structure is repeated in each area of a DEDB. Each area stores a different set of data base records.

The area approach makes it possible for the DBA to implement very large data bases. Each area is contained in a data set of a convenient size, and the area organization of the data base is transparent to the application program. Each area is independent of all other areas. If a failure occurs in one area, it can be taken out of service without affecting access to segment occurrences in the other areas.

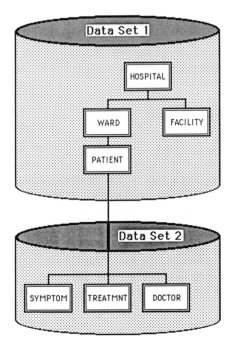

Figure 16.2. Multiple data sets with HDAM

Performance Features

The DEDB facility implements a number of performance features that improve the retrieval and update performance of a DEDB. A DEDB area is made up of three separate portions:

- Root-addressable portion
- Independent overflow portion
- Sequential dependent portion

The root-addressable and independent overflow portions of each area are managed in a similar way to an HDAM data base. As much as possible of a data base record is stored in the root-addressable area, with additional segment occurrences stored as necessary in the independent overflow portion. The sequential dependent portion is unique to a DEDB and is designed for applications that require fast insertion of large volumes of segment occurrences of a particular type. Certain segment types can be designated for storage in the sequential

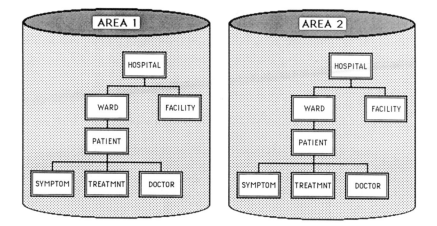

Figure 16.3. Multiple areas with DEDB

dependent portion of the DEDB. The sequential dependent portion is optimized for fast insertion of new segment occurrences. Sequential dependent segment occurrences are chained from the root segment in a last-in first-out manner. Sequential dependent segment occurrences are stored in the next available slot as they are inserted and are stored without regard to keeping related segment occurrences close to each other.

Each portion of a DEDB area can be optimized for performance separately from the other portions. For example, the DBA can choose a different VSAM control interval size for each portion of each DEDB area.

EXPEDITED MESSAGE HANDLING

In addition to the two data base options discussed above, the Fast Path feature also provides a facility called *Expedited Message Handling* that improves the performance of IMS-DC message processing programs. To enable the use of this feature, certain transaction types are declared to be Fast Path transaction types. Transactions of these types are intercepted by a user exit routine before being passed to IMS-DC for normal handling. The user exit routine then determines, based on the contents of the transactions themselves, whether they are to be passed directly to the appropriate message processing program or whether they are to be passed to IMS-DC for normal processing.

EXERCISES

1. Answer true or false to the following statements concerning the Fast Path feature:

   a. In a main storage data base, data base updates are processed as soon as the update calls are issued.
   b. Only the logical terminal that owns a terminal-related MSDB segment is allowed to update that segment.
   c. A dynamic terminal-related MSDB can be used to implement a scratch pad area for a Fast Path conversational transaction.
   d. Individual fields in an MSDB segment can be updated by issuing Change Field calls.
   e. A Verify Field call is used to verify that an update was successful.
   f. The ROLB call can be used to nullify the effects of a previously issued Change Field call.
   g. A data entry data base can be divided into areas, each of which holds occurrences of a single segment type.
   h. Each area in a DEDB is contained in a separate file.

Appendices

Appendix A
IMS JCL Coding

JCL coding for IMS programs can be complex and involved, especially for IMS DB/DC systems. For this reason, IMS JCL is normally handled by the data base administration group, and application programmers normally gain access to IMS through cataloged procedures. Some knowledge of IMS JCL, however, can provide some insight into how the various parts of IMS relate to one another. In this appendix, we introduce the subject of IMS JCL and look at some common JCL examples.

IMS/VS SYSTEM DATA SETS

There are many data sets that contain the components of IMS. The following are the IBM-supplied names for the more important of these data sets:

- IMSVS.RESLIB
- IMSVS.PGMLIB
- IMSVS.PSBLIB
- IMSVS.DBDLIB
- IMSVS.MACLIB
- IMSVS.PROCLIB
- IMSVS.ACBLIB

Each individual installation has the capability of changing the names of the various IMS system data sets. However, even if an installation does not use the names exactly as they appear in the list above, chances are they are similar. For example, many installations change the initial qualifier in each name but retain the last qualifier for ease of identification. This might be done in order to conform to installation naming conventions.

The IMSVS.RESLIB Data Set

This system data set contains all the load modules that make up the IMS software, including both DL/I and the data communications component. The operating system must have access to this data set, or its equivalent, via a STEPLIB or JOBLIB DD statement whenever an IMS program is executed.

The IMSVS.PGMLIB Data Set

In installations that follow IBM's standard, all IMS application program load modules are stored in this data set. The operating system must have access to this data set, as well as to IMSVS.RESLIB, whenever an IMS program is executed. Normally, the STEPLIB or JOBLIB statement specifies a concatenation of this data set with IMSVS.RESLIB. This standard is not followed in a lot of IMS installations, however, and in many cases, IMS application program load modules are stored in multiple load module libraries. The JCL that executes an IMS application must concatenate the appropriate IMS load module library with IMSVS.RESLIB, or its equivalent.

IMSVS.PSBLIB and IMSVS.DBDLIB

We have already discussed these two system data sets. They contain the DBDs and PSBs used by the installation. Again, many installations have multiple libraries for DBDs and PSBs—often a separate library for each application. It is important that execution JCL references the appropriate PSB and DBD libraries.

The IMSVS.MACLIB Data Set

This data set is normally used only by the data base administrator. It contains the definitions of the macros that are used to generate the IMS system and of other macros, such as the DBDGEN and PSBGEN macros.

The IMSVS.PROCLIB Data Set

The IMS cataloged procedures supplied with IMS are stored in this data set. Some installations store the IMS procedures used for application programs in this library. If this is the case, the reader procedure that is used to read in IMS jobs must reference this procedure library. In many cases, however, the IMS procedures are stored in the standard system procedure library, and

IMSVS.PROCLIB is not used in daily production. The cataloged procedures shown in this appendix are some of the ones received from IBM in the IMSVS.PROCLIB data set.

The IMSVS.ACBLIB Data Set

A JCL example in Chapter 3 showed that execution JCL must have access to the IMSVS.PSBLIB and IMSVS.DBDLIB data sets or their equivalents. There are exceptions to this rule. When an IMS application program is executed, IMS must combine the information in the DBD and PSB before the application program can be executed. To avoid causing IMS to do this each time a program runs, the DBA may choose to merge the DBD and PSB information in advance. To do this, a procedure called ACBGEN, which stands for *Application Control Block Generation*, is executed. The IMSVS.ACBLIB data set is used to store the combined DBDs and PSBs. The execution JCL then references IMSVS.ACBLIB (or its equivalent) rather than the PSBLIB and DBDLIB.

The use of the IMSVS.ACBLIB data set is optional for batch IMS programs but is required for MP and BMP programs. DBDs and PSBs must be merged ahead of time with an ACBGEN before MP or BMP programs can run. As with the other data sets, the installation may use other names for this data set, and there may be separate ACBLIBs available for different applications.

THE DBDGEN PROCEDURE

The set of JCL shown in Figure A.1 is an example of the JCL used to run the DBDGEN procedure. In the IMS/VS DBDGEN procedure, the two programs that are executed are the IFOX00 program and the DFSILNK0 program. These programs invoke the system assembler and the linkage editor respectively.

The DBDGEN statements that define a DBD actually consist of Assembler Language macros. The DBDGEN procedure first invokes the assembler to process the DBDGEN macros producing an object module. The second step invokes the linkage editor, which processes the object module passed from the assembler step. The linkage editor produces a DBD in load module form and stores it in DBDLIB.

A useful symbolic parameter in the above procedure is the MBR parameter. It allows the user to substitute a member name when invoking the procedure. Figure A.2 shows the JCL that might be used to invoke this procedure for the HOSPITAL DBD. The MBR=HOSPITAL parameter causes the procedure to store the DBD into DBDLIB under the member name HOSPITAL.

```
//          PROC  MBR=TEMPNAME,SOUT=A
//C         EXEC  PGM=IFOX00,REGION=120K,PARM='LOAD,NODECK'
//SYSLIB    DD    DSN=IMSVS.MACLIB,DISP=SHR
//SYSGO     DD    UNIT=SYSDA,DISP=(,PASS),SPACE=(80,(100,100),RLSE,
//                DCB=(BLKSIZE=400,RECFM=FB,LRECL=80)
//SYSPRINT  SYSOUT=&SOUT,DCB=(LRECL=121,RECFM=FBA,BLKSIZE=605),
//                SPACE=(121,(500,500),RLSE,,ROUND)
//SYSUT1    DD    UNIT=SYSDA,DISP=(,DELETE),SPACE=(1700,(100,50)
//SYSUT2    DD    UNIT=SYSDA,DISP=(,DELETE),SPACE=(1700,(100,50)
//SYSUT3    DD    UNIT=(SYSDA,SEP=(SYSLIB,SYSUT1,SYSUT2)),
//                SPACE=(1700,(100,50))
//L         EXEC  PGM=DFSILNKO,PARM='XREF,LIST',COND=(0,LT,C),REGION=120K
//STEPLIB   DD    DSN=IMSVS.RESLIB,DISP=SHR
//SYSLIN    DD    DSN=*.C.SYSGO,DISP=(OLD,DELETE)
//SYSPRINT  DD    SYSOUT=&SOUT.DCB=(LRECL=121,RECFM=FBA,BLKSIZE=605),
//                SPACE=(121,(100),RLSE)
//SYSLMOD   DD    DSN=IMSVS.DBDLIB(&MBR),DISP=SHR
//SYSUT1    DD    UNIT=(SYSDA,SEP=(SYSLMOD,SYSLIN)),DISP=(,DELETE),
//                SPACE=(1024,(100,10),RLSE)
```

Figure A.1. DBDGEN procedure

```
//DBD        EXEC  DBDGEN,MBR=HOSPITAL
//C.SYSIN    DD    *
                ---
                ---
                ---
           DBDGEN statements
                ---
                ---
                ---
```

Figure A.2. Executing the DBDGEN procedure

THE PSBGEN PROCEDURE

We have not included a copy of the PSBGEN procedure here because it is almost identical to the DBDGEN procedure. Its name is PBSGEN instead of DBDGEN, and the SYSLMOD data set in the linkage editor step is IMSVS.PSBLIB instead of IMSVS.DBDLIB. It uses the MBR symbolic parameter to assign a member name to the resulting PSB.

THE IMSCOBOL PROCEDURE

This procedure is similar to the standard procedure used to execute a COBOL compile and link edit job. The main differences are in the data sets referenced by the procedure. Let us look at the major differences between an IMS compile

```
//          PROC  MBR=,PAGES=60,SOUT=A
//C         EXEC  PGM=PARM='SIZE=130K,BUF=10K,LINECNT=50',REGION=150K
//SYSLIN    DD    DSN=&&LIN,DISP=(MOD,PASS),UNIT=SYSDA,
//                DCB=(LRECL=80,RECFM=FB,BLKSIZE=400),
//                SPACE=(CYL,(4,1),RLSE)
//SYSPRINT  SYSOUT=&SOUT,DCB=(LRECL=121,RECFM=FBA,BLKSIZE=605),
//                SPACE=(605,(&PAGES.0,&PAGES),RLSE,,ROUND)
//SYSUT1    DD    UNIT=SYSDA,DISP=(,DELETE),SPACE=(CYL,(10,1),RLSE)
//SYSUT2    DD    UNIT=SYSDA,DISP=(,DELETE),SPACE=(CYL,(10,1),RLSE)
//SYSUT3    DD    UNIT=SYSDA,DISP=(,DELETE),SPACE=(CYL,(10,1),RLSE)
//SYSUT4    DD    UNIT=SYSDA,DISP=(,DELETE),SPACE=(CYL,(10,1),RLSE)
//L         EXEC  PGM=DFSILNK0,REGION=120K,PARM='XREF,LET,LIST',
//                COND=(4,LT,C)
//STEPLIB   DD    DSN=IMSVS.RESLIB,DISP=SHR
//SYSLIB    DD    DSN=SYS1.COBLIB,DISP=SHR
//          DD    DSN=SYS1.PLILIB,DISP=SHR
//SYSLIN    DD    DSN=*.C.SYSGO,DISP=(OLD,DELETE)
//RESLIB    DD    DSN=IMSVS.RESLIB,DISP=SHR
//SYSLIN    DD    DSN=&&LIN,DISP=(OLD,DELETE),VOL=REF=*.C.SYSLIN
//          DD    DSN=IMSVS.PROCLIB(CBLTDLI),DISP=SHR
//          DD    DDNAME=SYSIN
//SYSLMOD   DD    DSN=IMSVS.PGMLIB(&MBR),DISP=SHR
//SYSPRINT  DD    SYSOUT=&SOUT.DCB=(LRECL=121,RECFM=FBA,BLKSIZE=605),
//                SPACE=(605,(&PAGES,PAGES),RLSE,,ROUND)
//SYSUT1    DD    UNIT=(SYSDA,SEP=(SYSLMOD,SYSLIN)),DISP=(,DELETE),
//                SPACE=(CYL,(10,1),RLSE)
```

Figure A.3. IMSCOBOL procedure

and link edit, and one for a non-IMS program. The IMSCOBOL procedure for IMS/VS is shown in Figure A.3.

The COBOL compile step is similar to any other COBOL compile. The main differences appear in the linkage editor step. The program being executed is DFSILNK0 instead of the normal IEWL. This program invokes the linkage editor.

Notice the RESLIB DD statement. It gives the linkage editor access to the IMSVS.RESLIB data set or its equivalent. The SYSLIN DD statement concatenates three data sets. The first one is the temporary object module passed by the COBOL compile step. The second one is a member of the IMSVS.PROCLIB data set. This member contains a few linkage editor control statements that, among other things, cause a load module in IMSVS.RESLIB to be combined with the object module passed by the compiler. This sets up the required linkages between the application program and IMS. The third data set is the standard DDNAME=SYSIN that allows additional input to be brought in from the input stream.

The rest of the JCL is similar to other linkage editor procedures. Notice that the SYSLMOD DD statement references the IMSVS.PGMLIB data set, and the MBR symbolic parameter assigns the load module name to the program.

```
//COMP      EXEC  IMSCOBOL,MBR=HOSPLOAD
//C.SYSIN   DD    *
            ---
            ---
            ---
    COBOL source program
            ---
            ---
            ---
```

Figure A.4. Executing the IMSCOBOL procedure

Figure A.4 shows the JCL that might be used to compile and link edit the HOSPLOAD program. Notice that the MBR symbolic parameter is used to assign the name HOSPLOAD to the resulting load module.

IMS EXECUTION JCL

Execution JCL for IMS programs is normally complex. We will look at three JCL examples to show the basics of execution JCL for batch IMS programs. IMS DB/DC JCL is beyond the scope of this book. Although it is helpful to look at examples of execution JCL, execution JCL for IMS programs is normally supplied by the DBA in the form of precoded cataloged procedures.

The first JCL example, in Figure A.5, shows JCL to execute a single IMS batch application program—the HOSPLOAD data base load program. This pro-

```
//LOAD       EXEC  PGM=DFSRRC00,PARM='DLI,HOSPLOAD'
//STEPLIB    DD    DSN=IMSVS.RESLIB,DISP=SHR
//           DD    DSN=IMSVS.PGMLIB,DISP=SHR
//IMS        DD    DSN=IMSVS.PSBLIB,DISP=SHR
//           DD    DSN=IMSVS.DBDLIB,DISP=SHR
//SYSUDUMP   DD    SYSOUT=A
//PRIME      DD    DSN=IMSVS.PRIME(PRIME),DISP=(,KEEP),
//                 SPACE=(CYL,(3,,CONTIG),VOL=SER=123456,
//                 UNIT=3350,DCB=DSORG=IS
//OVERFLOW   DD    DSN=IMSVS.OVFLW,DISP=(,KEEP),
//                 SPACE=(CYL,(3,,CONTIG),VOL=SER=654321,
//                 UNIT=3350
//OUTPUT     DD    SYSOUT=A,DCB=BLKSIZE=1330
//INPUT      DD    *
            ---
            ---
            ---
    input data base load statements
            ---
            ---
            ---
```

Figure A.5. Executing the HOSPLOAD program

gram reads an input file via a DD statement named INPUT and produces a report via a DD statement named OUTPUT. The data base is an HISAM data base that requires two DD statements named PRIME and OVERFLOW. These DD names are defined in the DATASET statement in the DBD for the data base.

In addition to the PRIME, OVERFLOW, INPUT, and OUTPUT DD statements, two other DD statements are required by IMS. These are the STEPLIB and IMS DD statements. The STEPLIB DD statement identifies the program libraries for this program. For batch IMS programs, the system must have access to the IMSVS.RESLIB and IMSVS.PGMLIB data sets or their equivalents. (A JOBLIB statement can, of course, take the place of the STEPLIB card.)

The IMS DD statement is used to tell IMS where the DBD and PSB for this program are stored. The IMS DD statement can specify the ACBLIB instead of the DBDLIB and PSBLIB concatenation if the DBA has combined the DBD and PSB by means of an ACBGEN.

The EXEC statement refers to the IMS region controller load module. The characters "DLI" in the first three positions of the PARM field tell IMS that this is an IMS batch application program. The second subparameter of PARM specifies the name of the application load module being executed. Since only one name is specified, the name of the application program load module and the name of the PSB must be the same. Additional information can be specified in the PARM parameter. An example of a PARM parameter is shown in the DLIBATCH procedure.

THE DLIBATCH PROCEDURE

IMS programs are seldom executed directly, as in the previous example. They are usually invoked through the use of cataloged procedures. The DLIBATCH procedure is one of those supplied with IMS and can be used to execute a batch IMS program. Figure A.6 shows an example of the DLIBATCH procedure. Notice that a number of parameters are provided for specifying additional information in the PARM parameter of the EXEC statement. These parameters are discussed in the IMS *System Programming Reference Manual*. Installation standards may also contain information about these parameters.

The three extra DD statements included in DLIBATCH are the IEFRDER, IEFRDER2, and IMSMON DD statements. These are used for various logging and monitoring functions. Installation standards generally contain information about these DD statements.

Figure A.7 shows an example of how the DLIBATCH procedure is invoked. Notice that the only additional DD statements required are the ones for the data base and for input and output files. The DD statements in the DLIBATCH procedure fulfill the standard IMS requirements.

```
//          PROC  MBR=TEMPNAME,SOUT=A,PSB=,BUF=,
//          SPIE=0,TEST=0,EXCPVR=0,RST=0,
//          PRLD=,SRCH0,CKPTID=,MON=N
//G         EXEC  PGM=DFSRRC00,REGION=192K,
//          PARM=(DLI,&MBR,&PSB,&BUF,
//          &SPIE&TEST&EXCPVR&RST,&PRLD,&SRCH,&CKPTID,&MON)
//STEPLIB DD  DSN=IMSVS.RESLIB,DISP=SHR
//        DD  DSN=IMSVS.PGMLIB,DISP=SHR
//IMS     DD  DSN=IMSVS.PSBLIB,DISP=SHR
//        DD  DSN=IMSVS.DBDLIB,DISP=SHR
//PROCLIB DD  DSN=IMSVS.PROCLIB,DISP=SHR
//IEFRDER DD  DSN=IMSLOG,DISP=(,KEEP),VOL=(,,,99),
//          UNIT=(2400,,DEFER,SEP=IEFRDER),
//          DCB=(RECFM=VBS,BLKSIZE=1920,LRECL=1916,BUFNO=2)
//SYSUDUMP DD  SYSOUT=&SOUT,DCB=(RECFM=FBA,LRECL=121,BLKSIZE=605),
//          SPACE=(605,(500,500),RLSE,,ROUND)
//IMSMON  DD  DUMMY
```

Figure A.6. DLIBATCH procedure

```
//LOAD        EXEC  DLIBATCH,MBR=HOSPLOAD
//G.PRIME     DD  DSN=IMSVS.PRIME(PRIME),DISP=(,KEEP),
//            SPACE=(CYL,(3,,CONTIG),VOL=SER=123456,
//            UNIT=3350,DCB=DSORG=IS
//G.OVERFLOW  DD  DSN=IMSVS.OVFLW,DISP=(,KEEP),
//            SPACE=(CYL,(3,,CONTIG),VOL=SER=654321,
//            UNIT=3350
//G.OUTPUT    DD  SYSOUT=A,DCB=BLKSIZE=1330
//G.INPUT     DD  *
            ---
            ---
            ---
        input data base load statements
            ---
            ---
            ---
```

Figure A.7. Executing the DLIBATCH procedure for HOSPLOAD

Appendix B
IMS Debugging Techniques

This appendix discusses techniques that can be used to locate the problem when an IMS application program terminates abnormally (ABENDs) and produces a virtual storage dump. These hints apply to IMS/VS programs running under all versions of the VS1, MVS, and MVS/XA operating systems. We will not cover debugging for VSE DL/I systems.

In general, the hints in this appendix provide information on finding the CALL statement parameter list, PCBs, and a data area that gives information about the last few IMS calls issued by the program. Finding these areas in the dump generally helps in diagnosing and fixing the problem.

LOCATING THE PARAMETER LIST

The parameter list of the last IMS call that was issued is useful during debugging. Two different techniques are used to locate the parameter list. One applies to batch IMS programs; the other applies to message processing or BMP programs.

IMS Batch Programs

To locate the parameter list in a batch IMS program, a particular IMS load module in the dump must first be located. The name of this load module is DFSPRPX0. This module is located using conventional dump-reading techniques that apply to the operating system being used. Add hex "104" to the entry point address (EPA) of DFSPRPX0. This points to a fullword address that points directly to the first word of the parameter list. Figure B.1 summarizes this procedure. After the parameter list is located, the addresses in that list can be used to find the IMS-related data areas in the program.

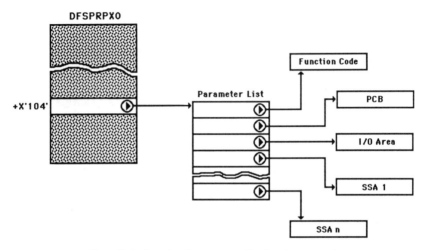

Figure B.1. Locating the parameter list (batch programs)

MP and BMP Programs

To find the parameter list in an MP or BMP program, locate the save area trace portion of the dump. Then locate the register printout corresponding to the first occurrence of DFSPR020 WAS ENTERED VIA CALL in the PROCEEDING BACK VIA REG 13 portion of the save area trace. Register 1 in that register printout points directly to the CALL statement parameter list. Figure B.2 summarizes this procedure.

LOCATING THE PCBS

One of the addresses in the CALL statement parameter list points to the PCB referenced by that call. If the program uses more than one PCB, it is often useful

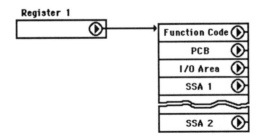

Figure B.2. Locating the parameter list (MP and BMP programs)

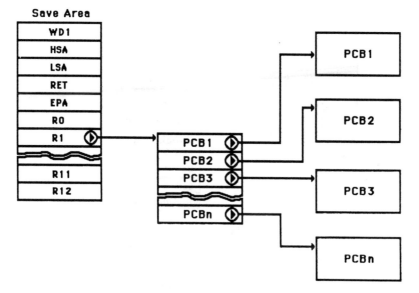

Figure B.3. Locating the PCBs

to locate one or more of the other PCBs as well. This is especially true for MP or BMP programs.

Figure B.3 summarizes a technique that can be used to locate all of the PCBs. The contents of register 1 can be used to locate a list of PCBs. This time, however, locate the *save area trace* portion of the dump. The particular save area that is desired is the one used the first time the load module was entered via a LINK. Register 1 within that save area points to a list of addresses of all the program's PCBs. (Note that it does not point to a PCB, but to a list of addresses of the PCBs.) The addresses are in the same order as the PCB mask names in the program's entry coding.

LOCATING INFORMATION ABOUT RECENT IMS CALLS

IMS saves two bytes of information about each of the six most recent IMS calls that the program has issued. Figure B.4 summarizes the procedure for finding information about recent calls. The fifth word in the PCB contains a pointer to a system control block called the JCB. An area within the JCB describes the six most recent calls. To locate this area, find the PCB by one of the methods discussed above. Then add hex "20" to the beginning address of the JCB to locate the twelve-byte area that contains information about the last six calls.

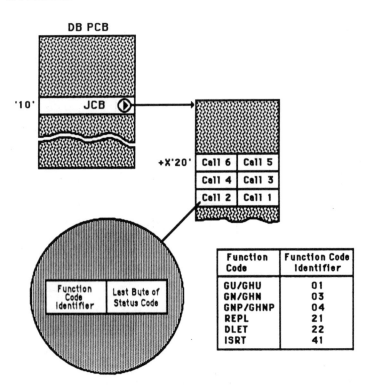

Figure B.4. Finding information about recent calls

The first two-byte field in that area describes the oldest call, and the last describes the most recent call. The first byte of each two-byte area contains a code that indicates the call's function code. The table in Figure B.4 lists the codes and their corresponding function codes. The second byte of each two-byte area contains the last byte of the status code that IMS has returned for that call.

Appendix C
GSAM Programming

The *Generalized Sequential Access Method* (GSAM) allows an application program to access either a standard sequential data set or a VSAM ESDS through IMS calls. These IMS calls are similar to standard data base calls; however, the GSAM parameter list is somewhat different.

ACCESS METHODS USED WITH GSAM

The physical access method used by GSAM depends on the type of data set the application program is accessing. If the program is accessing a standard sequential data set, GSAM uses BSAM. If the program is accessing a VSAM ESDS, GSAM uses VSAM.

GSAM RECORD FORMATS

One of the unique features of GSAM is that it allows an IMS program to access files that use any of the standard operating system record formats. By using GSAM, the program can access files that are organized with fixed-length records, fixed-length blocked records, variable-length records, variable-length blocked records, and undefined records.

GSAM FUNCTIONS SUPPORTED

Only a few of the normal data base function codes are supported with GSAM. A few additional function codes are unique to GSAM. A program can sequentially load a GSAM data base from scratch, and it can retrieve a segment sequentially from it. Records can also be added to a GSAM data base; however, new records must be added to the end of the data base. A program can randomly retrieve segments from the data base; but, as we will see, random retrieval capabilities are somewhat limited.

GSAM DIFFERENCES FROM STANDARD DATA BASES

As mentioned above, a GSAM data base consists of a standard operating system sequential data set or a VSAM ESDS. No provision is made in GSAM to define different segment types, nor is a hierarchical structure defined. The units of data that are retrieved when using GSAM are *records*, just as with normal operating system data sets. Since the concept of *segment* does not exist in GSAM data bases, there are no search fields or key fields defined in GSAM records.

GSAM DBD AND PSB STATEMENTS

Figure C.1 shows an example of a DBD and a PSB for a GSAM data base. Notice that in some ways the GSAM DBD and PSB statements are similar to those for HSAM. Because there is no concept of segments in GSAM, there are no SEGM or FIELD macros in the DBD, and no SENSEG statements in the PSB. Notice that in the DATASET statement in the DBD statements, two DD names are specified. These DD names are used in a similar manner to the DD names in an HSAM DBD. One DD name specifies an input GSAM data base for retrieval and the other DD name specifies an output GSAM data base for sequential loading. A program reads an old version of the GSAM data base, processes updates to it, and loads a new version using the output DD statement.

Notice in the PSB that there are two PCB statements. One PCB statement is used to retrieve segments from the old GSAM data base and the other is used to load segments into a new GSAM data base. A PSB for a GSAM data base can contain a single PCB statement if the program only retrieves or only loads segments.

```
DBD       NAME=GSAMDBD,ACCESS=(GSAM,VSAM)
DATASET   DD1=INPUT,DD2=OUTPUT,RECFM=F,RECORD=80
DBDGEN
FINISH
END


PCB       TYPE=GSAM,PROCOPT=G,DBDNAME=GSAMDBD
PCB       TYPE=GSAM,PROCOPT=L,DBDNAME=GSAMDBD
PSBGEN    LANG=COBOL,PSBNAME=GSAMPSB
END
```

Figure C.1. DBD and PSB coding for GSAM

```
WORKING-STORAGE SECTION.
01  GSAM-RSA.
    03  RSA-WORD1      PIC S9(5) COMP.
    03  RSA-WORD2      PIC S9(5) COMP.
        .
        .

    CALL  'CBLTDLI'  USING  GET-NEXT
                            GSAM-PCB
                            I-O-AREA
                            GSAM-RSA.
```

Figure C.2. GSAM CALL statement

GSAM IMS CALLS

Figure C.2 shows the COBOL coding for a typical GSAM CALL statement and its associated parameter list. The first parameter specifies the function codes that will be used with the GSAM call, the second parameter specifies the PCB mask, and the third parameter specifies the I/O area. The fourth parameter specifies the address of a *Record Search Argument* (RSA). The RSA is optional for all but Get-Unique calls.

THE RECORD SEARCH ARGUMENT

The RSA provides a means for locating individual records in a GSAM data base. It consists of a doubleword whose specific format depends on the type of device used to store the GSAM data base. Because the format of the RSA varies, it is not recommended that application programs normally attempt to format the data in the RSA. The *Application Programming Reference Manual* contains information about the RSA format for individual device types. We will next see how the RSA is used with GSAM calls.

GSAM FUNCTION CODES

The following is a list of the function codes that can be used with GSAM calls:

- GU   —Retrieve a unique record
- GN   —Retrieve next sequential record
- ISRT —Add a record to the end
- OPEN —Open a GSAM data base
- CLSE —Close a GSAM data base

- CHKP —Write a checkpoint record
- XRST —Restart from a checkpoint
- DUMP—Used for debugging
- SNAP —Used for debugging

We will discuss three of the above function codes: GU, GN, and ISRT. The OPEN and CLSE function codes are optional and are used to explicitly open or close the GSAM data base. These are not normally used because opens and closes are automatically performed when they are required. The CHKP and XRST function codes are used in conjunction with the IMS checkpoint/restart facilities. The DUMP or SNAP function codes are used to send GSAM control blocks to special IMS data sets for debugging purposes.

The GN Function Code

Get-Next calls are used with GSAM to sequentially retrieve records. The use of the RSA in a Get-Next call parameter list is optional. If an RSA is included in the parameter list, the GSAM routines store information in the RSA about the location of the record just retrieved. After a Get-Next call, the contents of the RSA can be moved to some other area for future use.

The GU Function Code

A Get-Unique call can be used to retrieve segments randomly from a GSAM data base. The Get-Unique call is the only call that requires an RSA in the parameter list. Random retrievals are normally made by first saving the value that was stored in an RSA by a previous Get-Next or Insert call. The contents of the saved RSA field are then used in a Get-Unique call.

In one instance, it is useful to place an explicit value in an RSA. An RSA that contains a binary 1 in the first fullword and a binary 0 in the second fullword always refers to the first record in the GSAM data base, no matter what type of device it is stored on. An RSA with this value can be used in a Get-Unique call to retrieve the first record in a GSAM data base.

The ISRT Function Code

The Insert call can be used in two ways: to load a GSAM data base from scratch or to add segments to the end of an existing GSAM data base. The DISP parameter that is coded in the DD statement for the output data set determines which function is performed by the Insert call. DISP=NEW or DISP=OLD indicates that the data base is being loaded; DISP=MOD indicates that segments will be added to the end of an existing GSAM data base.

As with Get-Next calls, the RSA is optional when used with the Insert call. If an RSA is included, IMS returns information in the RSA about the location of the segment that was just inserted. This RSA value can then be saved for future use in a Get-Unique call.

Appendix D
The HOSPITAL Data Base

This appendix summarizes in one place all the information about the HOSPITAL data base that is needed to complete the coding problems in this book. Figure D.1 is a copy of the HOSPITAL data base hierarchy chart. Figure D.2 shows the segment description coding, in COBOL, that can be stored in a source statement library. Figures D.3 and D.4 repeat that coding in PL/I and Assembler Language. Figure D.5 shows the DBD coding for the HOSPITAL data base. Assume that this is the DBD in effect for the data base that the sample solutions will access. Each exercise has its own PSB, but a sample PSB, allowing all calls but Insert in the load mode for all seven segment types, is shown in Figure D.6.

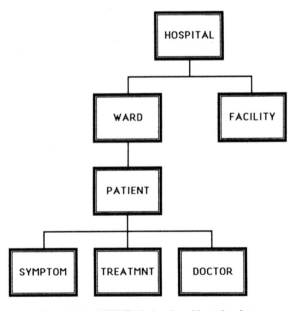

Figure D.1. HOSPITAL data base hierarchy chart

```
01  HOSPITAL
    03  HOSPNAME          PIC  X(20).
    03  HOSP-ADDRESS      PIC  X(30).
    03  HOSP-PHONE        PIC  X(10).
    03  ADMIN             PIC  X(20).

01  WARD.
    03  WARDNO            PIC  XX.
    03  TOT-ROOMS         PIC  XXX.
    03  TOT-BEDS          PIC  XXX.
    03  BEDAVAIL          PIC  XXX.
    03  WARDTYPE          PIC  X(20).

01  PATIENT.
    03  PATNAME           PIC  X(20).
    03  PAT-ADDRESS       PIC  X(30).
    03  PAT-PHONE         PIC  X(10).
    03  BEDIDENT          PIC  X(4).
    03  DATEADMT          PIC  X(6).
    03  PREV-STAY-FLAG    PIC  X.
    03  PREV-HOSP         PIC  X(20).
    03  PREV-DATE         PIC  X(4).
    03  PREV-REASON       PIC  X(30).

01  SYMPTOM.
    03  DIAGNOSE          PIC  X(20).
    03  SYMPDATE          PIC  X(6).
    03  PREV-TREAT-FLAG   PIC  X.
    03  TREAT-DESC        PIC  X(20).
    03  SYMP-DOCTOR       PIC  X(20).
    03  SYMP-DOCT-PHONE   PIC  X(10).

01  TREATMNT.
    03  TRTYPE            PIC  X(20).
    03  TRDATE            PIC  X(6).
    03  MEDICATION-TYPE   PIC  X(20).
    03  DIET-COMMENT      PIC  X(30).
    03  SURGERY-FLAG      PIC  X.
    03  SURGERY-DATE      PIC  X(6).
    03  SURGERY-COMMENT   PIC  X(30).

01  DOCTOR.
    03  DOCTNAME          PIC  X(20).
    03  DOCT-ADDRESS      PIC  X(30).
    03  DOCT-PHONE        PIC  X(10).
    03  SPECIALT          PIC  X(20).

01  FACILITY.
    03  FACTYPE           PIC  X(20).
    03  TOT-FACIL         PIC  XXX.
    03  FACAVAIL          PIC  XXX.
```

Figure D.2. COBOL segment description coding

```
DCL     HOSPITAL_PTR    POINTER;
DCL  1  HOSPITAL        BASED (HOSPITAL_PTR),
        3  HOSPNAME              CHAR (20),
        3  HOSP_ADDRESS          CHAR (30),
        3  HOSP_PHONE            CHAR (10);
        3  ADMIN                 CHAR (20);
DCL  WARD-PTR           POINTER;
DCL  1  WARD            BASED (WARD_PTR),
        3  WARDNO                CHAR (2),
        3  TOT_ROOMS             CHAR (3),
        3  TOT_BEDS              CHAR (3),
        3  BEDAVAIL              CHAR (3),
        3  WARDTYPE              CHAR (20);
DCL  PATIENT_PTR        POINTER;
DCL  1  PATIENT         BASED (PATIENT_PTR),
        3  PATNAME               CHAR (20),
        3  PAT_ADDRESS           CHAR (30),
        3  PAT_PHONE             CHAR (10),
        3  BEDIDENT              CHAR (4),
        3  DATEADMT              CHAR (6),
        3  PREV_STAY_FLAG        CHAR (1),
        3  PREV_HOSP             CHAR (20),
        3  PREV_DATE             CHAR (4),
        3  PREV_REASON           CHAR (30);
DCL  SYMPTOM_PTR        POINTER;
DCL  1  SYMPTOM         BASED (SYMPTOM_PTR),
        3  DIAGNOSE              CHAR (20),
        3  SYMPDATE              CHAR (6),
        3  PREV_TREAT_FLAG       CHAR (1),
        3  TREAT_DESC            CHAR (20),
        3  SYMP_DOCTOR           CHAR (20),
        3  SYMP_DOCT_PHONE       CHAR (10);
DCL  TREATMNT_PTR       POINTER;
DCL  1  TREATMNT        BASED (TREATMNT_PTR),
        3  TRTYPE                CHAR (20),
        3  TRDATE                CHAR (6),
        3  MEDICATION_TYPE       CHAR (20),
        3  DIET_COMMENT          CHAR (30),
        3  SURGERY_FLAG          CHAR (1),
        3  SURGERY_DATE          CHAR (6),
        3  SURGERY_COMMENT       CHAR (30);
DCL  DOCTOR-PTR         POINTER;
DCL  1  DOCTOR          BASED (DOCTOR_PTR),
        3  DOCTNAME              CHAR (20),
        3  DOCT_ADDRESS          CHAR (30),
        3  DOCT_PHONE            CHAR (10),
        3  SPECIALT              CHAR (20);
DCL  FACILITY_PTR       POINTER;
DCL  1  FACILITY        BASED (FACILITY_PTR),
        3  FACTYPE               CHAR (20),
        3  TOT_FACIL             CHAR (3),
        3  FACAVAIL              CHAR (3);
```

Figure D.3. PL/I segment description coding

```
HOSPITAL DS    0CL60           HOSPITAL SEGMENT
HOSPNAME DS    CL20              UNIQUE KEY
HOSPADDR DS    CL30
HOSPPHON DS    CL10
ADMIN    DS    CL20

WARD     DS    0CL31           WARD SEGMENT
WARDNO   DS    CL2               UNIQUE KEY
TOTROOMS DS    CL3
TOTBEDS  DS    CL3
BEDAVAIL DS    CL3               SEARCH
WARDTYPE DS    CL20

PATIENT  DS    0CL125          PATIENT SEGMENT
PATNAME  DS    CL20              SEARCH
PATADDR  DS    CL30
PATPHONE DS    CL10
BEDIDENT DS    CL4               UNIQUE KEY
DATEADMT DS    CL6               SEARCH
PREVSTAY DS    C
PREVHOSP DS    CL20
PREVDATE DS    CL4
PREVREAS DS    CL30

SYMPTOM  DS    0CL77           SYMPTOM SEGMENT
DIAGNOSE DS    CL20              SEARCH
SYMPDATE DS    CL6               KEY
PREVTRT  DS    C
TREATDES DS    CL20
SYMPDOCT DS    CL20
SYMPPHON DS    CL10

TREATMNT DS    0CL113          TREATMNT SEGMENT
TRTYPE   DS    CL20              SEARCH
TRDATE   DS    CL6               KEY
MEDICAT  DS    CL20
DIETCOMM DS    CL30
SURGFLAG DS    C
SURGDATE DS    CL6
SURGCOMM DS    CL30

DOCTOR   DS    0CL80           DOCTOR SEGMENT
DOCTNAME DS    CL20              SEARCH
DOCTADDR DS    CL30
DOCTPHON DS    CL10
SPECIALT DS    CL20              SEARCH

FACILITY DS    0CL26           FACILITY SEGMENT
FACTYPE  DS    CL20              SEARCH
TOTFACIL DS    CL3
FACAVAIL DS    CL3               SEARCH
```

Figure D.4. Assembler Language segment description coding

```
        PRINT NOGEN
        DBD      NAME=HOSPDBD,ACCESS=(HISAM,ISAM)
        DATASET  DD1=PRIME,OVFLW=OVERFLOW,DEVICE=3350
*
        SEGM     NAME=HOSPITAL,PARENT=0,BYTES=80
         FIELD    NAME=(HOSPNAME,SEQ,U),BYTES=20,START=1,TYPE=C
         FIELD    NAME=ADMIN,BYTES=20,START=61,TYPE=C
*
        SEGM     NAME=WARD,PARENT=HOSPITAL,BYTES=31
         FIELD    NAME=(WARDNO,SEQ,U),BYTES=2,START=1,TYPE=C
         FIELD    NAME=BEDAVAIL,BYTES=3,START=9,TYPE=C
         FIELD    NAME=WARDTYPE,BYTES=20,START=12,TYPE=C
*
        SEGM     NAME=PATIENT,PARENT=WARD,BYTES=125
         FIELD    NAME=(BEDIDENT,SEQ,U),BYTES=4,START=61,TYPE=C
         FIELD    NAME=PATNAME,BYTES=20,START=1,TYPE=C
         FIELD    NAME=DATEADMT,BYTES=6,START=65,TYPE=C
*
        SEGM     NAME=SYMPTOM,PARENT=PATIENT,BYTES=77
         FIELD    NAME=(SYMPDATE,SEQ),BYTES=6,START=21,TYPE=C
         FIELD    NAME=DIAGNOSE,BYTES=20,START=1,TYPE=C
*
        SEGM     NAME=TREATMNT,PARENT=PATIENT,BYTES=113
         FIELD    NAME=(TRDATE,SEQ),BYTES=6,START=21,TYPE=C
         FIELD    NAME=TRTYPE,BYTES=20,START=1,TYPE=C
*
        SEGM     NAME=DOCTOR,PARENT=PATIENT,BYTES=80
         FIELD    NAME=DOCTNAME,BYTES=20,START=1,TYPE=C
         FIELD    NAME=SPECIALT,BYTES=20,START=61,TYPE=C
*
        SEGM     NAME=FACILITY,PARENT=HOSPITAL,BYTES=26
         FIELD    NAME=FACTYPE,BYTES=20,START=1,TYPE=C
         FIELD    NAME=FACAVAIL,BYTES=3,START=24,TYPE=C
*
        DBDGEN
        FINISH
        END
```

Figure D.5. HOSPITAL data base DBD coding

```
        PRINT    NOGEN
        PCB      TYPE=DB,DBNAME=HOSPDBD,PROCOPT=A,KEYLEN=32
*
        SENSEG   NAME=HOSPITAL,PARENT=0
        SENSEG   NAME=WARD,PARENT=HOSPITAL
        SENSEG   NAME=PATIENT,PARENT=WARD
        SENSEG   NAME=SYMPTOM,PARENT=PATIENT
        SENSEG   NAME=TREATMNT,PARENT=PATIENT
        SENSEG   NAME=DOCTOR,PARENT=PATIENT
        SENSEG   NAME=FACILITY,PARENT=HOSPITAL
*
        PSBGEN   LANG=COBOL,PSBNAME=SAMPLE
        END
```

Figure D.6. HOSPITAL data base PSB coding

Appendix E
Exercise Solutions

This appendix contains solutions to the exercises found at the end of each chapter. Solutions are also provided for the coding problems at the end of Chapter 5 and Chapter 11. All solutions that require actual coding are provided in COBOL. Sample PL/I programs are found in Appendix F, and sample Assembler Language programs are found in Appendix G.

SOLUTIONS TO CHAPTER 1 EXERCISES

1. Increase data independence, reduce data redundancy, and provide facilities for data communications.

2. A–a, B–d, C–c, D–e, E–b

SOLUTIONS TO CHAPTER 2 EXERCISES

1. A–g, B–k, C–c, D–l, E–j, F–i, G–b, H–d, I–f, J–h, K–e, L–a

2. a. A, B, C, D, E, and F
   b. A
   c. A—B—C; A—B—D; A—E—F
   d. E
   e. C and D
   f. Three
   g. Six

SOLUTIONS TO CHAPTER 3 EXERCISES

1. A–c, B–d, C–b, D–j, E–i, F–g, G–e, H–h, I–a, J–f

2. a. EMPLOYEE, 100 bytes.

    TASK, 42 bytes.
    TIME, 20 bytes.
    PERSONNL, 56 bytes.

  b. EMPNO, 8 bytes long, starting in position 1, unique.

    TASKNO, 6 bytes long, starting in position 1, unique.

    DATA, 6 bytes long, starting in position 15, nonunique.

  c. EMPNAME, 25 bytes long, starting in position 30.

    TASKNAME, 25 bytes long, starting in position 7.

  d. PAYROLL.
  e. Figure E.1 shows the solution to 2e.

3. a. EMPLOYEE, TASK, TIME.
  b. Figure E.2 shows the solution to 3b.
  c. One.
  d. HOURCALC.
  e. PAYROLL.
  f. TASK, TIME.

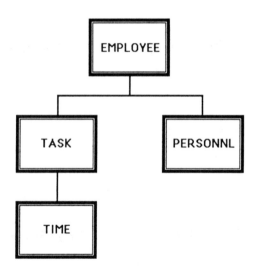

Figure E.1. Solution to chapter 3—Exercise 2e

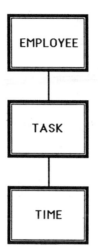

Figure E.2. Solution to chapter 3—Exercise 3b

SOLUTIONS TO CHAPTER 4 EXERCISES

1. a–5, b–1, c–4, d–3, e–2

2. a—3, blanks; b—10, blanks; c—none, GE; d—21, blanks

3.   a.   GU   HOSPITAL(HOSPNAME =MAC NEAL   )

                  WARD   (WARDTYPE =INTENSIVE   )

                  PATIENT (PATNAME =WHEELER   )

    b.   GU   HOSPITAL

        WARD   (BEDAVAIL >100)

        or

        GU   WARD   (BEDAVAIL >100)

    c.   GU   PATIENT (PATNAME =BAILEY   )

                  DOCTOR (DOCTNAME =ROGERS   )

```
    d.    GU      HOSPITAL(HOSPNAME =MAC NEAL                    )
          ^^^^    ^^^^^^^^^^^^^^^^^^^^^^^^^^^^^^^^^^^^^^^^^^^^^^^^^

                  FACILITY(FACTYPE  =COBALT                     )
                  ^^^^^^^^^^^^^^^^^^^^^^^^^^^^^^^^^^^^^^^^^^^^^^^^
```

4. The blank status code means the segment was retrieved successfully. The GE status code means the segment could not be found.

SOLUTIONS TO CHAPTER 5 EXERCISES

The listing in Figure E.3 shows a possible COBOL solution to the Chapter 5 coding problem. See Appendix F for a PL/I solution; see Appendix G for an Assembler Language solution. The solutions shown, of course, are not the only possible solutions. Evaluate your solution against the ones given here in determining whether yours is correct.

```
000100 ID DIVISION.
000200 PROGRAM-ID. CHAP5C.
000300 AUTHOR.      DAN KAPP.
000500 DATE-COMPILED.
000610 REMARKS.
000700          THE OUTPUT OF THIS PROGRAM IS A LIST OF PATIENTS WHO
000800          ARE IN QUARANTINE WARDS PRESENTLY AND HAVE ALSO
000900          BEEN IN A HOSPITAL PREVIOUSLY WITHIN THE PAST YEAR.
001100
001200 ENVIRONMENT DIVISION.
001900 INPUT-OUTPUT SECTION.
002000 FILE-CONTROL.
002200 SELECT HOSPITAL-NAME-FILE  ASSIGN TO UT-S-INPUT.
002300 SELECT PRINT-FILE          ASSIGN TO UT-S-OUTPUT.
002500
002600 DATA DIVISION.
002800 FILE SECTION.
002900
003000 FD HOSPITAL-NAME-FILE      BLOCK CONTAINS 0 RECORDS
003300                            RECORDING MODE IS F
003400                            LABEL RECORDS ARE STANDARD
003500                            DATA RECORD IS PARM-INPUT.
003700 01  PARM-INPUT.
003800     05  FILLER             PIC XX.
003900     05  HOSPNAME-INPUT     PIC X(20).
004000     05  FILLER             PIC X(58).
004100
004300 FD  PRINT-FILE             BLOCK CONTAINS 0 RECORDS
004600                            RECORDING MODE IS F
004700                            LABEL RECORD ARE STANDARD
004800                            DATA RECORD IS PRINT-LINE.
005000 01  PRINT-LINE.
005100     05  CARR-CNTRL     PIC X.
005200     05  PRINT-AREA     PIC X(132).
005300
005400 WORKING-STORAGE SECTION.
005500
005600 77  NO-HOSPITAL        PIC X      VALUE '0'.
005700 77  NO-WARDS           PIC X      VALUE '0'.
005800 77  NO-PATIENTS        PIC X      VALUE '0'.
005900 77  TOP-PAGE           PIC X      VALUE '1'.
006000 77  DOUBLE-SPACE       PIC X      VALUE '0'.
006100 77  SINGLE-SPACE       PIC X      VALUE ' '.
006500 77  GET-UNIQUE         PIC XXXX   VALUE 'GU  '.
006700 77  GET-NEXT-P         PIC XXXX   VALUE 'GNP '.
006800 77  LINE-CNT           PIC 99     VALUE 45.
006900 77  PAGE-CNT           PIC 9999   VALUE ZERO.
007100 01  NEW-DATE
007300     05  NEW-MONTH      PIC S99.
007400     05  NEW-YEAR       PIC S99.
007700 01  CURR-DATE.
007800     05  CURR-MONTH     PIC S99.
007900     05  FILLER         PIC X      VALUE '/'.
008000     05  CURR-DAY       PIC S99.
008100     05  FILLER         PIC X      VALUE '/'.
008200     05  CURR-YEAR      PIC S99.
008400 01  PREV-DATE-SAVE.
008500     05  PREV-MONTH-SAVE    PIC S99.
008600     05  PREV-YEAR-SAVE     PIC S99.
```

Figure E.3. COBOL solution to Chapter 5 coding problem (page 1 of 7)

```
008700
008800 01  HOSPITAL-I-O-AREA        COPY    HOSPITAL.
009000 01  WARD-I-O-AREA            COPY    WARD.
009200 01  PATIENT-I-O-AREA         COPY    PATIENT.
009300
009400 01  HOSPITAL-SSA.
009500     05  FILLER               PIC X(8)   VALUE 'HOSPITAL'.
009600     05  FILLER               PIC X      VALUE '('.
009700     05  FILLER               PIC X(8)   VALUE 'HOSPNAME'.
009800     05  FILLER               PIC XX     VALUE 'EQ'.
009900     05  HOSPNAME-SSA         PIC X(20).
010000     05  FILLER               PIC X      VALUE ')'.
010100
010200 01  WARD-SSA.
010400     05  FILLER               PIC X(8)   VALUE 'WARD    '.
010500     05  FILLER               PIC X      VALUE '('.
010600     05  FILLER               PIC X(8)   VALUE 'WARDNAME'.
010700     05  FILLER               PIC XX     VALUE 'EQ'.
010800     05  WARDTYPE-SSA         PIC X(20).
010900     05  FILLER               PIC X      VALUE ')'.
010905
010920 01  PATIENT-SSA             PIC X(9)   VALUE 'PATIENT  '.
011000
011100 01  HEAD-LINE-TITLE.
011300     05  FILLER               PIC X(26) VALUE SPACES.
011400     05  TITLE                PIC X(106) VALUE
011500             'P R E V I O U S   S T A Y   R E P O R T'.
011700
011800 01  HEAD-LINE-PAGE.
012100     05  FILLER               PIC X(5)   VALUE 'PAGE'.
012200     05  HPAGE-CTR            PIC ZZZ9.
012300     05  FILLER               PIC X(123) VALUE SPACES.
012400
012500 01  HEAD-LINE-HOSPITAL.
012800     05  FILLER               PIC X(25)  VALUE 'HOSPITAL NAME'.
013000     05  FILLER               PIC X(35)  VALUE 'HOSPITAL ADDRESS'.
013200     05  FILLER               PIC X(10)  VALUE 'HOSP PHONE'.
013300     05  FILLER               PIC X(62)  VALUE SPACES.
013400
013500 01  HEAD-LINE-WARD.
013800     05  FILLER               PIC X(12)  VALUE 'WARD NO'.
013900     05  FILLER               PIC X(14)  VALUE 'TOT ROOMS'.
014000     05  FILLER               PIC X(13)  VALUE 'TOT BEDS'.
014100     05  FILLER               PIC X(15)  VALUE 'BEDS AVAIL'.
014200     05  FILLER               PIC X(20)  VALUE 'WARD TYPE'.
014300     05  FILLER               PIC X(58)  VALUE SPACES.
014400
014500 01  HEAD-LINE-PATIENT.
014800     05  FILLER               PIC X(21)  VALUE 'PATIENT NAME'.
014900     05  FILLER               PIC X(6)   VALUE 'BED'.
015000     05  FILLER               PIC X(12)  VALUE 'ADMIT DATE'.
015100     05  FILLER               PIC X(11)  VALUE 'PREV DATE'.
015200     05  FILLER               PIC X(21)  VALUE 'PREVIOUS HOSPITAL'.
015400     05  FILLER               PIC X(30)  VALUE 'PREVIOUS REASON'.
015500     05  FILLER               PIC X(31)  VALUE SPACES.
015600
```

Figure E.3. COBOL solution to Chapter 5 coding problem (page 2 of 7)

```
015700 01  DETAIL-LINE-HOSPITAL.
015800
016000      05  HOSPNAME-LINE      PIC X(20).
016100      05  FILLER             PIC X(5)    VALUE SPACE.
016200      05  HOSP-ADDRESS-LINE  PIC X(30).
016300      05  FILLER             PIC X(5)    VALUE SPACE.
016400      05  HOSP-PHONE-LINE    PIC X(10).
016500      05  FILLER             PIC X(62)   VALUE SPACE.
016600
016700 01  DETAIL-LINE-WARD.
016800
016900      05  FILLER             PIC X(3)    VALUE SPACE.
017000      05  WARDNO-LINE        PIC 99.
017100      05  FILLER             PIC X(10)   VALUE SPACE.
017200      05  TOT-ROOMS-LINE     PIC 999.
017300      05  FILLER             PIC X(11)   VALUE SPACE.
017400      05  TOT-BEDS-LINE      PIC 999.
017500      05  FILLER             PIC X(10)   VALUE SPACE.
017600      05  BEDAVAIL-LINE      PIC 999.
017700      05  FILLER             PIC X(9)    VALUE SPACE.
017800      05  WARDTYPE-LINE      PIC X(20).
017900      05  FILLER             PIC X(58)   VALUE SPACE.
018000
018100 01  DETAIL-LINE-PATIENT.
018200
018400      05  PATNAME-LINE       PIC X(20).
018500      05  FILLER             PIC X       VALUE SPACE.
018600      05  BEDIDENT-LINE      PIC 9999.
018700      05  FILLER             PIC X(4)    VALUE SPACE.
018800      05  DATEADMT-LINE      PIC X(6).
018900      05  FILLER             PIC X(6)    VALUE SPACE.
019000      05  PREV-DATE-LINE     PIC X(4).
019100      05  FILLER             PIC X(5)    VALUE SPACE.
019200      05  PREV-HOSP-LINE     PIC X(20).
019300      05  FILLER             PIC X       VALUE SPACE.
019400      05  PREV-REASON-LINE   PIC X(30).
019500      05  FILLER             PIC X(31)   VALUE SPACE.
019600
019700 01  NO-HOSP-LINE.
019800
020100      05  HOSPNAME-ERROR     PIC X(20).
020110      05  FILLER             PIC X(5)    VALUE SPACE.
020200      05  FILLER             PIC X(107) VALUE
020300          '****  HOSPITAL NOT FOUND  ****'.
020310
020311 01  NO-WARD-LINE            PIC X(132) VALUE
020312          '****  NO QUARANTINE WARDS ****'.
020313
020314 01  NO-PAT-LINE             PIC X(132) VALUE
020315      '****  NO PATIENTS WITH PREVIOUS STAY  ****'.
020316
020500 LINKAGE SECTION.
020520
020600 01  DB-PCB-HOSPITAL  COPY  MASKC.
020700
```

Figure E.3. COBOL solution to Chapter 5 coding problem (page 3 of 7)

```
020800 PROCEDURE DIVISION.
020900
021000 ENTRY-LINKAGE.
021100
021200     ENTRY  'DLITCBL'  USING  DB-PCB-HOSPITAL.
021300
021220 PROGRAM-START.
021240
021300     OPEN  INPUT  HOSPITAL-NAME-FILE  OUTPUT  PRINT-FILE.
021500     MOVE CURRENT-DATE TO CURR-DATE.
021600
021700 READ-INPUT.
021800
021900     READ HOSPITAL-NAME-FILE  AT END GO TO END-OF-JOB.
022000     MOVE HOSPNAME-INPUT  TO  HOSPNAME-SSA.
022100     MOVE 45             TO  LINE-CNT.
022200
022300     CALL  'CBLTDLI'  USING  GET-UNIQUE
022400                             DB-PCB-HOSPITAL
022500                             HOSPITAL-I-O-AREA
022600                             HOSPITAL-SSA.
022700
022800     IF STATUS-CODE NOT EQUAL '  '
023000         PERFORM HOSPITAL-NOT-FOUND
023100         GO TO READ-INPUT.
023200
023300     MOVE HOSPNAME     TO  HOSPNAME-LINE.
023400     MOVE HOSP-ADDRESS TO  HOSP-ADDRESS-LINE.
023500     MOVE HOSP-PHONE   TO  HOSP-PHONE-LINE.
023600
023700     CALL  'CBLTDLI'  USING  GET-UNIQUE
023800                             DB-PCB-HOSPITAL
023900                             WARD-I-O-AREA
024000                             HOSPITAL-SSA
024100                             WARD-SSA.
024200
024300     IF STATUS-CODE NOT EQUAL '  '
024500         PERFORM WARD-NOT-FOUND
024600         GO TO READ-INPUT.
024700
024710     MOVE WARDNO     TO  WARDNO-LINE.
024800     MOVE TOT-ROOMS  TO  TOT-ROOMS-LINE.
024900     MOVE TOT-BEDS   TO  TOT-BEDS-LINE.
025000     MOVE BEDAVAIL   TO  BEDAVAIL-LINE.
025100     MOVE WARDTYPE   TO  WARDTYPE-LINE.
025200     MOVE '0'        TO  NO-PATIENTS.
025300
025400     PERFORM  GET-PATIENT THRU GET-PATIENT-EXIT
025600                          UNTIL STATUS-CODE = 'GE'.
025610
025700     IF NO-PATIENTS EQUAL '0'
025800
025900         MOVE NO-PAT-LINE  TO   DETAIL-LINE-PATIENT
026000         PERFORM WRITE-RTN THRU WRITE-RTN-EXIT
026100         MOVE SPACE        TO   DETAIL-LINE-PATIENT.
026200
026300     MOVE '0' TO NO-PATIENTS.
026400     GO TO READ-INPUT.
026500
```

Figure E.3. COBOL solution to Chapter 5 coding problem (page 4 of 7)

```
026600 GET-PATIENT.
026700
026800     CALL  'CBLTDLI'  USING  GET-NEXT-P
026900                             DB-PCB-HOSPITAL
027000                             PATIENT-I-O-AREA
027010                             PATIENT-SSA.
027100
027200     IF STATUS-CODE EQUAL 'GE' GO TO GET-PATIENT-EXIT.
027300     IF STATUS-CODE NOT EQUAL '  '
027400
027500         MOVE DB-PCB-HOSPITAL TO   DETAIL-LINE-PATIENT
027600         PERFORM WRITE-RTN    THRU WRITE-RTN-EXIT
027700         MOVE SPACE           TO   DETAIL-LINE-PATIENT
027800         GO TO READ-INPUT.
027900
028000     IF PREV-STAY-FLAG NOT EQUAL '1' GO TO GET-PATIENT-EXIT.
028100
028200     MOVE     PREV-DATE       TO   PREV-DATE-SAVE.
028300     SUBTRACT PREV-MONTH-SAVE FROM CURR-MONTH GIVING NEW-MONTH.
028500     SUBTRACT PREV-YEAR-SAVE  FROM CURR-YEAR GIVING NEW-YEAR.
028700
029000     IF NEW-YEAR GREATER THAN 1 GO TO GET-PATIENT-EXIT.
029100     IF NEW YEAR EQUAL 0
029200
029300         PERFORM WRITE-PATIENT-DATA
029400         MOVE '1' TO NO-PATIENTS
029500         GO TO GET-PATIENT-EXIT.
029600
029700     IF NEW-YEAR EQUAL 1 AND NEW-MONTH LESS THAN 1
029900
030000         PERFORM WRITE-PATIENT-DATA
030100         MOVE 1 TO NO-PATIENTS.
030110
030200 GET-PATIENT-EXIT.
030300     EXIT.
030400
```

Figure E.3. COBOL solution to Chapter 5 coding problem (page 5 of 7)

```
030500 WRITE-RTN.
030520
030600     IF LINE-CNT LESS THAN 44 GO TO WRITE-PATIENT-LINE.
030700
030800     MOVE 1              TO  LINE-CNT.
030900     MOVE HEAD-LINE-TITLE TO  PRINT-AREA.
031000     WRITE PRINT-LINE AFTER POSITIONING TOP-PAGE.
031010
031100     ADD 1              TO  PAGE-CNT.
031200     MOVE PAGE-CNT       TO  HPAGE-CTR.
031300     MOVE HEAD-LINE-PAGE TO  PRINT-AREA.
031400     WRITE PRINT-LINE AFTER POSITIONING DOUBLE-SPACE.
031410
031500     MOVE HEAD-LINE-HOSPITAL TO PRINT-AREA.
031600     WRITE PRINT-LINE AFTER POSITIONING DOUBLE-SPACE.
031610
031700     MOVE DETAIL-LINE-HOSPITAL TO PRINT-AREA.
031800     WRITE PRINT-LINE AFTER POSITIONING DOUBLE-SPACE.
031900
032000     IF NO-HOSPITAL EQUAL '1' GO TO WRITE-RTN-EXIT.
032010
032200     MOVE HEAD-LINE-WARD TO PRINT-AREA.
032300     WRITE PRINT-LINE AFTER POSITIONING DOUBLE-SPACE.
032310
032400     MOVE DETAIL-LINE-WARD TO PRINT-AREA.
032500     WRITE PRINT-LINE AFTER POSITIONING DOUBLE-SPACE.
032600
032700     IF NO-WARDS EQUAL '1' GO TO WRITE-RTN-EXIT.
032710
032900     MOVE HEAD-LINE-PATIENT TO PRINT-AREA.
033000     WRITE PRINT-LINE AFTER POSITIONING DOUBLE-SPACE.
033010
033100     MOVE SPACE TO PRINT-AREA.
033200     WRITE PRINT-LINE AFTER POSITIONING SINGLE-SPACE.
033210
033220 WRITE-PATIENT-LINE.
033300
033400     MOVE DETAIL-LINE-PATIENT TO PRINT-AREA.
033500     WRITE PRINT-LINE AFTER POSITIONING SINGLE-SPACE.
033600     ADD 1 TO LINE-CNT.
033700
033800 WRITE-RTN-EXIT.
033900     EXIT.
034900
034100 WRITE-PATIENT-DATA.
034200
034300     MOVE PATNAME       TO  PATNAME-LINE.
034400     MOVE BEDIDENT      TO  BEDIDENT-LINE.
034500     MOVE DATEADMT      TO  DATEADMT-LINE.
034600     MOVE PREV-HOSP     TO  PREV-HOSP-LINE.
034700     MOVE PREV-DATE     TO  PREV-DATE-LINE.
034800     MOVE PREV-REASON   TO  PREV-REASON-LINE.
034900     PERFORM WRITE-RTN THRU WRITE-RTN-EXIT.
035000
```

Figure E.3. COBOL solution to Chapter 5 coding problem (page 6 of 7)

```
035100 HOSPITAL-NOT-FOUND.
035200
035300     MOVE '1'             TO   NO-HOSPITAL.
035310     MOVE HOSPNAME-INPUT  TO   HOSPNAME-ERROR.
035400     MOVE NO-HOSP-LINE    TO   DETAIL-LINE-HOSPITAL.
035500     PERFORM WRITE-RTN    THRU WRITE-RTN-EXIT.
035510     MOVE SPACE           TO   DETAIL-LINE-HOSPITAL.
035600     MOVE '0'             TO   NO-HOSPITAL.
035700
035800 WARD-NOT-FOUND.
035900
036000     MOVE '1'             TO   NO-WARDS.
036100     MOVE NO-WARD-LINE    TO   DETAIL-LINE-WARD.
036200     PERFORM WRITE-RTN    THRU WRITE-RTN-EXIT.
036210     MOVE SPACE           TO   DETAIL-LINE-WARD.
036300     MOVE '0'             TO   NO-WARDS.
036400
036500 END-OF-JOB.
036600
036700     CLOSE  HOSPITAL-NAME-FILE  PRINT-FILE.
036800     GOBACK.
```

Figure E.3. COBOL solution to Chapter 5 coding problem (page 7 of 7)

SOLUTIONS TO CHAPTER 6 EXERCISES

1. A–a, B–d, C–e, D–b, E–f, F–c

2.　　ISRT　PATIENT

3.　　ISRT　HOSPITAL(HOSPNAME =MAC NEAL　　　　　)

　　　　　WARD　(WARDNO　=04)

　　　　　PATIENT

4. a. Insert rule FIRST—11.
　　 Insert rule LAST—14.
　　 Insert rule HERE—11.
　 b. Insert rule FIRST—15.
　　 Insert rule LAST—18.
　　 Insert rule HERE—15.

SOLUTIONS TO CHAPTER 8 EXERCISES

1. A–b, B–i, C–f, D–g, E–c, F–a, G–e, H–h, I–j, J–d

2.　　GHU　HOSPITAL*DN(HOSPNAME =MAC NEAL　　　　　)

　　　　　WARD　*D-(WARDNO　=04)

　　　　　PATIENT *N(BEDIDENT =0002)

3.　　GU　WARD　*C(RIVEREDGE　　　08)

4.　　GU　HOSPITAL*P(HOSPNAME =MAC NEAL　　　　)

　　　　　WARD　(WARDTYPE =RECOVERY　　　)

　　　　　PATIENT *L

SOLUTIONS TO CHAPTER 10 EXERCISES

1. IMS control region, message processing region, batch message processing region.

2. Data Base PCB, used for accessing a IMS data base; I/O PCB, used to receive messages and send messages back to the originating terminal; Alternate PCB, used to

send messages to terminals other than the originating terminal or to the message queues.

3. A–d, B–c, C–f, D–g, E–i, F–e, G–h, H–j, I–b, J–a

SOLUTIONS TO CHAPTER 11 EXERCISES

The listing in Figure E.4 shows a possible COBOL solution to the Chapter 11 coding problem.

```
000100 ID DIVISION.
000200 PROGRAM-ID.  CHAP11C.
000300 AUTHOR.      JOE LEBEN.
000400 DATE-COMPILED.
000600 REMARKS.  THIS IS A SIMPLE IMS-DC PROGRAM.  IT READS AN INPUT
000700           TRANSACTION HAVING THE FOLLOWING FORMAT:
000900
001000           POSITIONS   1 -  2  TRANSACTION LENGTH
001100                       3 -  4  ZZ FIELD
001200                       5 - 24  HOSPITAL NAME
001300                      25 - 26  WARD NUMBER
001400                      27 - 46  PATIENT NAME
001500
001600           FOR EACH TRANSACTION, THE PROGRAM ISSUES A DL/I CALL
001700           FOR THE PATIENT SEGMENT IDENTIFIED IN THAT TRANSACTION
001800           AND SENDS A COPY OF THAT PATIENT SEGMENT TO I/O PCB.
002600 DATA DIVISION.
002800 WORKING STORAGE SECTION.
003000 01  TERM-IN.
003200     03  IN-LENGTH         PIC S9999    COMP.
003300     03  IN-ZZ             PIC XX.
003400     03  HOSPNAME-TERM     PIC X(20).
003500     03  WARDNO-TERM       PIC X(2).
003600     03  PATNAME-TERM      PIC X(20).
003800 01  TERM-OUT.
004000     03  OUT-LENGTH        PIC S9999    VALUE +129   COMP.
004100     03  OUT-ZZ            PIC XX.
004200     03  PATIENT-INFO      PIC X(125).
004400 01  GET-UNIQUE           PIC X(4)    VALUE 'GU  '.
004500 01  INSERT-FUNCTION      PIC X(4)    VALUE 'ISRT'.
004600 01  SPACE-DATA           PIC X       VALUE SPACE.
004610 01  BAD-DATA REDEFINES SPACE-DATA.
004620     03  FILLER            PIC S9.
004700 01  PACKED-ONE           PIC S9      VALUE +1.
004900 01  HOSPITAL-SSA.
005000     03  FILLER      PIC X(19)   VALUE 'HOSPITAL(HOSPNAME ='.
005100     03  HOSPNAME-SSA PIC X(20).
005200     03  FILLER      PIC X       VALUE ')'.
005400 01  WARD-SSA.
005500     03  FILLER      PIC X(19)   VALUE 'WARD     (WARDNO   ='.
005600     03  WARDNO-SSA  PIC X(2).
005700     03  FILLER      PIC X       VALUE ')'.
005900 01  PATIENT-SSA.
006000     03  FILLER      PIC X(19)   VALUE 'PATIENT (PATNAME   ='.
006100     03  PATNAME-SSA PIC X(20).
006200     03  FILLER      PIC X       VALUE ')'.
006400 01  I-O-AREA  COPY  PATIENT.
006500
006600 LINKAGE SECTION.
006700 01  DB-PCB  COPY  MASKC.
006900 01  I-O-PCB.
007000     03  LTERM-NAME        PIC X(8).
007100     03  FILLER            PIC XX.
007200     03  I-O-STAT-CODE     PIC XX.
007300     03  INPUT-PREFIX.
007400         05  PREF-DATE     PIC S9(7)   COMP-3.
007500         05  PREF-TIME     PIC S9(7)   COMP-3.
007510         05  PREF-SEQ      PIC S9(7)   COMP.
```

Figure E.4. COBOL solution to Chapter 11 coding problem (page 1 of 2)

```
007700 PROCEDURE DIVISION.
007800
007900 ENTRY-LINKAGE.
008000
008100     ENTRY  'DLITCBL'  USING  I-O-PCB  DB-PCB.
008120
008140 MAIN-PROGRAM.
008160
008200     PERFORM GET-MESSAGE-RTN THRU GET-MESSAGE-RTN-EXIT
008210                         UNTIL I-O-STAT-CODE EQUAL 'QC' OR 'QD'.
008300     GOBACK.
008400
008500 GET-MESSAGE-RTN.
008600
008700     CALL  'CBLTDLI'  USING  GET-UNIQUE
008800                             I-O-PCB
008900                             TERM-IN.
008910
009000     IF I-O-STAT-CODE EQUAL 'QC' GO TO GET-MESSAGE-RTN EXIT.
009020
009100     IF I-O-STAT-CODE NOT EQUAL SPACE
009110
009200         MOVE I-O-PCB TO PATIENT INFO
009300         PERFORM SEND-MESSAGE-RTN
009400         GO TO GET-MESSAGE-RTN EXIT.
009410
009500     MOVE HOSPNAME-TERM TO HOSPNAME-SSA.
009600     MOVE WARDNO-TERM   TO WARDNO-SSA.
009700     MOVE PATNAME-TERM  TO PATNAME-SSA.
009710  .
009800     CALL  'CBLTDLI'  USING  GET-UNIQUE
009900                             DB-PCB
010000                             I-O-AREA
010100                             HOSPITAL-SSA
010200                             WARD-SSA
010300                             PATIENT-SSA.
010310
010400     IF STATUS-CODE NOT EQUAL SPACE
010410
010500         MOVE DB-PCB TO PATIENT-INFO
010600         PERFORM SEND-MESSAGE-RTN
010700         GO TO GET-MESSAGE-RTN-EXIT.
010710
010800     MOVE I-O-AREA TO PATIENT-INFO.
010900     PERFORM SEND-MESSAGE-RTN.
011000
011100 GET-MESSAGE-RTN-EXIT.
011200     EXIT.
011300
011400 SEND-MESSAGE-RTN.
011500
011600     CALL  'CBLTDLI'  USING  INSERT-FUNCTION
011700                             I-O-PCB
011800                    .        TERM-OUT.
011810
011900     IF I-O-STAT-CODE NOT EQUAL SPACE
011910
012100         ADD PACKED-ONE TO BAD-DATA.
```

Figure E.4. COBOL solution to Chapter 11 coding problem (page 2 of 2)

SOLUTIONS TO CHAPTER 12 EXERCISES

1. a—HISAM, HIDAM; b—HSAM; c—HDAM, HIDAM; d—HSAM, HISAM; e—HSAM, HISAM; f—HDAM; g—HSAM, HISAM; h—HIDAM; i—HDAM, HIDAM; j—HDAM; k—HSAM; l—HISAM; m—HDAM; n—HDAM, HIDAM

2. A–c, B–f, C–a, D–e, E–b, F–d

SOLUTIONS TO CHAPTER 13 EXERCISES

1. a—False—the index pointer segment points to the segments being indexed.
   b—True
   c—False—the indexed field can also be referenced when the INDICES parameter is coded in the segment's SENSEG statement.
   d—False—the index target segment can be any segment.
   e—False the index source segment and index target segment can be the same or different segment types.
   f—True; g—True; h—True
   i—False—the secondary processing sequence can be used by referencing an appropriate PCB without referencing the indexed field in an SSA.

2. a–B; b–C; c–D; d–a; e–E

3. GN   PATIENT
    ∿∿∿∿ ∿∿∿∿∿∿∿∿∿

4. GU   HOSPITAL (XADMIN = LUKENS   )
    ∿∿∿∿ ∿∿∿

SOLUTIONS TO CHAPTER 14 EXERCISES

1. A–a, B–e, C–d, D–g, E–c, F–j, G–b, H–f, I–h, J–i

SOLUTIONS TO CHAPTER 15 EXERCISES

1. a—False—the DBA can choose to place only the logical child, only the logical parent, or both in the I/O area.
   b—True; c—True
   d—False—the DBA can choose a symbolic pointer, a direct pointer, or both.
   e—True
   f—False—only the virtual logical child can have a scattered key field.

2. b

3. b

SOLUTIONS TO CHAPTER 16 EXERCISES

1.a—False—updates are processed only after the issuing program reaches a synchronization point.

b—True; c—True; d—True

e—False—a Verify Field call is used to determine whether a segment has been updated between the time an update call was issued and the time that a synchronization point was reached.

f—True

g—False—each area of a DEDB contains segments of all types

h—True

Appendix F
PL/I Coding Examples

This appendix contains the information required to code IMS programs in PL/I. Figure F.1 summarizes the PL/I conventions that must be followed for entry linkage, PCB masks, and CALL statements. Notice that the PCB mask must be set up as a based variable, and the name used in the entry linkage is the pointer name that has been declared in the PCB mask coding.

We don't show any SSA examples because any type of PL/I structure can be used to define SSAs. SSAs can be defined as any of the following:

- A major structure
- An array
- A fixed-character string
- An adjustable character string
- A pointer to any of the above
- A pointer to a minor structure

There is one major difference between the CALL statement parameter list in PL/I and the parameter list in COBOL. In PL/I, the function code is the second parameter in the list rather than the first. In a PL/I parameter list, the first parameter points to a fullword binary number that gives the number of parameters which follow the first parameter in the list. This parameter count field can be used in COBOL and Assembler Language programs, but in those languages it is optional. In PL/I, the parameter-count field is required.

This appendix also contains two complete PL/I programs. Figure F.2 is a PL/I version of the PATIENT segment retrieval program from Chapter 4. Figure F.3 is a PL/I solution to the coding problem in Chapter 5.

```
/*                                                    */
/*  PL/I ENTRY LINKAGE                                */
/*                                                    */
    DLITPLI: PROC (PCB_MASK) OPTIONS (MAIN);

/*                                                    */
/*  PL/I PCB MASK CODING                              */
/*                                                    */
    DCL  1  PCB_NAME              BASED (PCB_MASK),
            2  DBD_NAME           CHAR (8),
            2  LEVEL_NUMBER       CHAR (2),
            2  STATUS_CODE        CHAR (2),
            2  PROC_OPTIONS       CHAR (4),
            2  JCB_ADDRESS        FIXED BIN (31,0),
            2  SEGMENT_NAME       CHAR (8),
            2  KEY_LENGTH         FIXED BIN (31,0),
            2  NUMBER_SEGS        FIXED BIN (31,0),
            2  KEY                CHAR (26),
    DCL     KEY_PTR    POINTER;
    DCL  1  KEY_FEEDBACK          BASED (KEY_PTR),
            2  HOSPNAME_KEY       CHAR (20),
            2  WARDNO_KEY         CHAR (2)
            2  BEDIDENT_KEY       CHAR (4)
    KEY_PTR = ADDR (KEY);
/*                                                    */
/*  FUNCTION CODE, PARM COUNT, I/O AREA               */
/*                                                    */
    DCL     GET_UNIQUE    CHAR (4) INIT ('GU ');
    DCL     PARMCNT       FIXED BIN (31,0) INIT (6);
    DCL     I_O_AREA      CHAR (200);
/*                                                    */
/*  PL/I CALL STATEMENT                               */
/*                                                    */
    CALL  PLITDLI   (PARMCNT,
                     GET_UNIQUE,
                     PCB_MASK,
                     I_O_AREA,
                     SSA_ONE,
                     SSA_TWO,
                     SSA_THREE);
```

Figure F.1. PL/I coding conventions

```
DLITPLI: PROC (PCB_MASK) OPTIONS (MAIN):                      00000100
                                                             00000200
     /*        THIS IS A SIMPLE LIST PROGRAM.  IT DOES VERY LITTLE   00000300
               ERROR CHECKING.  IT READS AN INPUT DATA SET WHOSE     00000400
               RECORDS HAVE THE FOLLOWING FORMAT:                    00000500
                                                             00000600
               POSITIONS    1 - 20  HOSPITAL NAME           00000700
                           21 - 22  WARD NUMBER             00000800
                           23 - 42  PATIENT NAME            00000900
                           43 - 80  SPACES                  00001000
                                                             00001100
          FOR EACH RECORD READ, THE PROGRAM ISSUES A DL/I CALL    00001200
          FOR THE PATIENT SEGMENT IDENTIFIED IN THAT RECORD.      00001300
          IT THEN PRINTS OUT THAT PATIENT SEGMENT.           */ 00001400
                                                             00001500
DCL INPUT FILE RECORD SEQUENTIAL;                            00001600
DCL OUTPUT FILE RECORD SEQUENTIAL;                           00001700
                                                             00001800
                                                             00001900
DCL   PLITDLI   ENTRY;                                       00002000
                                                             00002100
DCL   1  INPUT-AREA,                                         00002200
         3  HOSPNAME_INPUT          CHAR (20),               00002300
         3  WARDNO_INPUT            CHAR (2),                00002400
         3  PATNAME_INPUT           CHAR (20),               00002500
         3  INPUT_AREA_PAD          CHAR (38);               00002600
                                                             00002700
DCL   1  PRINT_LINE,                                         00002800
         3  CARR_CNTL               CHAR (1),                00002900
         3  PATIENT_INFO            CHAR (125),              00003000
         3  PRINT_LINE_PAD          CHAR (7);                00003100
                                                             00003200
DCL   TOP_PAGE             CHAR (1),      INIT ('1');        00003300
DCL   SINGLE_SPACE         CHAR (1)       INIT (' ');        00003400
DCL   GET_UNIQUE           CHAR (4)       INIT ('GU  ');     00003500
DCL   LINE_COUNT           FIXED BIN (31) INIT (50);         00003600
DCL   SIX                  FIXED BIN (31) INIT (6);          00003700
                                                             00003800
DCL   1  HOSPITAL_SSA,                                       00003900
         3  ST_HOSP_SSA    CHAR (19)  INIT ('HOSPITAL(HOSPNAME ='), 00004000
         3  HOSPNAME_SSA   CHAR (20),                        00004100
         3  END_HOSP_SSA   CHAR (1)   INIT (')');            00004200
                                                             00004300
DCL   1  WARD_SSA,                                           00004400
         3  ST_WARD_SSA    CHAR (19)  INIT ('WARD     (WARDNO  ='), 00004500
         3  WARDNO_SSA     CHAR (2),                         00004600
         3  END_WARD_SSA   CHAR (1)   INIT (')');            00004700
                                                             00004800
DCL   1  PATIENT_SSA,                                        00004900
         3  ST_PAT_SSA     CHAR (19)  INIT ('PATIENT (PATNAME ='), 00005000
         3  PATNAME_SSA    CHAR (20),                        00005100
         3  END_PAT_SSA    CHAR (1)   INIT (')');            00005200
                                                             00005300
     DCL PATIENT_STRING BASED (PATIENT_PTR) CHAR (125);      00005400
     %INCLUDE PPATIENT;                                      00005500
                                                             00005600
     DCL PCB_STRING BASED (PCB_MASK) CHAR (62);              00005700
     %INCLUDE MASKP;                                         00005800
                                                             00005900
     DCL ADDR BUILTIN;                                       00006000
```

Figure F.2. PATIENT segment retrieval program in PL/I (page 1 of 2)

```
START_OF_PROGRAM:                                           00006200
    OPEN FILE (INPUT)    INPUT;                              00006400
    OPEN FILE (OUTPUT)   OUTPUT;                             00006500
    ON ENDFILE (INPUT) GO TO END_OF_JOB;                    00006600
    PATIENT_PTR = ADDR (PATIENT);                           00006700
                                                            00006800
READ_INPUT:                                                 00006900
    READ FILE (INPUT) INTO (INPUT_AREA);                    00007100
    HOSPNAME_SSA = HOSPNAME_INPUT;                          00007200
    WARDNO_SSA   = WARDNO_INPUT;                            00007300
    PATNAME_SSA  = PATNAME_INPUT;                           00007400
                                                            00007500
    CALL    PLITDLI   (SIX,                                 00007600
                       GET_UNIQUE,                          00007700
                       PCB_MASK,                            00007800
                       PATIENT,                             00007900
                       HOSPITAL_SSA,                        00008000
                       WARD_SSA,                            00008100
                       PATIENT_SSA);                        00008200
                                                            00008300
    IF STATUS_CODE  ^= ' '   THEN                           00008400
    DO;                                                     00008500
        CALL BAD_STATUS;                                    00008700
        GO TO READ_INPUT;                                   00008800
    END;                                                    00008900
                                                            00009000
    CALL PRINT_ROUTINE;                                     00009100
    GO TO READ_INPUT;                                       00009200
                                                            00009300
BAD_STATUS:  PROC;                                          00009400
    PATIENT_STRING = PCB_STRING;                            00009700
    CALL PRINT_ROUTINE;                                     00009800
    RETURN;                                                 00009900
END;                                                        00010000
                                                            00010100
PRINT_ROUTINE: PROC;                                        00010200
    IF LINE_COUNT = 50 THEN                                 00010400
    DO;                                                     00010500
        LINE_COUNT = 0;                                     00010700
        PATIENT_INFO = '          P A T I E N T  L I S T';  00010800
        CARR_CNTL  = TOP_PAGE;                              00010900
        WRITE FILE (OUTPUT) FROM (PATIENT_INFO);            00011000
        PATIENT_INFO = ' ';                                 00011100
        CARR_CNTL  = SINGLE_SPACE;                          00011200
        WRITE FILE (OUTPUT) FROM (PRINT_LINE);              00011300
    END;                                                    00011400
                                                            00011500
    PATIENT_INFO = PATIENT_STRING;                          00011600
    WRITE FILE (OUTPUT) FROM (PRINT_LINE);                  00011700
    LINE_COUNT = 1;                                         00011800
    RETURN;                                                 00011900
END;                                                        00012000
                                                            00012100
END_OF_JOB:                                                 00012200
    CLOSE FILE (INPUT), FILE (OUTPUT);                      00012400
    RETURN;                                                 00012500
END;                                                        00012600
```

Figure F.2. PATIENT segment retrieval program in PL/I (page 2 of 2)

```
DLITPLI: PROC (PCB_MASK) OPTIONS (MAIN);                          00000100
                                                                 00000200
/*      THE OUTPUT OF THIS PROGRAM IS A LIST OF PATIENTS WHO      00000300
        ARE IN QUARANTINE WARDS PRESENTLY AND ALSO HAVE          00000400
        BEEN IN A HOSPITAL WITHIN THE PAST YEAR.         */       00000500
                                                                 00000600
DCL HOSPITAL_NAME_FILE FILE RECORD SEQUENTIAL;                   00000700
                                                                 00000800
DCL 1  HOSPITAL_INPUT,                                           00000900
       5  PAD01             CHAR (2),                            00001000
       5  HOSPNAME_INPUT    CHAR (20),                           00001100
       5  PAD02             CHAR (58);                           00001200
                                                                 00001300
DCL PRINT_FILE  FILE RECORD SEQUENTIAL;                          00001400
                                                                 00001500
DCL 1  PRINT_LINE,                                              00001600
       5  CARR_CTL          CHAR (1),                            00001700
       5  PRINT_AREA        CHAR (132);                          00001800
                                                                 00001900
DCL  PLITDLI               ENTRY;                                00002000
DCL  ADDR                  BUILTIN;                              00002100
DCL  THREE                 FIXED BIN (31) INIT (3);              00002200
DCL  FOUR                  FIXED BIN (31) INIT (4);              00002300
DCL  FIVE                  FIXED BIN (31) INIT (5);              00002400
DCL  NO_HOSPITAL           CHAR (1)   INIT ('0');                00002500
DCL  NO_WARDS              CHAR (1)   INIT ('0');                00002600
DCL  NO_PATIENTS           CHAR (1)   INIT ('0');                00002700
DCL  TOP_PAGE              CHAR (1)   INIT ('1');                00002800
DCL  DOUBLE_SPACE          CHAR (1)   INIT ('0');                00002900
DCL  SINGLE_SPACE          CHAR (1)   INIT (' ');                00003000
DCL  GET_UNIQUE            CHAR (4)   INIT ('GU  ');             00003400
DCL  GET_NEXT_P            CHAR (4)   INIT ('GNP ');             00003600
DCL  LINE_CNT              FIXED BIN (31) INIT (52);             00003700
DCL  PAGE_CNT              FIXED BIN (31) INIT (0);              00003800
                                                                 00003900
DCL 1  NEW_DATE,    5  NEW_MONTH            DECIMAL FIXED (2,0),  00004200
       5  NEW_YEAR            DECIMAL FIXED (2,0);               00004300
DCL 1  CURR_DATE,               .                               00004600
       5   CURR_MONTH      PIC '99',                            00004700
       5   PAD03           CHAR (1)   INIT ('/'),                00004800
       5   CURR_DAY        PIC '99',                            00004900
       5   PAD04           CHAR (1)   INIT ('/'),                00005000
       5   CURR_YEAR       PIC '99';                            00005100
                                                                 00005200
DCL  PREV_DATE_PTR         POINTER;                              00005300
DCL  PREV_DATE_STRING      BASED (PREV_DATE_PTR)  CHAR (4);      00005400
DCL 1  PREV_DATE_SAVE      BASED (PREV_DATE_PTR),                00005500
       5  PREV_MONTH_SAVE  PIC '99',                            00005600
       5  PREV_YEAR_SAVE   PIC '99';                            00005700
                                                                 00005800
PREV_DATE_PTR = ADDR (PREV_DATE_SAVE);                          00005900
                                                                 00006000
%INCLUDE PHOSPITA;                                              00006100
%INCLUDE PWARD;                                                00006300
%INCLUDE PPATIENT;                                             00006500
                                                                 00006600
```

Figure F.3. PL/I Solution to Chapter 5 Problem (page 1 of 8)

```
DCL  1  HOSPITAL_SSA,                                        00006700
                                                             00006800
        5  PAD05              CHAR (8)  INIT ('HOSPITAL'),    00006900
        5  PAD06              CHAR (1)  INIT ('('),           00007000
        5  PAD07              CHAR (8)  INIT ('HOSPNAME'),    00007100
        5  PAD08              CHAR (1)  INIT ('EQ'),          00007200
        5  HOSPNAME_SSA       CHAR (20),                      00007300
        5  PAD09              CHAR (1)  INIT (')');           00007400
                                                             00007500
DCL  1  WARD_SSA,                                            00007600
                                                             00007650
        5  PAD10              CHAR (8)  INIT ('WARD    '),    00007700
        5  PAD11              CHAR (1)  INIT ('('),           00007800
        5  PAD12              CHAR (8)  INIT ('WARDTYPE'),    00007900
        5  PAD13              CHAR (1)  INIT ('EQ'),          00008000
        5  WARDTYPE_SSA       CHAR (20) INIT ('QUARANTINE'), 00008100
        5  PAD14              CHAR (1)  INIT (')');           00008200
                                                             00008300
DCL     PATIENT_SSA             CHAR (9)  INIT ('PATIENT');  00008400
DCL     HEAD_LINE_TITLE_PTR     POINTER;                     00008500
DCL     HEAD_LINE_TITLE_STRING  BASED (HEAD_LINE_TITLE_PTR) CHAR (132);  00008800
DCL  1  HEAD_LINE_TITLE         BASED (HEAD_LINE_TITLE_PTR), 00008900
                                                             00009000
        5  PAD15              CHAR (26) INIT (' '),          00009100
        5  TITLE              CHAR (106)                     00009200
           INIT   (P R E V I O U S   S T A Y   R E P O R T');  00009300
                                                             00009400
        HEAD_LINE_TITLE_PTR = ADDR (HEAD_LINE_TITLE);        00009500
                                                             00009600
DCL     HEAD_LINE_PAGE_PTR     POINTER;                      00009700
DCL     HEAD_LINE_PAGE_STRING  BASED (HEAD_LINE_PAGE_PTR) CHAR (132);  00009800
DCL  1  HEAD_LINE_PAGE         BASED (HEAD_LINE_PAGE_PTR),   00009900
                                                             00010000
        5  PAD16              CHAR (5)   INIT ('PAGE'),      00010100
        5  HPAGE_CTR          PIC 'ZZZ9',                    00010200
        5  PAD17              CHAR (123) INIT (' ');         00010300
                                                             00010400
        HEAD_LINE_PAGE_PTR = ADDR (HEAD_LINE_PAGE);          00010500
                                                             00010600
DCL     HEAD_LINE_HOSP_PTR     POINTER;                      00010700
DCL     HEAD_LINE_HOSP_STRING  BASED (HEAD_LINE_HOSP_PTR) CHAR (132);  00010800
DCL  1  HEAD_LINE_HOSP         BASED (HEAD_LINE_HOSP_PTR),   00010900
                                                             00011000
        5  PAD18              CHAR (25) INIT ('HOSPITAL NAME'),     00011100
        5  PAD19              CHAR (35) INIT ('HOSPITAL ADDRESS'),  00011200
        5  PAD20              CHAR (10) INIT ('HOSPITAL PHONE'),    00011300
        5  PAD21              CHAR (62) INIT (' ');          00011400
                                                             00011500
        HEAD_LINE_HOSP_PTR = ADDR (HEAD_LINE_HOSP);          00011700
                                                             00011800
```

Figure F.3. PL/I Solution to Chapter 5 Problem (page 2 of 8)

```
DCL     HEAD_LINE_WARD_PTR       POINTER;                                    00011900
DCL     HEAD_LINE_WARD_STRING    BASED (HEAD_LINE_WARD_PTR) CHAR (132);      00012000
DCL 1   HEAD_LINE_WARD           BASED (HEAD_LINE_WARD_PTR),                 00012100
                                                                             00012200
        5  PAD22                 CHAR (12) INIT ('WARD NO'),                 00012300
        5  PAD23                 CHAR (14) INIT ('TOT ROOMS'),               00012400
        5  PAD24                 CHAR (13) INIT ('TOT BEDS'),                00012500
        5  PAD25                 CHAR (15) INIT ('BEDS AVAIL'),              00012600
        5  PAD26                 CHAR (20) INIT ('WARD TYPE'),               00012700
        5  PAD27                 CHAR (58) INIT (' ');                       00012800
                                                                             00012900
        HEAD_LINE_WARD_PTR = ADDR (HEAD_LINE_WARD);                          00013000
                                                                             00013100
DCL     HEAD_LINE_PAT_PTR        POINTER;                                    00013200
DCL     HEAD_LINE_PAT_STRING     BASED (HEAD_LINE_PAT_PTR);                  00013300
DCL 1   HEAD_LINE_PAT            BASED (HEAD_LINE_PAT_PTR),                  00013400
                                                                             00013500
        5  PAD28                 CHAR (21) INIT ('PATIENT NAME'),            00013600
        5  PAD29                 CHAR (6)  INIT ('BED'),                     00013700
        5  PAD30                 CHAR (12) INIT ('ADMIT DATE'),              00013800
        5  PAD31                 CHAR (11) INIT ('PREV DATE'),               00013900
        5  PAD32                 CHAR (21) INIT ('PREVIOUS HOSPITAL'),       00014000
        5  PAD33                 CHAR (30) INIT ('PREVIOUS REASON'),         00014100
        5  PAD34                 CHAR (31) INIT (' ');                       00014200
                                                                             00014300
        HEAD_LINE_PAT_PTR = ADDR (HEAD_LINE_PAT);                           00014400
                                                                             00014500
DCL     DETAIL_HOSP_PTR          POINTER;                                    00014800
DCL     DETAIL_HOSP_STRING       BASED (DETAIL_HOSP_PTR)  CHAR (132);        00014900
DCL 1   DETAIL_HOSP              BASED (DETAIL_HOSP_PTR),                    00015000
                                                                             00015100
        5  HOSPNAME_LINE         CHAR (20),                                  00015200
        5  PAD35                 CHAR (5)  INIT (' '),                       00015300
        5  HOSP_ADDRESS_LINE     CHAR (30),                                  00015400
        5  PAD36                 CHAR (5)  INIT (' '),                       00015500
        5  HOSP_PHONE_LINE       CHAR (10),                                  00015600
        5  PAD37                 CHAR (62) INIT (' ');                       00015700
                                                                             00015800
        DETAIL_HOSP_PTR = ADDR (DETAIL_HOSP_;                                00015900
                                                                             00016000
DCL     DETAIL_WARD_PTR          POINTER;                                    00016100
DCL     DETAIL_WARD_STRING       BASED (DETAIL_WARD_PTR) CHAR (132);         00016200
DCL 1   DETAIL_WARD              BASED (DETAIL_WARD_PTR),                    00016300
                                                                             00016400
        5  PAD38                 CHAR (3)  INIT (' '),                       00016500
        5  WARDNO_LINE           CHAR (2),                                   00016600
        5  PAD39                 CHAR (10) INIT (' '),                       00016700
        5  TOT_ROOMS_LINE        CHAR (3),                                   00016800
        5  PAD40                 CHAR (11) INIT (' '),                       00016900
        5  TOT_BEDS_LINE         CHAR (3),                                   00017000
        5  PAD41                 CHAR (10) INIT (' '),                       00017100
        5  BEDAVAIL_LINE         CHAR (3),                                   00017200
        5  PAD42                 CHAR (9)  INIT (' '),                       00017300
        5  WARDTYPE_LINE         CHAR (20),                                  00017400
        5  PAD43                 CHAR (58) INIT (' '),                       00017500
                                                                             00017600
        DETAIL_WARD_PTR = ADDR (DETAIL_WARD);                               00017700
                                                                             00017800
```

Figure F.3. PL/I Solution to Chapter 5 Problem (page 3 of 8)

```
DCL     DETAIL_PAT_PTR           POINTER;                                       00017900
DCL     DETAIL_PAT_STRING        BASED (DETAIL_PAT_PTR);                        00018000
DCL 1   DETAIL_PAT               BASED (DETAIL_PAT_PTR),                        00018100
                                                                                00018200
        5  PATNAME_LINE          CHAR (20),                                     00018300
        5  PAD44                 CHAR (1)  INIT (' '),                          00018400
        5  BEDIDENT_LINE         CHAR (4),                                      00018500
        5  PAD45                 CHAR (4)  INIT (' '),                          00018600
        5  DATEADMT_LINE         CHAR (6),                                      00018700
        5  PAD46                 CHAR (6)  INIT (' '),                          00018800
        5  PREV_DATE_LINE        CHAR (4),                                      00018900
        5  PAD47                 CHAR (5)  INIT (' '),                          00019000
        5  PREV_HOSP_LINE        CHAR (20),                                     00019100
        5  PAD48                 CHAR (1)  INIT (' '),                          00019200
        5  PREV_REASON_LINE      CHAR (30),                                     00019300
        5  PAD49                 CHAR (31) INIT (' ');                          00019400
                                                                                00019500
        DETAIL_PAT_PTR = ADDR (DETAIL_PAT);                                     00019600
                                                                                00019700
DCL     NO_HOSP_LINE_PTR         POINTER;                                       00020000
DCL     NO_HOSP_LINE_STRING      BASED (NO_HOSP_LINE_PTR)  CHAR (132);          00020100
DCL 1   NO_HOSP_LINE             BASED (NO_HOSP_LINE_PTR),                      00020200
                                                                                00020300
        5  HOSPNAME_ERROR        CHAR (20),                                     00020600
        5  PAD50                 CHAR (5) INIT (' '),                           00020610
        5  PAD51                 CHAR (107)                                     00020700
              INIT ('**** HOSPITAL NOT FOUND  ****');                           00020800
                                                                                00021300
DCL     NO_WARD_LINE             CHAR (132)                                     00021400
              INIT ('*** NO QUARANTINE WARDS ***');                            00021410
                                                                                00021600
DCL     NO_PAT_LINE              CHAR (132)                                     00021700
              INIT ('*** NO PATIENTS WITH RECENT STAY ***');                   00021800
                                                                                00021900
DCL     PCB_STRING               BASED (PCB_MASK)  CHAR (62);                   00022000
                                                                                00022050
%INCLUDE MASKP;                                                                 00022100
                                                                                00022300
```

Figure F.3. PL/I Solution to Chapter 5 Problem (page 4 of 8)

```
ENTRY_POINT:                                                          00022400
      OPEN FILE    (HOSPITAL_NAME_FILE)  INPUT;                       00022600
      OPEN FILE    (PRINT_FILE)          OUTPUT;                      00022700
      ON ENDFILE   (HOSPITAL_NAME_FILE)  GO TO END_OF_JOB;            00022800
      CALL DATE_RTN;                                                  00022900
                                                                      00023000
READ_INPUT:                                                           00023100
      READ FILE (HOSPITAL_NAME_FILE) INTO (HOSPITAL_INPUT);          00023300
      HOSPNAME_SSA = HOSPNAME_INPUT;                                  00023400
      LINE_CNT     = 45;                                              00023500
                                                                      00023600
      CALL  PLITDLI        (FOUR,  GET_UNIQUE,                        00023800
                            PCB_MASK,                                 00023900
                            HOSPITAL,                                 00024000
                            HOSPITAL_SSA);                            00024100
                                                                      00024200
      IF STATUS_CODE ^= ' ' THEN                                     00024300
         DO;                                                          00024500
              CALL   HOSPITAL_NOT_FOUND;                              00024600
              GO TO READ_INPUT;                                       00024700
         END;                                                         00024800
                                                                      00024900
      HOSPNAME_LINE       = HOSPNAME;                                 00025000
      HOSP_ADDRESS_LINE   = HOSP_ADDRESS;                             00025100
      HOSP_PHONE_LINE     = HOSP_PHONE;                               00025200
                                                                      00025300
      CALL  PLITDLI        (FIVE,  GET_UNIQUE,                        00025500
                            PCB_MASK,                                 00025600
                            WARD,                                     00025700
                            HOSPITAL_SSA,                             00025800
                            WARD_SSA);                                00025900
                                                                      00026000
      IF STATUS_CODE ^= ' ' THEN                                     00026100
         DO;                                                          00026300
              CALL WARD_NOT_FOUND;                                    00026400
              GO TO READ_INPUT;                                       00026500
         END;                                                         00026600
                                                                      00026700
      WARDNO_LINE     =  WARDNO;                                      00026710
      TOT_ROOMS_LINE  =  TOT_ROOMS;                                   00026800
      TOT_BEDS_LINE   =  TOT_BEDS;                                    00026900
      DBEDAVAIL_LINE  =  BEDAVAIL;                                    00027000
      WARDTYPE_LINE   =  WARDTYPE;                                    00027100
      NO_PATIENTS     =  '0';                                        00027200
                                                                      00027300
      DO WHILE (STATUS_CODE ^= 'GE';                                 00027400
         CALL  CALL_PATIENT;                                          00027600
      END;                                                            00027800
                                                                      00027900
      IF NO_PATIENTS = '0' THEN                                      00028000
         DO;                                                          00028200
              DETAIL_PAT_STRING = NO_PAT_LINE;                        00028400
              CALL WRITE_RTN;                                         00028500
              DETAIL_PAT_STRING = ' ';                               00028600
         END;                                                         00028700
                                                                      00028800
      NO_PATIENTS = '0';                                             00028900
      GO TO READ_INPUT;                                               00029000
```

Figure F.3. PL/I Solution to Chapter 5 Problem (page 5 of 8)

```
                                                            00029100
CALL_PATIENT:  PROC;                                        00029200
                                                            00029300
    CALL  PLITDLI          (FOUR,  GET_NEXT_P,              00029500
                            PCB_MASK,                       00029600
                            PATIENT,                        00029700
                            PATIENT_SSA);                   00029800
                                                            00029900
    IF STATUS_CODE = 'GE' THEN RETURN;                      00030000
                                                            00030050
    IF STATUS_CODE ^= '   ' THEN                            00030100
        DO;                                                 00030300
            DETAIL_PAT_STRING = PCB_STRING;                 00030500
            CALL WRITE_RTN;                                 00030600
            DETAIL_PAT_STRING = ' ';                        00030700
            GO TO READ_INPUT;                               00030800
        END;                                                00030900
                                                            00031000
    IF    PREV_STAY_FLAG ^= '1'  THEN  RETURN;              00031100
                                                            00031200
    PREV_DATE_STRING  =  PREV_DATE;                         00031400
    NEW_MONTH         =  CURR_MONTH - PREV_MONTH_SAVE;      00031500
    NEW_YEAR          =  CURR_YEAR - PREV_YEAR_SAVE;        00031600
                                                            00031700
    IF   NEW_YEAR  > 1 THEN RETURN;                         00031800
                                                            00031850
    IF   NEW_YEAR  = 0 THEN                                 00031900
        DO;                                                 00032100
            CALL WRITE_PAT_DATA;                            00032200
            NO_PATIENTS = ^1';                              00032300
            RETURN;                                         00032400
        END;                                                00032500
                                                            00032600
    IF   NEW_YEAR  = 1 & NEW_MONTH < 1 THEN                 00032700
        DO;                                                 00032900
            CALL WRITE_PAT_DATA;                            00033000
            NO_PATIENTS = ^1';                              00033100
        END;                                                00033200
                                                            00033300
    RETURN;                                                 00033400
                                                            00033500
END;                                                        00033600
```

Figure F.3. PL/I Solution to Chapter 5 Problem (page 6 of 8)

```
                                                                     00033700
WRITE_RTN:  PROC;                                                    00033800
                                                                     00033900
    IF LINE_CNT > 44 THEN                                            00034000
        DO;                                                          00034100
            LINE_CNT    = 1;                                         00034200
            PRINT_AREA  = HEAD_LINE_TITLE_STRING;                    00034400
            CARR_CTL    = TOP_PAGE;                                  00034500
            WRITE FILE (PRINT_FILE) FROM (PRINT_LINE);               00034600
                                                                     00034700
            PAGE_CNT    = PAGE_CNT + 1;                              00034800
            HPAGE_CTR   = PAGE_CNT;                                  00034900
            PRINT_AREA  = HEAD_LINE_PAGE_STRING;                     00035100
            CARR_CTL    = DOUBLE_SPACE;                              00035200
            WRITE FILE (PRINT_FILE) FROM (PRINT_LINE);               00035300
                                                                     00035400
            PRINT_AREA  = HEAD_LINE_HOSP_STRING;                     00035600
            CARR_CTL    = DOUBLE_SPACE;                              00035700
            WRITE FILE (PRINT_FILE) FROM (PRINT_LINE);               00035800
                                                                     00035900
            PRINT_AREA  = DETAIL_HOSP_STRING;                        00036100
            CARR_CTL    = DOUBLE_SPACE;                              00036200
            WRITE FILE (PRINT_FILE) FROM (PRINT_LINE);               00036300
                                                                     00036400
            IF NO_HOSPITAL = '1' THEN RETURN;                        00036500
                                                                     00036600
            PRINT_AREA  = HEAD_LINE_WARD_STRING;                     00036800
            CARR_CTL    = DOUBLE_SPACE;                              00036900
            WRITE FILE (PRINT_FILE) FROM (PRINT_LINE);               00037000
                                                                     00037100
            PRINT_AREA  = DETAIL_WARD_STRING;                        00037300
            CARR_CTL    = DOUBLE_SPACE;                              00037400
            WRITE FILE (PRINT_FILE) FROM (PRINT_LINE);               00037500
                                                                     00037600
            IF NO_WARDS = '1' THEN RETURN;                           00037700
                                                                     00037800
            PRINT_AREA  = HEAD_LINE_PAT_STRING;                      00038000
            CARR_CTL    = DOUBLE_SPACE;                              00038100
            WRITE FILE (PRINT_FILE) FROM (PRINT_LINE);               00038200
                                                                     00038300
            PRINT_AREA  = ' ';                                       00038400
            CARR_CTL    = SINGLE_SPACE;                              00038500
            WRITE FILE (PRINT_FILE) FROM (PRINT_LINE);               00038600
        END;                                                         00038700
                                                                     00038800
    PRINT_AREA = DETAIL_PAT_STRING;                                  00039000
    CARR_CTL   = SINGLE_SPACE;                                       00039100
    WRITE FILE (PRINT_FILE) FROM (PRINT_LINE);                       00039200
                                                                     00039300
    LINE_CNT   = LINE_CNT + 1;                                       00039400
                                                                     00039500
RETURN;                                                              00039600
                                                                     00039700
END;                                                                 00039800
```

Figure F.3. PL/I Solution to Chapter 5 Problem (page 7 of 8)

```
WRITE_PAT_DATA:   PROC;                                          00039900
                                                                 00040000
                                                                 00040100
     PATNAME_LINE        = PATNAME;                              00040200
     BEDIDENT_LINE       = BEDIDENT;                             00040300
     DATEADMT_LINE       = DATEADMT;                             00040400
     PREV_HOSP_LINE      = PREV_HOSP;                            00040500
     PREV_DATE_LINE      = PREV_DATE;                            00040600
     PREV_REASON_LINE    = PREV_REASON;                         00040700
     CALL    WRITE_RTN;                                          00040800
                                                                 00040900
RETURN;                                                          00041000
                                                                 00041100
END;                                                             00041200
                                                                 00041300
HOSPITAL_NOT_FOUND:    PROC;                                     00041400
                                                                 00041500
     NO_HOSPITAL         = '1';                                  00041600
     HOSPNAME_ERROR      = HOSPNAME_INPUT;                       00041700
     NO_HOSP_LINE_PTR    = ADDR (NO_HOSP_LINE);                 00041900
     DETAIL_HOSP_STRING  = NO_HOSP_LINE_STRING;                 00042000
     CALL   WRITE_RTN;                                           00042100
     DETAIL_HOSP_STRING  = ' ';                                 00042200
     NO_HOSPITAL         = '0';                                 00042300
                                                                 00042400
RETURN;                                                          00042500
                                                                 00042600
END;                                                             00042700
                                                                 00042800
WARD_NOT_FOUND:   PROC;                                          00042900
                                                                 00043000
     NO_WARDS            = '1';                                  00043100
     NO_HOSP_LINE_PTR    = ADDR (NO_WARD_LINE);                 00043300
     DETAIL_WARD_STRING  = NO_HOSP_LINE_STRING;                 00043400
     CALL WRITE_RTN;                                             00043500
     DETAIL_WARD_STRING  = ' ';                                 00043600
     NO_WARDS            = '0';                                 00043700
                                                                 00043800
RETURN;                                                          00043900
                                                                 00044000
END;                                                             00044100
                                                                 00044200
DATE_RTN:  PROC;                                                 00044300
                                                                 00044400
     CURR_MONTH  =  06;                                          00044500
     CURR_DAY    =  27;                                          00044600
     CURR_YEAR   =  87;                                          00044700
                                                                 00044800
RETURN;                                                          00044900
                                                                 00045000
END;                                                             00045100
                                                                 00045200
END_OF_JOB:                                                      00045300
                                                                 00045400
     CLOSE FILE (HOSPITAL_NAME_FILE), FILE (PRINT_FILE);        00045500
                                                                 00045600
     RETURN;                                                     00045700
                                                                 00045800
END;                                                             00045900
```

Figure F.3. PL/I Solution to Chapter 5 Problem (page 8 of 8)

Appendix G
Assembler Language
Coding Examples

This appendix contains information that will be helpful in coding IMS programs in Assembler Language. Figure G.1 summarizes the Assembler Language conventions that must be followed for entry coding, PCB masks, and CALL statements. This appendix also contains two complete Assembler Language programs. Figure G.2 is an Assembler Language version of the PATIENT segment retrieval program from Chapter 4. Figure G.3 is an Assembler Language solution to the coding problem in Chapter 5.

```
*
*          ASSEMBLER LANGUAGE ENTRY LINKAGE
*
DLITASM  CSECT
         SAVE  (14,12)
         BALR  12,0        REG 12 -- PROG BASE REGISTER
         USING *,12
         LA    11,SAVE
         ST    11,8(0,13)
         ST    13,SAVE+4
         LR    13,11
         L     11,0(0,1)   REG 11 -- PCB BASE REGISTER
         USING PCBMASK,11
            .


*
*          ASSEMBLER LANGUAGE CALL STATEMENT
*
         CALL  ASMTDLI,(GU,(11),IOAREA,SSA1,SSA2,SSA3),VL
            .
            .

*
*          FUNCTION CODE, I/O AREA
*
GU       DC    CL4'GU '
IOAREA   DC    CL200' '
            .
            .


*
*          PCB MASK
*
PCBMASK  DSECT
DBDNAME  DS    CL8
LEVELNO  DS    CL2
STATCODE DS    CL2
PROCOPT  DS    CL4
JCBADDR  DS    F
SEGMENT  DS    CL8
KEYLNGTH DS    F
NOSEGS   DS    F
KEYFEED  DS    OCL26
HOSPKEY  DS    CL20
WARDKEY  DS    CL2
BEDKEY   DS    CL4
         END   DLITASM
```

Figure G.1. Assembler Language coding conventions

```
          PRINT NOGEN                                                00000100
CHAP4A    START 0                                                    00000200
DLITCBL   EQU   *                                                    00000210
          ENTRY DLITCBL                                              00000211
          SAVE  (14,12)                                              00000300
          BALR  12,0                                                 00000400
          USING *,12                                                 00000500
          LA    2,SAVE                                               00000600
          ST    2,8(0,13)                                            00000700
          ST    13,SAVE+4                                            00000800
          LR    13,2                                                 00000900
          L     3,0(0,1)                                             00001000
          USING PCBMASK,3                                            00001100
          OPEN  (INPUT,(INPUT),OUTPUT,(OUTPUT))                      00001300
*                                                                    00001400
READINPT  GET   INPUT,INPTDATA                                       00001500
          MVC   HNAMSSA,HNAMINPT                                     00001600
          MVC   WNOSSA,WNOINPT                                       00001700
          MVC   PNAMSSA,PNAMINPT                                     00001800
*                                                                    00001900
          CALL  CBLTDLI,(GU,(3),IOAREA,HOSPSSA,WARDSSA,PATSSA),VL    00002000
*                                                                    00002100
          CLC   STATCODE,=' '                                        00002200
          BNE   BADSTAT                                              00002300
          MVC   PATINFO,IOAREA                                       00002400
*                                                                    00002500
PRINT     LH    2,LINECNT                                            00002600
          CH    2,=H'50'                                             00002700
          BL    NOHEAD                                               00002800
          LA    2,0                                                  00002900
          STH   2,LINECNT                                            00003000
          MVC   PRNTLINE(33),=C'1         P A T I E N T  L I S T '   00003100
          PUT   OUTPUT,PRNTLINE                                      00003200
          MVI   PRNTLINE,C' '                                        00003300
          MVC   PRNTLINE+1,PRNTLINE                                  00003400
          PUT   OUTPUT,PRNTLINE                                      00003500
*                                                                    00003600
NOHEAD    MVC   PATINFO,IOAREA                                       00003700
          PUT   OUTPUT,PRNTLINE                                      00003800
          LH    2,LINECNT                                            00003900
          AH    2,=H'1'                                              00004000
          STH   2,LINECNT                                            00004100
          B     READINPT                                             00004200
*                                                                    00004300
EOFINPT   CLOSE (INPUT)                                              00004400
          CLOSE (OUTPUT)                                             00004410
          L     13,SAVE+4                                            00004500
          RETURN (14,12),RC=0                                        00004600
*                                                                    00004700
BADSTAT   MVI   IOAREA,C' '                                          00004800
          MVC   IOAREA+1(124),IOAREA                                 00004900
          MVC   IOAREA(62),PCBMASK                                   00005000
          B     PRINT                                                00005100
```

Figure G.2. PATIENT retrieval program in Assembler Language (page 1 of 2)

```
INPUT     DCB   DSORG=PS,MACRF=GM,EODAD=EOFINPT,LRECL=80,RECFM=FB,   *00005300
                DDNAME=INPUT                                          00005310
*                                                                     00005400
OUTPUT    DCB   DSORG=PS,MACRF=PM,LRECL=133,RECFM=FBA,               *00005500
                DDNAME=OUTPUT                                         00005510
*                                                                     00005600
INPTDATA  DS    0CL80                                                 00005700
HNAMINPT  DS    CL20                                                  00005800
WNOINPT   DS    CL2                                                   00005900
PNAMINPT  DS    CL20                                                  00006000
          DS    CL38                                                  00006100
*                                                                     00006200
PRNTLINE  DS    0CL133                                                00006300
CARRCNTL  DS    C                                                     00006400
PATINFO   DS    CL125                                                 00006500
          DS    CL7                                                   00006600
*                                                                     00006700
TOPPAGE   DC    C'1'                                                  00006800
SNGLSPCE  DC    C' '                                                  00006900
GU        DC    CL4'GU '                                              00007000
LINECNT   DC    H'60'                                                 00007100
*                                                                     00007200
HOSPSSA   DS    0CL40                                                 00007300
          DC    CL19'HOSPITAL(HOSPNAME ='                             00007400
HNAMSSA   DS    CL20                                                  00007500
          DC    C')'                                                  00007600
*                                                                     00007700
WARDSSA   DS    0CL22                                                 00007800
          DC    CL19'WARD    (WARDNO  ='                              00007900
WNOSSA    DS    CL2                                                   00008000
          DC    C')'                                                  00008100
*                                                                     00008200
PATSSA    DS    0CL40                                                 00008300
          DC    CL19'PATIENT (PATNAME  ='                             00008400
PNAMSSA   DS    CL20                                                  00008500
          DC    C')'                                                  00008600
SAVE      DS    18F                                                   00008610
*                                                                     00008700
IOAREA    DS    0CL125                                                00008810
          COPY  APATIENT                                              00008900
*                                                                     00009000
PCBMASK   DSECT                                                       00009100
          COPY  MASKA                                                 00009200
          END   CHAP4A                                                00009300
```

Figure G.2. PATIENT retrieval program in Assembler Language (page 2 of 2)

```
          PRINT NOGEN                                          00000100
CHAP5A    START 0                                              00000200
DLITCBL   EQU   *                                              00000300
          ENTRY DLITCBL                                        00000400
          SAVE  (14,12)                                        00000500
          BALR  12,0                                           00000600
          USING *,12                                           00000700
          LA    2,SAVE                                         00000800
          ST    2,8(0,13)                                      00000900
          ST    13,SAVE+4                                      00001000
          LR    13,2                                           00001100
          L     2,0(0,1)                                       00001200
          USING PCBMASK,2                                      00001300
*                                                              00001600
START     OPEN  (HOSPFILE,(INPUT),PRINTER,(OUTPUT))            00001700
          BAL   11,DATE                                        00001800
*                                                              00001900
READINPT  GET   HOSPFILE,HOSPINPT                              00002000
          MVC   SSAHNAME,IHOSPNAM                              00002100
          MVC   LINECNT,=H'45'                                 00002200
*                                                              00002300
          CALL  CBLTDLI,(GU,(2),HOSPITAL,SSAHOSP),VL           00002400
*                                                              00002500
          CLC   STATCODE,=C' '                                 00002600
          BE    AHEAD1                                         00002700
          BAL   11,HOSPNFND                                    00002800
          B     READINPT                                       00002900
*                                                              00003000
AHEAD1    MVC   DHOSPNAM,HOSPNAME                              00003100
          MVC   DHOSPADR,HOSPADDR                              00003200
          MVC   DHOSPHON,HOSPPHON                              00003300
*                                                              00003400
          CALL  CBLTDLI,(GU,(2),WARD,SSAHOSP,SSAWARD),VL       00003500
*                                                              00003600
          CLC   STATCODE,=C' '                                 00003700
          BE    AHEAD2                                         00003800
          BAL   11,WARDNFND                                    00003900
          B     READINPT                                       00004000
*                                                              00004100
AHEAD2    MVC   DWARDNO,WARDNO                                 00004200
          MVC   DTOTRMS,TOTROOMS                               00004300
          MVC   DTOTBEDS,TOTBEDS                               00004400
          MVC   DBDSAVAI,BEDAVAIL                              00004500
          MVC   DWARDTYP,WARDTYPE                              00004600
          MVI   NOPAT,C'0'                                     00004700
LOOP1     CLC   STATCODE,=C'GE'                                00004800
          BE    AHEAD3                                         00004900
          BAL   11,CALLPAT                                     00005000
          B     LOOP1                                          00005100
*                                                              00005200
AHEAD3    CLI   NOPAT,C'0'                                     00005300
          BNE   AHEAD4                                         00005400
          MVC   DTPAT,NOPATLN                                  00005500
          BAL   11,WRITERTN                                    00005600
          MVI   DTPAT,C' '                                     00005700
          MVC   DTPAT+1(131),DTPAT                             00005800
*                                                              00005900
AHEAD4    MVI   NOPAT,C'0'                                     00006000
          B     READINPT                                       00006100
```

Figure G.3.   Chapter 5 coding problem in Assembler Language (page 1 of 7)

```
CALLPAT  ST    11,PATSAVE                                    00006300
*                                                            00006400
         CALL  CBLTDLI,(GNP,(2),PATIENT,SSAPAT),VL           00006500
*                                                            00006600
         CLC   STATCODE,=C'GE'                               00006700
         BE    PATEXIT                                       00006800
*                                                            00006900
         CLC   STATCODE,=C'  '                               00007000
         BE    AHEAD5                                        00007100
*                                                            00007200
         MVI   DTPAT+61,C' '                                 00007300
         MVC   DTPAT+62(69),DTPAT+61                         00007400
         MVC   DTPAT(62),PCBMASK                             00007500
         BAL   11,WRITERTN                                   00007600
         MVI   DTPAT,C' '                                    00007700
         MVC   DTPAT+1(131),DTPAT                            00007800
         B     READINPT                                      00007900
*                                                            00008000
AHEAD5   CLI   PREVSTAY,C'1'                                 00008100
         BNE   PATEXIT                                       00008200
*                                                            00008300
         MVC   WSPREVDT,PREVDATE                             00008400
         PACK  DATEWK1,CURRMO                                00008500
         PACK  DATEWK2,PREVMO                                00008600
         ZAP   NEWMONTH,DATEWK1                              00008700
         SP    NEWMONTH,DATEWK2                              00008800
         PACK  DATEWK1,CURRYR                                00008900
         PACK  DATEWK2,PREVYR                                00009000
         ZAP   NEWYEAR,DATEWK1                               00009100
         SP    NEWYEAR,DATEWK2                               00009200
*                                                            00009300
         CP    NEWYEAR,=P'1'                                 00009400
         BH    PATEXIT                                       00009500
         BE    CHKMO                                         00009600
         BL    WPAT                                          00009700
*                                                            00009800
CHKMO    CP    NEWMONTH,=P'1'                                00009900
         BNL   PATEXIT                                       00010000
*                                                            00010100
WPAT     BAL   11,WPATDATA                                   00010200
         MVI   NOPAT,C'1'                                    00010300
*                                                            00010400
PATEXIT  L     11,PATSAVE                                    00010500
         BR    11                                            00010600
*                                                            00010700
PATSAVE  DS    F                                             00010800
*                                                            00010900
WPATDATA ST    11,WPATSAVE                                   00011000
         MVC   DPATNAM,PATNAME                               00011100
         MVC   DBEDID,BEDIDENT                               00011200
         MVC   DDATADMI,DATEADMT                             00011300
         MVC   DPREHOSP,PREVHOSP                             00011400
         MVC   DPREVDTE,PREVDATE                             00011500
         MVC   DPREVREA,PREVREAS                             00011600
         BAL   11,WRITERTN                                   00011700
         L     11,WPATSAVE                                   00011800
         BR    11                                            00011900
*                                                            00012000
WPATSAVE DS    F                                             00012100
```

Figure G.3. Chapter 5 coding problem in Assembler Language (page 2 of 7)

```
HOSPNFND ST     11,HOSPSAVE                          00012400
         MVI    NOHOSP,C'1'                          00012500
         MVC    ERRHNAM,IHOSPNAM                     00012600
         MVC    DTHOSP,NOHOSPLN                      00012700
         BAL    11,WRITERTN                          00012800
         MVI    NOHOSP,C'0'                          00012900
         MVI    DTHOSP,C' '                          00013000
         MVC    DTHOSP+1(131),DTHOSP                 00013100
         L      11,HOSPSAVE                          00013200
         BR     11                                   00013300
*                                                    00013400
HOSPSAVE DS     F                                    00013500
*                                                    00013600
*                                                    00013700
WARDNFND ST     11,WARDSAVE                          00013800
         MVI    NOWARD,C'1'                          00013900
         MVC    DTWARD,NOWARDLN                      00014000
         BAL    11,WRITERTN                          00014100
         MVI    NOWARD,C'0'                          00014200
         MVI    DTWARD,C' '                          00014300
         MVC    DTWARD+1(131),DTWARD                 00014400
         L      11,WARDSAVE                          00014500
         BR     11                                   00014600
*                                                    00014700
WARDSAVE DS     F                                    00014800
*                                                    00014900
*                                                    00015000
ENDJOB   CLOSE  (HOSPFILE)                           00015100
         CLOSE  (PRINTER)                            00015200
         L      13,SAVE+4                            00015300
         RETURN (14,12),RC=0                         00015400
```

Figure G.3. Chapter 5 coding problem in Assembler Language (page 3 of 7)

```
*                                                           00015500
DATE      MVC   CURRDATE,=C'06/26/77'                       00015600
          BR    11                                          00015700
*                                                           00015800
WRITERTN  ST    11,WRITSAVE                                 00016000
          LH    10,LINECNT                                  00016100
          CH    10,=H'45'                                   00016200
          BL    AHEAD6                                      00016300
*                                                           00016400
          MVC   LINECNT,=H'1'                               00016500
          MVC   PRAREA,HDTITLE                              00016600
          MVC   PRCTL,TOPPAGE                               00016700
          PUT   PRINTER,PRNTLINE                            00016800
*                                                           00016900
          MVC   PRAREA,HDSPC                                00017000
          MVC   PRCTL,DOUBSPC                               00017100
          PUT   PRINTER,PRNTLINE                            00017200
*                                                           00017300
          MVC   PRAREA,HDHOSP                               00017400
          PUT   PRINTER,PRNTLINE                            00017500
          MVC   PRAREA,DTHOSP                               00017600
          PUT   PRINTER,PRNTLINE                            00017700
*                                                           00017800
          CLI   NOHOSP,C'1'                                 00017900
          BE    WRITEXIT                                    00018000
*                                                           00018100
          MVC   PRAREA,HDWARD                               00018200
          PUT   PRINTER,PRNTLINE                            00018300
*                                                           00018400
          MVC   PRAREA,DTWARD                               00018500
          PUT   PRINTER,PRNTLINE                            00018600
*                                                           00018700
          CLI   NOWARD,C'1'                                 00018800
          BE    WRITEXIT                                    00018900
*                                                           00019000
          MVC   PRAREA,HDPAT                                00019100
          PUT   PRINTER,PRNTLINE                            00019200
*                                                           00019300
          MVC   PRCTL,SINGSPC                               00019400
          MVI   PRAREA,C' '                                 00019500
          MVC   PRAREA+1(131),PRAREA                        00019600
          PUT   PRINTER,PRNTLINE                            00019700
*                                                           00019800
AHEAD6    MVC   PRAREA,DTPAT                                00019900
          MVC   PRCTL,SINGSPC                               00020000
          PUT   PRINTER,PRNTLINE                            00020100
*                                                           00020200
          LH    10,LINECNT                                  00020300
          LA    10,1(0,10)                                  00020400
          STH   10,LINECNT                                  00020500
*                                                           00020600
WRITEXIT  L     11,WRITSAVE                                 00020700
          BR    11                                          00020800
*                                                           00020900
WRITSAVE  DS    F                                           00021000
```

Figure G.3. Chapter 5 coding problem in Assembler Language (page 4 of 7)

```
SAVE       DS    18F                                                     00021200
*                                                                        00021300
HOSPFILE DCB    DSORG=PS,MACRF=GM,EODAD=ENDJOB,RECFM=FB,LRECL=80,       *00021400
                DDNAME=INPUT                                             00021500
*                                                                        00021600
PRINTER    DBC   DSORG=PS,MACRF=PM,RECFM=FBA,LRECL=133,                 *00021700
                DDNAME=OUTPUT                                            00021800
*                                                                        00021900
*                                                                        00022000
HOSPINPT DS     0CL133                                                   00022100
         DS     CL2                                                      00022200
IHOSPNAM DS     CL20                                                     00022300
         DS     CL58                                                     00022400
*                                                                        00022500
PRNTLINE DS     0CL133                                                   00022600
PRCTL    DS     C                                                        00022700
PRAREA   DS     CL132                                                    00022800
*                                                                        00022900
NOHOSP   DC     C'0'                                                     00023100
NOWARD   DC     C'0'                                                     00023200
NOPAT    DC     C'0'                                                     00023300
TOPPAGE  DC     C'1'                                                     00023400
DOUBSPC  DC     C'0'                                                     00023500
SINGSPC  DC     C' '                                                     00023700
GU       DC     CL4'GU  '                                               00023800
GNP      DC     CL4'GNP '                                               00024000
LINECNT  DC     H'52'                                                    00024100
PAGECNT  DC     H'0'                                                     00024200
NEWMONTH DS     PL2                                                      00024300
NEWYEAR  DS     PL2                                                      00024400
WRDTYPE  DC     CL20' '                                                  00024500
DATEWK1  DS     PL2                                                      00024600
DATEWK2  DS     PL2                                                      00024700
*                                                                        00024800
CURRDATE DS     0CL8                                                     00024900
CURRMO   DS     CL2                                                      00025000
         DC     C'/'                                                     00025100
CURRDAY  DS     CL2                                                      00025200
         DC     C'/'                                                     00025300
CURRYR   DS     CL2                                                      00025400
*                                                                        00025500
WSPREVDT DS     0CL4                                                     00025600
PREVMO   DS     CL2                                                      00025700
PREVYR   DS     CL2                                                      00025800
         COPY   AHOSPITA                                                 00026000
*                                                                        00026100
         COPY   AWARD                                                    00026200
*                                                                        00026300
         COPY   APATIENT                                                 00026400
*                                                                        00026500
SSAHOSP  DC     C'HOSPITAL(HOSPNAME ='                                   00026600
*                                                                        00026700
SSAHNAME DS     CL20                                                     00026800
         DC     C')'                                                     00026900
*                                                                        00027000
SSAWARD  DC     C'WARD    (WARDTYPE =QUARANTINE            '             00027100
*                                                                        00027200
SSAPAT   DC     CL9'PATIENT '                                            00027300
*                                                                        00027400
```

Figure G.3. Chapter 5 coding problem in Assembler Language (page 5 of 7)

```
HDTITLE  DS    OCL132                                          00027500
         DC    CL26' '                                         00027600
         DC    CL106' P R E V I O U S   S T A Y   R E P O R T' 00027700
*                                                              00027800
HDSPC    DS    CL132' '                                        00027900
*                                                              00028000
HDHOSP   DS    OCL132                                          00028100
         DC    CL25'HOSPITAL NAME'                             00028200
         DC    CL35'HOSPITAL ADDRESS'                          00028300
         DC    CL10'HOSP PHONE'                                00028400
         DC    CL62' '                                         00028500
*                                                              00028600
HDWARD   DS    OCL132                                          00028700
         DC    CL12'WARD NO'                                   00028800
         DC    CL14'TOT ROOMS'                                 00028900
         DC    CL13'TOT BEDS'                                  00029000
         DC    CL15'BEDS AVAIL'                                00029100
         DC    CL20'WARD TYPE'                                 00029200
         DC    CL58' '                                         00029300
*                                                              00029400
HDPAT    DS    OCL132                                          00029500
         DC    CL21'PATIENT NAME'                              00029600
         DC    CL6'BED'                                        00029700
         DC    CL12'ADMIT DATE'                                00029800
         DC    CL11'PREV DATE'                                 00029900
         DC    CL21'PREVIOUS HOSPITAL'                         00030000
         DC    CL30'PREVIOUS REASON'                           00030100
         DC    CL31' '                                         00030200
```

Figure G.3. Chapter 5 coding problem in Assembler Language (page 6 of 7)

```
DTHOSP    DS   OCL132                                                00030400
DHOSPNAM  DS   CL20                                                  00030500
          DC   CL5' '                                               00030600
DHOSPADR  DS   CL30                                                  00030700
          DC   CL5' '                                               00030800
DHOSPHON  DS   CL10                                                  00030900
          DC   CL62' '                                              00031000
*                                                                   00031100
DTWARD    DS   OCL132                                               00031200
          DC   CL3' '                                               00031300
DWARDNO   DS   CL2                                                  00031400
          DC   CL10' '                                              00031500
DTOTRMS   DS   CL3                                                  00031600
          DC   CL11' '                                              00031700
DTOTBEDS  DS   CL3                                                  00031800
          DC   CL10' '                                              00031900
DBDSAVAI  DS   CL3                                                  00032000
          DC   CL9' '                                               00032100
DWARDTYP  DS   CL20                                                 00032200
          DC   CL58' '                                              00032300
*                                                                   00032400
DTPAT     DS   OCL132                                               00032500
DPATNAME  DS   CL20                                                 00032600
          DC   C' '                                                 00032700
DBEDID    DS   CL4                                                  00032800
          DC   CL4' '                                               00032900
DDATADMI  DS   CL6                                                  00033000
          DC   CL6' '                                               00033100
DPREVDTE  DS   CL4                                                  00033200
          DC   CL5' '                                               00033300
DPREHOSP  DS   CL20                                                 00033400
          DC   C' '                                                 00033500
DPREVREA  DS   CL30                                                 00033600
          DC   CL31' '                                              00033700
*                                                                   00033800
NOHOSPLN  DS   OCL132                                               00033900
ERRHNAM   DS   CL20                                                 00034000
          DC   CL5' '                                               00034100
          DC   CL107'**** HOSPITAL NOT FOUND  ****'                 00034200
*                                                                   00034300
NOWARDLN  DC   CL132'**** NO QUARANTINE WARDS  ****'                00034400
*                                                                   00034500
NOPATLN   DC   CL132'**** NO PATIENTS WITH PREVIOUS STAY ****'      00034600
*                                                                   00034700
PCBMASK   DSECT                                                     00034800
          COPY MASKA                                                00034900
          END  DLITCBL                                              00035000
```

Figure G.3. Chapter 5 coding problem in Assembler Language (page 7 of 7)

Appendix H
IMS Reference Manuals

There are a number of manuals that are useful to people working in the IMS environment—a different set for IMS/VS and for DL/I VSE. All of the manuals listed below are available from International Business Machines Corporation, White Plains, New York 10604. Since IBM changes manual names and order numbers from time to time, it is a good idea to check manual GC20-0001, *IBM System/370 and 4300 Processors Bibliography* before placing a manual order.

IMS/VS REFERENCE MANUALS

The following is a list of the manuals that are most useful in IMS/VS installations:

GH20-1260	*General Information*
GH20-9069	*Fast Path Feature General Information*
SH20-9025	*Data Base Administration Guide*
SH20-9026	*Application Programming: Design and Coding*
SH20-9027	*System Programming Reference*
SH20-9028	*Operator's Reference*
SH20-9029	*Utilities Reference*
SH20-9030	*Messages and Codes Reference*
SH20-9053	*Message Format Service User's Guide*
SH20-9054	*Programming Guide for Remote SNA Systems*
SH20-9081	*Installation Guide*
SH20-9145	*Primer*
SH20-9178	*System Administration Guide*

DL/I VSE REFERENCE MANUALS

The following is a list of the manuals that are most useful in DL/I VSE installations:

GH20-1246 *General Information*
SH12-5412 *Utilities and Guide for the System Programmer*
SH12-5413 *System/Application Design Guide*
SH12-5414 *Messages and Codes*
SH12-5415 *Application Programming Reference*
SH12-5417 *Application Programmer's Reference Summary*
SH12-5418 *Utilities Reference Summary*

Index

UNDER
A SILENT
MOON